— ADVANCED —
SHAMANISM

". . . a rich and fascinating journey intended to culminate in increasing levels of shamanic mastery. As the title implies, this is not a book for dabblers but is for advanced practitioners who have the grounding and patience necessary to work through and digest these exercises and resulting experiences over a period of months, even years."

HILLARY S. WEBB, PH.D., AUTHOR OF *TRAVELING BETWEEN THE WORLDS: CONVERSATIONS WITH CONTEMPORARY SHAMANS*

"James Endredy births another book that provides theory, personal background, and teaching stories that illuminate shamanic practices and exercises that can produce a meaningful path in life. It makes for 'powerful medicine,' if you use what he offers in a respectful and humble way. He expands our notions of 'self' and what is possible at a time of cultural crisis that calls for us to meet the challenges of today's world with expanded vision and empowerment to create life-affirming ways of living with all our relations."

TOM PINKSON, PH.D., AUTHOR OF *THE SHAMANIC WISDOM OF THE HUICHOL* AND *FRUITFUL AGING*

"This remarkable book provides readers already proficient in basic shamanism a rare glimpse into the deeper universe of traditional healers and their most powerful practices. With precision and integrity Endredy provides step-by-step guidance for learning the advanced healing arts of world shamanism, such as interacting with Sacred Fire, recapitulating energy drains, creating animal-spirit jicara bowls, a personal death/rebirth ceremony, lucid-shamanic dreaming, and "quantum" healing through direct shamanic viewing. If you are ready to fully step through the portal of conscious transformation, this book will be your treasured companion and guide."

JEFF NIXA, J.D., M.DIV., FOUNDER OF GREAT PLAINS
SHAMANIC PROGRAMS AND AUTHOR OF
THE LOST ART OF HEART NAVIGATION

"James Endredy's *Advanced Shamanism* weaves together practices he has learned and used over many years, and his transparency about their origins adds to their validity. There are skills for improving your ability to practice shamanism as well as valuable tools for benefiting your community. A must-have for any shamanic practitioner seeking a solid practical text to learn from."

LUPA, AUTHOR OF *NATURE SPIRITUALITY FROM THE
GROUND UP* AND CREATOR OF *THE TAROT OF BONES*

— ADVANCED —
SHAMANISM

THE PRACTICE OF CONSCIOUS
TRANSFORMATION

JAMES ENDREDY

Bear & Company
Rochester, Vermont • Toronto, Canada

Bear & Company
One Park Street
Rochester, Vermont 05767
www.BearandCompanyBooks.com

Bear & Company is a division of Inner Traditions International

Library of Congress Cataloging-in-Publication Data

Names: Endredy, James, author.
Title: Advanced Shamanism : the practice of conscious transformation / JamesEndredy.
Description: Rochester, VT : Bear & Company, 2018. | Includes bibliographical references and index.
Identifiers: LCCN 2017026433 (print) | LCCN 2017028065 (e-book) | ISBN 9781591432838 (pbk.) | ISBN 9781591432845 (e-book)
Subjects: LCSH: Shamanism.
Classification: LCC BF1611 .E6548 2018 (print) | LCC BF1611 (e-book) | DDC 201/.44—dc23
LC record available at https://lccn.loc.gov/2017026433

Printed and bound in the United States by P. A. Hutchison Company

10 9 8 7 6 5 4 3 2 1

Text design by Priscilla H. Baker and layout by Virginia Scott Bowman
This book was typeset in Garamond Premier Pro and Frutiger with Cheddar Gothic, Corporative, Kepler, Frutiger, and Texta used as display typefaces

To send correspondence to the author of this book, mail a first-class letter to the author c/o Inner Traditions • Bear & Company, One Park Street, Rochester, VT 05767, and we will forward the communication, or contact the author directly at **www.JamesEndredy.com**.

Contents

PART THREE

THE SHAMANIC DREAMSCAPE

PART FOUR
SHAMANIC PRACTICES FOR QUANTUM HEALING

Why Advanced Shamanism?

My father, who was truly my hero, passed away when I was fourteen years old. It was tragic, a battle with brain cancer that he gallantly lost. A Hungarian immigrant new to this country, my father went from sweeping floors to becoming president of a multinational corporation. Probably because of his driven and protective nature, he loved his family with the ferocity of a mountain lion. I loved him back in the same roaring way. So when he died, I was devastated on both a cellular and a psychic level. The deep questions prevailed in my adolescent heart: Who am I? Why do I exist? What am I to do with my life?

With this in my head, I took off for the freedom of the road, and by the time I was eighteen, I had been through more than twenty-five states—seeking shelter in stolen cars, mountain shacks, and cheap hotels. Through all my travels, I maintained my continuous love for nature, which both my parents had instilled in me. I attribute this passion for the outdoors for saving me from the downward spiral I was experiencing after such loss and for keeping me from being pulled into *el camino perdido* (the lost path).

My mother was my grounding force during this time and still is: I talk on the phone to her daily. Her feminine energy is an inspiration in my work. She has this effect on folks, particularly as an eighty-one-year-old voluntary caregiver at numerous nursing homes. She is, in my opinion, the embodiment of Tatai Urianka (Huichol for "Grandmother Growth"). As I grew up and settled more on accepting my father's passing, I learned the importance of healing oneself on a quantum level. Since then, I have been a student of the existential, seeking answers to those deeper questions only humans ask. In trying to find answers, I learned many useful things.

I quickly decided organized religion was not for me, and I became drawn to more esoteric teachings and also the type of nature-based spirituality that indigenous cultures practice. During this period, I traveled extensively throughout the United States—then Mexico, South and Central America, and Europe. For many years I was a seeker, a sponge for knowledge of other cultures and how they dealt with these big questions I was asking myself. Year after year—practice after practice—I gradually came to know on a deep level the lessons taught to me by elders of the Seneca, Lenni Lenape, Apurimac Inca, Arapaho, Minneconjou Sioux, Kanaka Maoli, Tuscarora, Tukano, Mazatek, Yurok, Navaho, Hopi, Yucatec Maya, and Huichol/Wirrarika tribes. It is from these tribes I developed the practices for this book, *Advanced Shamanism*.

During the past thirty years of my life, I have been privileged to be accepted and learn from shamans of many different cultures. With their shamanic vision they could see that even though I was a white Western man I was gifted with a spirit in my heart that could help make the world a better place. I came to know healers, shamans, *kawiteros, lamas, siddhas,* roadmen, and leaders in the modern fields of ecopsychology, bioregionalism, and sustainable living. I was especially interested in those that retained their ancestral traditions and were still directly connected to nature; they were the most fascinating, grounded, and mature humans I have ever encountered.

In 1998, while visiting the peyote desert with the Huichol, I received a direct message from the spirit of the desert concerning one of the tasks for my life. (Finding a path for their life is the main reason the Huichol make pilgrimages to the peyote desert on their first quests.) The message was delivered to me by the small sparrows that winter in the Chihuahuan desert as I sat in the shade of a tree. The experience was so amazing that at first I thought it couldn't possibly be real. But as I continued to listen, I realized the magic of the peyote desert was speaking to me through the little birds fluttering around. It wasn't a booming voice, like you might imagine the voice of God would be; it was a powerful telepathic message from a form I had never encountered before. The message was that I was to write a book. This was a rather confusing message because I wasn't a writer and never even thought about writing a book; and the message did not include what the book was to be about. I struggled for more than two years with the task of writing a book—I had no idea what to write about—until during a day of rock climbing I had a near-death experience in which I received another message, this time from the spirit of a mountain in the Gunks of Upstate New York. I wrote about this encounter in my book *Ecoshamanism: Sacred Practices of Unity, Power & Earth Healing.*

> As I climbed higher and higher up the sheer face of the mountain I knew that I was in big trouble. The route I was trying to climb was above my skill level of technical rock climbing experience, and in this remote area of wilderness I was about to pay the ultimate price for my foolishness. I hadn't placed my safety gear properly and the safety rope was dragging me down. But even worse, for fear of more rope drag I stopped placing safety gear in the rock as I climbed, so now the rope was useless and if I fell I would surely drop to my death. My arms were burning from fatigue and my feet were continuously slipping off of the tiny crevices that were holding me upright. I couldn't climb any higher, I couldn't go back, and I couldn't stay where I was. I had come to the end of the road and I knew it. I was completely exhausted and it was physically impossible for me to hang on any longer.[1]

At that moment, the spirit of the Gunks took me. I felt myself flying like Ebenezer Scrooge trapped in Christmas past. My perception was dual. On the one hand, I could clearly feel myself about to slip off the cliff and I could "see" my life blast before my eyes. On the other hand, I also felt myself hovering—watching the whole incident with a feeling of detached awe. Meanwhile, during this duality I had a silent conversation with the ancient spirit of the mountain that was about to end my life. Everything happened so rapidly that I didn't have time to mentally analyze what was going on. I instinctively knew that this was the same spirit that had spoken to me during a three-day vision quest I had done a few months earlier on the same exact mountain in the Gunks. The spirit had spoken to me during the vision quest ceremony, when I had given the Gunks my offerings of blood, breath, and soul and had granted my vision of being one with Tatai Urianaka— Grandmother Growth. The mountain knew my task in life even better than I did.

Now as I hung precariously, the spirit of the mountain made me a deal: my life would be spared if I would stop goofing around with childish games and get busy accomplishing my task in life. I silently agreed and suddenly found myself resting safely on a wide ledge— way, way above where I believed I was destined to land, becoming an instant corpse.

On that ledge I learned many things. The spirit of the mountain told me that because of my years of dedication in trying to find my true path—which enabled me to accept and believe this important message from the spirit—my own spirit was able to take the control of my body away from my mind and deliver me safely to the ledge. Even more valuable, the spirit told me that it wasn't necessary to knock on death's door for my spirit to take control. I could learn to use this capacity even during the course of my everyday life. If I simply walked the path of my true calling, I would learn how to do it.

Fortunately, I had already learned about my path with heart years before from the message I received in the peyote desert. However, knowing it and walking it are two different things. The mountain spirit reminded me that I had let my own spirit guide my actions countless times before, such as when I connected with the spirits of nature during ceremonies with indigenous shamans and while I was learning the purpose and properties of medicinal herbs, flowers, and plants. Yet I had not learned to will my spirit of my own volition. I realized then the way to do this was to make my everyday life just as magical, mysterious, and urgent as those times when a crisis coaxed my spirit to emerge.

The mountain spirit's most important message was that actual experience, in the moment, was the key to knowledge. I know now—from over thirty years of shamanic learning, practice, teaching, and healing—that no amount of visualization or guided imagery will further your progress as a shamanic healer or actually get "the work" done. I can imagine that I'm going to write a book, but unless I actually write it, the book won't exist. To fully experience the practices I have laid out in this book, you have to do them. I have learned these practices from indigenous shamans and then personally expanded them. I have written them here for shamanic practice and healing. In our Western culture we do have the capacity to utilize shamanic practice and change our life as well as help change the lives of others. That is the gift of these practices.

I consider the practices in this book to be advanced due to the rigors and fortitude necessary to accomplish them. In this book, my eleventh on shamanic study, research, and practice, I begin with fundamental and then advanced studies and practices that will support you on your journey toward becoming an advanced level shamanic healer. All of these practices, even the fundamentals, are absolutely required for my own advanced shamanic students, and my hope is that you will use these exercises and complete all of them to really feel what it is to be a deeply rooted shamanic healer. It is my goal to pass on—in the most respectful and accurate way—shamanic techniques that can enrich the lives of modern people toward healthy and holistic states of being.

It is my genuine hope that this book will provide you with solid, personal, "time-tested" practices that will enable you to move forward on your shamanic path for your own benefit and knowledge. If you are a shamanic practitioner, these practices will help you to better heal your clients. As an offering, I would like to share my personal translation of a Huichol Indian prayer chant:

Bless our path Grandfather Fire
Bless our food Grandmother Growth
Bless our voice Brother Wind
Bless our rain Sister Water
We send our prayers to Reu'unar (Sacred Spirits of the East)
We send our prayers to Tatai Haramara (Sacred Spirits of the West)
We send our prayers to Hauxamanaka (Sacred Spirits of the North)
We send our prayers to Tatai Xapawiyeme (Sacred Spirits of the South)
We send our prayers to Teakata (Sacred Land of Our Center)
May you bless us as we walk our Sacred Path

Many blessings on your journey!

PART ONE

THE PHENOMENA OF SHAMANISM

1

The Shamanic Worldview

Although the majority of people buying this book will probably be in some way familiar with the term *shamanism*, I still think it's important to briefly review the topic. Shamans were the earliest initiators of spiritual knowledge and were widely dispersed throughout the globe. Ancient shamans were generally associated with northern and central Asia, but they were also located in Africa, Australia, Europe, and the Americas, which is basically where they can still be found today among the few existing societies that have been able to preserve this ancient sacred tradition.

These shamans function in an extraordinarily wide range of roles, performing many activities. They are healers, visionaries, singers, dancers, psychologists, rainmakers, food finders, and, most importantly, intermediaries between the human and nonhuman world. As spiritual leaders, their expertise is both cosmic and physical, their knowledge covering the ways of spirits, deities, plants, and animals. Today, they also commonly function as a guide for younger generations; they are intermediaries between their community's culture and the modern world.

As both a cultural platform and a discipline of consciousness, shamanism is an ancient system, perhaps the oldest known to humankind. The masked dancing shamans depicted in Paleolithic caves are the ancestors of the world's earliest religions. Ancient and classic shamanism was not characterized by the worship of a single god or through codified scriptures but comprised specific techniques and ideology through which spiritual issues as well as ecological realities could be addressed. The shaman's role is to honor the integrity of natural systems and maintain balance between society and nature and to deal with the community as a social unit and heal individual community members. Consequently, the shaman personifies the healer, mystic, and intellectual, which is in marked contrast to our contemporary fragmented view of the world, where "civilized" Western consciousness splits the mind, body, and spirit. This creates rigid and separate roles in the community. You can't go to just one source for healing; in our society you need to see a therapist, a physician, and a pastor or priest.

Shamanism as practiced throughout the world shares many basic elements. These include the following:

- A shaman, whether male or female, is always chosen because of his or her specific talents, which can be hereditary, learned, or spontaneously attained, depending on the culture and circumstances.
- Shamans always go through a period of initiation. They attain the power and knowledge to enter into altered states of consciousness through their work with elder shamans, with nature, and with spirits.
- The spirits that a shaman works with can be guides and helpers, sometimes companions and even lovers; other times the spirits can be antagonistic and harmful to the shaman.
- Shamans are often experts in working with indigenous plants and the spirits of powerful special plants or entheogens; these plants of the gods are often employed in their rituals to heal others or themselves.
- Shamans use various tools, such as feathers, healing stones, and plants, during their rituals and ceremonies to help their consciousness travel to the realms of the unknown and to perceive the great mysteries of life and death.

The most we can do as healers on this path is enter the world of the shaman with an open mind. Although many modern people are now open to shamanism and interested in understanding better this fascinating subject, it took centuries of intolerance gradually giving way to observation and investigation and finally appreciation before Westerners could get to a place of acceptance and respect.

2

States of Consciousness

ALTERED STATES OF CONSCIOUSNESS

The term *altered state of consciousness* (ASC) was popularized in 1969 by transpersonal psychologist Charles Tart in his book *Altered States of Consciousness,* which is a collection of thirty-five scientific papers describing various altered states. An altered state of consciousness can be described as a change in one's normal mental state to a different, temporary state, without loss of consciousness. Altered states of consciousness can be created intentionally, or they can happen by accident or due to illness.

Accidental or pathological circumstances that can induce altered states of consciousness include traumatic experiences on either a physical or mental level, near-death experiences, seizures, extended sleep deprivation, bodily infections, and extended lack of food or water. Some forms of spontaneous psychosis happen with no apparent cause.

Intentional activities that stimulate these altered states of consciousness include meditation, dreaming, lucid dreaming, sex, hypnosis, fasting, the use of mind-altering drugs and plant entheogens, sensory deprivation, and contemplation of art, music, and nature. Attuning with nature provides sensory stimulation, with deep connections to natural energies, such as fire, wind, water, earth, and animals. Other avenues for these sorts of ASC are also brought forth in parapsychological or psi faculties or activities, such as telepathy, psychokinesis, remote viewing, and shamanic viewing.

Shamanic state of consciousness. The term *shamanic state of consciousness* (SSC) was coined by Michael Harner in 1982 with his famous book *The Way of the Shaman*. Unfortunately, although many of the topics covered in Harner's book are shamanic, since the publication of that book, many people have used, and still are using, the term SSC for activities that are not shamanic. For example, I have been to classes on "shamanic journeying" where the leader sits everyone in a circle and, after doing some drumming, tells participants to "close your eyes and imagine that you are in a beautiful meadow, or on top of a mountain, or in a cave." This is not shamanism. This is a useful therapeutic technique more aptly described as guided visualization, often employed by a trained practitioner in treating social anxiety, depression, bipolar disorder, and post-traumatic stress disorder, among others.

Integrative state of consciousness. Integrative state of consciousness (ISC) is the term I use because I think it best describes the states of consciousness that the practices in this book will produce. An ISC involves enhanced access to normally unconscious information through integration of different brain systems, which induces emotional, behavioral, and cognitive integration, passive manipulation of our autonomic nervous system, and psychic-energetic integration with our environment via our holographic fields and phase-conjugate mirrors. (In chapter 4, I explain holographic fields and phase-conjugate mirrors.)

During the practices in this book the ISC will be experienced in various *modes*. Modes of consciousness are experienced within all states of consciousness. For example, in a normal state of consciousness riding a bike is a mode of experience much different from swimming, as is reading a different mode from cooking. ASC have modes as well; for example, lucid dreaming is not ecstatic dance, although they can both be experienced as an ASC. An ISC can have many modes as well, as we will experience during the practices in this book.

THE AUTONOMIC NERVOUS SYSTEM AND PASSIVE VOLITION—GATEWAYS TO ISC

Our nervous system is divided into two main systems. The central nervous system is the command center of our human organism and includes the brain and spinal cord. The peripheral nervous system (PNS) consists of the nerves and ganglia outside the brain and spinal cord. The PNS is further divided into the somatic nervous system and the autonomic nervous system (ANS). The somatic nervous system is the part of the PNS associated with the voluntary control of body movements via skeletal muscles. The ANS, also known as the visceral nervous system or involuntary nervous system, is the part of the peripheral nervous system that functions largely below the level of consciousness to control visceral functions such as digestion, breathing, and heart rate. Most autonomous functions are involuntary, but they can often work in conjunction with the somatic nervous, which provides voluntary control.

Within the brain, the ANS is located in the medulla oblongata in the lower brainstem. The medulla's major ANS functions include the respiratory control center, cardiac regulation, vasomotor activity, and certain reflex actions such as sneezing. These are then subdivided into other areas and are linked to autonomic nervous subsystems and nervous systems external to the brain. The hypothalamus, just above the brain stem, acts as an integrator for autonomic functions, receiving ANS regulatory input from the limbic system to do so.

Here is the part we are most interested in for the practices in this book. The ANS is divided into two main subsystems: the parasympathetic nervous system and the sympathetic nervous system. Depending on the circumstances, these subsystems may operate independently of each other or interact cooperatively.

The sympathetic nervous system is often considered the "fight or flight" system, while the parasympathetic nervous system is often considered the "rest and digest" or "feed and breed" system. In many cases both nervous systems have opposite actions wherein one system activates a physiological response and the other inhibits it. The modern characterization is that the sympathetic nervous system is a quick response mobilizing system and the parasympathetic is a more slowly activated dampening system, but even this has exceptions, such as in sexual arousal and orgasm, wherein both play a role.

It's very important for us as shamanic healers to understand that a person can augment physiological activity within the autonomic nervous system and enter deep states of ISC through practices of *passive volition* (PV). Throughout the practices in this book, one of the most important aspects is PV, so complete understanding and experience of this state of consciousness are vital to progressing.

The way that I teach people how best to experience passive volition is through a technique called autogenic training (AT). In my last book, *Advanced Autogenic Training and Primal Awareness: Techniques for Wellness, Deeper Connection to Nature, and Higher Consciousness,* I detail forty training practices of AT and primal awareness. Even though AT is not a shamanic practice, it provides modern people a gateway to ISC by learning PV and gaining access to the ANS. I encourage all modern people interested in shamanic practices to engage in PV as much as possible, to the point where it becomes second nature, and to learn and master AT.

Autogenic training is a perfect vehicle for learning PV because volition is definitely applied but not the *will* of action. In attempting to explain this better, I have found the work of some researchers in the field of biofeedback to be helpful. For example, Elmer and Alyce Green in their book *Beyond Biofeedback* make this comment about PV: "A metaphoric way of putting it is to say that the cortex plants the idea in the subcortex and then allows nature to take its course without interference."[1] The Greens go on to explain that PV can be seen as analogous to farming. The analogy goes like this:

1. A farmer desires and visualizes a crop of corn.
2. He carefully plants his seed in the earth.
3. He allows nature to take its course.
4. He obtains the corn.

Correspondingly, employing passive volition to affect our normally involuntary or unconscious processes looks like this:

1. We desire a certain mental or physiological behavior, which is a conscious cortical process.
2. So we plant the idea in the psychological earth of our being, which is our subcortical area.
3. Then we let nature take its course without interfering (if the farmer digs up his seeds to check on them they will never grow).
4. And finally we reap an enhanced experience of life.

Passive volition is a kind of paradox for modern people, who have been taught their whole lives to be in control—the more control we have within ourselves and our surroundings, the more successful we will be. To plant an idea or process or practice in our mind and then "let nature take its course" is a very foreign idea to most people. But the more we engage in this state of consciousness, the more comfortable it becomes, and the more we experience this state as healers, the more we will begin to find extraordinary results in our shamanic practice. In chapter 9 we will delve deeper into this subject during the practices.

3

Psi and Shamanism

Psi is the twenty-third letter in the Greek alphabet, and the letter psi is now commonly used in physics to represent wave functions in quantum mechanics, such as in the Schrödinger equation and bra–ket notation. In recent times psi is also used and understood to represent parapsychological or psychic faculties or phenomena such as psychokinesis, telepathy, and clairvoyance.

That psi is now used both in science and in understanding psychic experiences is not an accident. Physics, especially quantum theory, and research on psychic phenomena are now coming together in ways never imagined before. The most important discovery to both fields is best described as entanglement. Erwin Schrödinger, father of quantum mechanics, coined the term *entanglement* when referring to connections between separated particles that persisted regardless of distance. These connections are apparently instantaneous and operating outside the usual flow of time. He states that entanglements "imply that at very deep levels, the separations that we see between ordinary isolated objects are, in a sense, illusions created by our limited perceptions."[1] In terms of psi, many experiments have been conducted over the past forty years that conclude the existence of entangled brains. This phrase describes the similarities of quantum-psi phenomena—that our minds are physically entangled with the universe and that quantum theory is relevant to understanding psi.

The theory of quantum entanglement would explain in scientific terms many psi phenomena.

THE HISTORY OF PSI

A short history of psi research follows.

Psi Phenomena in Ancient History

The earliest indication that people were aware of psychic phenomena occurred in ancient Egypt. Around 2000 BCE Egyptians practiced dream incubation, which entailed repeating incantations and prayers to encourage a dream that would help solve a particular problem the dreamer was having. In the Shang Dynasty, circa 1600–1046 BCE, oracle bones were used in pyromancy, a kind of divination. The oracle of Delphi in Greece, who was a Pythian priestess infused with the spirit of the god, provided advice and made prophecies, a practice that lasted seven hundred years, beginning around 650 BCE.

In 1486, the *Malleus Maleficarum* (Hammer of Witches) by Catholic clergyman Heinrich Kramer, was published, endorsing the prosecution and extermination of witches in Europe. The existence of this book indicates that a number of people in Europe, particularly women, were practicing shaman-like arts during this time, enough to be considered a direct threat to Christianity, the prevailing religion.

The Seventeenth through the Nineteenth Centuries

By the seventeenth century, with the start of the scientific revolution, interest in and study of psi phenomena was not as persecuted or vilified. In 1627, *Sylva Sylvarum* by Francis Bacon was published posthumously; in it, Bacon proposed studies of "binding thoughts," what we now call telepathy. Bacon's interest in psi testing was among the very first proposed uses of science. In 1774 Franz Anton Mesmer introduced "animal magnetism" and set the stage for hypnosis, psychoanalysis, and psychosomatic medicine. Marquis de Puységur, a student of Mesmer, showed that "magnetic somnambulism," which we now call hypnosis, includes a full range of paranormal skills, such as telepathy, clairvoyance, and precognition. Mesmer's and Puységur's methods outraged the physicians of the day.

In the early 1850s, séances (people meeting in small groups to connect with the dead) became hugely popular after Margaretta and Catherine Fox reported communications with spirits. Scottish medium Daniel Dunglas Home regularly levitated in front of audiences at this time and was never caught cheating. His feats are still a mystery today. German physicist Gustav Theodor Fechner demonstrated relationships between mind and matter and that both arise from the same nonmaterial spiritual force. In 1867, Sir William F. Barrett presented his research on "thought transfer" to the Royal College of Science. Later, Barrett would help found the Society for Psychical Research in London. During this time French physiologist Charles Richet published the first paper using statistical inference for studying telepathy. Richet's card experiments resulted in odds of one in twenty-five thousand.

Twentieth-Century Psi Research

In 1903 Frederic W. H. Myers, a member of the Society for Psychical Research, wrote *Human Personality and Its Survival of Bodily Death*. This book raised many eyebrows as one of the first scholarly volumes investigating this subject. Thomas Welton Stanford, brother of the founder of Stanford University, donated hundreds of thousands of dollars to Stanford for the investigation and advancement of the knowledge of psychic phenomena and occult sciences. One result was a 640-page volume called *Experiments in Psychical Research at Leland Stanford Junior University*, published in 1917. Around this same time Leonard T. Troland at Harvard University obtained successful results with one of the first automated ESP testing machines.

Around 1929 biologist Joseph Banks Rhine began psi research at Duke University, which continued until 1965. Rhine also established the Foundation for Research on the Nature of Man with the assistance of Chester Carlson, the founder of the Xerox Corporation. Rhine later (1937) began publishing the *Journal of Parapsychology*. Upton Sinclair published the widely popular book *Mental Radio* in 1930 describing successful mental telepathy tests. He later coined the term *extrasensory perception* (ESP) and published a book of the same name. In the late 1940s Albert Einstein was comparing quantum theory's prediction about entangled particles to telepathy.

The Parapsychology Foundation, a nonprofit organization, was founded in 1951 by the medium Eileen J. Garrett and Frances Payne Bolton, Ohio's then congresswoman. Today, the foundation is based in New York and offers grants and scholarships to those undertaking studies in the paranormal. The Parapsychological Association was formed in 1957 as a professional society for scientists, scholars, and parapsychologists. Its purpose has been "to advance parapsychology as a science, to disseminate knowledge of the field, and to integrate the findings with those of other branches of science."

Leonid Vasiliev published the popular book *Experiments in Mental Suggestion* in 1963, which furthered the topic of "remote hypnosis." Two years later the notion of entangled minds was solidified with the publication of "Extrasensory electroencephalographic induction between identical twins," in the journal *Science*. These findings of the researchers from the Department of Ophthalmology of Thomas Jefferson University Hospital in Philadelphia were reviewed as nothing less than "spooky."

In 1969, the Parapsychological Association became an official affiliate of the American Association for the Advancement of Science, a big step in legitimizing psi research on a scientific level. The Institute of Noetic Sciences, cofounded in 1973 by former astronaut Edgar Mitchell, is an American nonprofit parapsychological research institute. Mitchell, the sixth man to walk on the moon, reportedly conducted a successful ESP card experiment while flying inside the Apollo 14 space capsule. The Princeton Engineering Anomalies Research program, a research program at Princeton University established in 1979 by then dean of engineering Robert G. Jahn, became one of the world's premiere research groups on psi phenomena.

In 1981 the U.S. Congress through the Congressional Research Service began to study psi. For the next fifteen years the American Institutes for Research (by way of the CIA), the U.S. Army Research Institute, and the National Research Council prepared reports and all concluded that due to experimental evidence the study of psi should continue. In England the University of Edinburgh established the chair of parapsychology in 1985. American psychologist Robert Morris held the chair until his death in 2004. During his tenure close to fifty students earned their doctorates and went on to further legitimize psi research.

Interestingly, the 1990s began with Sony's ESPER (Extrasensory Perception and Excitation Research) lab researching ESP. The lab closed when one of the founders, Masaru Ibuka, died. A Sony Labs spokesperson reportedly commented that "we found out experimentally that yes, ESP exists, but that any practical application of this knowledge is not likely in the foreseeable future." In 1995 the CIA made public the secret, and now terminated, StarGate project, which began in 1978 to investigate the potential for psychic phenomena in military and domestic applications. The CIA report concluded that it was never useful in any intelligence operation. The first patent for a psi-operated switch was granted in 1998 based on mind-matter research by the Princeton Engineering Anomalies Research laboratory.

Psi Research in the Twenty-First Century

Since 2005, the Parapsychological Association has supported students and researchers with scholarships and grants-in-aid to help meet the research costs for experimental, phenomenological, sociological, and historical investigations into psychic phenomena. A number of other organizations formed in the nineteenth and twentieth centuries have continued their research into the twenty-first century, among them the Institute of Noetic Sciences (IONS), the American Society for Psychical

Research (ASPR), the Society for Psychical Research (SPR), and the International Association for Near Death Studies (IANDS).

From its inception in 1973, IONS has blazed new trails in exploring big questions: Who are we? What is consciousness, and how does it impact the physical world? What are our human potentials, and how can we achieve those potentials? What leads to personal and societal healing and transformation?

Because limitations in our human consciousness underlie many of the problems we face as a global community, research at IONS focuses on exploring the fundamental nature of consciousness, investigating how it interacts with the physical world, and studying how consciousness can dramatically transform in beneficial ways. IONS research focuses on three primary program areas: (1) Consciousness and healing: What role does consciousness play in health and healing? (2) Worldview transformation: How does consciousness transform? How can we support individual and collective transformation? (3) Extended human capacities or the science of interconnectedness: How does consciousness interact with the physical world?

IONS conducts basic science and laboratory research on mind-matter interactions, social science investigations of transformational experiences and practices and their impact on individual and collective wellness, and clinical and applied studies testing the real-world effectiveness of consciousness-based interventions. IONS synthesizes bodies of knowledge, such as the science of meditation or the role of compassion in healing; disseminates these summaries; and uses that learned knowledge to identify next steps. Peer-reviewed scientific journals and scholarly meetings translate the findings into educational products and curricula for targeted audiences and the general public.

ASPR is the oldest psychical research organization in the United States. For more than a century, its mission has been to explore extraordinary or as yet unexplained phenomena that have been called psychic or paranormal and their implications for our understanding of consciousness and the nature of existence. Current research by ASPR examines ESP functioning in an altered state of consciousness. New case reports of personal experiences include premonitions of 9/11, as well as reports bearing on the survival hypothesis from a survey of near-death experiences, apparitions, awareness of death at a distance, and unusual experiences in the presence of the dying. The ASPR library and archives are a leading repository of significant aspects of American and scientific history, including the earliest history of psychology and psychiatry in the United States, early studies of multiple personality, the evolution of mind-body medicine, Eastern and Western religious philosophy, the mental healers movement, and American visionary traditions.

SPR, founded in 1882, is a nonprofit organization in the United Kingdom. Its stated purpose is to understand "events and abilities commonly described as psychic or paranormal by promoting and supporting important research in this area" and to "examine allegedly paranormal phenomena in a scientific and unbiased way."

IANDS is a nonprofit organization based in Durham, North Carolina, and associated with the academic field of near-death studies. The association was founded in the United States in 1981 to study and provide information on the phenomena of the near-death experience. Today, it has grown into an international organization, which includes a network of more than fifty local interest groups and approximately eight hundred and fifty members worldwide. Local chapters and support groups are established in major U.S. cities. IANDS also supports and assists folks who have had near-death experiences and people close to them. In one of its publications the organization has formulated its vision as one of building "global understanding of near-death and near-death-like experiences through research, education, and support."

Throughout my many years working with shamans and psi phenomena, I've collected many stories. Here is one of my favorite short ones, excerpted from my book *Lightning in My Blood: A Journey into Shamanic Healing and the Supernatural*.[2]

Personal Story of Psi Phenomena

Old John Redcorn was of the Lenni Lenape tribe of Oklahoma. But when I first met John he was living in Pennsylvania, as he had wanted to live for a spell in the woods where his ancestors once lived.

One day in my early twenties I saw in the newspaper an advertisement for a local event about Indian culture at a state park near the Delaware River. As I flipped through the pamphlet of programs, I saw there was a fire-making course starting in a few minutes, so I headed over to that area and that's where I first met Old John Redcorn. He was the first person to ever really teach me how to make a fire without matches. John's preferred method was the bow-drill, at which he was a master. The old man was so passionate and so good at teaching that I have never forgotten what he taught me, and I have actually taught many others over the years what John shared with me about making fire.

Remarkably, after that first meeting John and I kept in touch even though not very often. Looking back on the years now John had an uncanny way of writing me a letter just before I was about to move somewhere. It was because of this, some fifteen years later, that my girlfriend Sue and I were on our way to his house in Missouri while visiting Arizona from the East Coast.

As we pulled into the driveway John must have been waiting because he came dashing out motioning for us to be quiet and to follow him. It was a dark but clear night, and John led us to the back of his rural house seemingly situated in a large hay field. But as my eyes adjusted to the dark I began to see that there were many fruit trees and also a large garden (yes, probably with some red corn) off to the left of the house.

Anyway, after only a minute or so it became apparent what John wanted to show us. His nephew John (for ease in identification I'll refer to him as John Jr. even though he was probably in his fifties then) was out back as well, and he joined us as we all watched four coyotes and a single badger toying with a squirrel that was badly injured by the gang of carnivores but was still alive. For whatever reason, right then neither the coyotes nor the badger seemed in a hurry for a meal of squirrel; they preferred to just play with the unfortunate squirrel, tossing it into the air, picking it up lightly, and shaking and pawing at it.

This was the first time I ever saw a badger "playing." I had seen coyotes do all kinds of strange and funny things before but never a badger. I looked intently at John Redcorn and he whispered to us with a snicker, "That badger is drunk from all the rotten fruit he ate earlier." And the more I watched the badger it seemed that John was right; the badger was kind of stumbling around and seemed to lack coordination.

Well the poor squirrel finally died and the coyotes made a quick meal of him. The badger didn't seem to mind that they didn't share it with him. He just turned and started to amble away. Just then, one of the larger coyotes perked up, and I could swear I saw a mischievous or even malicious gleam in his eye. From the look of it the taste of blood had gotten him riled up, and the squirrel was nothing more than a snack. He was licking his lips and paws while eying the badger as he walked away.

But Mr. Coyote was not going to let him go. He snuck up on the badger and bit him square on the backside. The badger turned fiercely and puffed himself up, teeth unfurled. He was more than a formidable opponent even for four coyotes, and they all knew it. However, the lead coyote must have sensed that there was something a bit off about this badger tonight, just like John had said, because it proceeded to rally its friends, and after a fierce but fairly quick fight the coyotes killed the badger, ripped open his belly, and began to feed on him.

Old John Redcorn said he wanted the badger pelt, so he grabbed a garden shovel and scared off the coyotes. The rest of us walked over to the slain badger where John was kneeling over it and saying some prayers in a language I didn't understand. The moon was about half full that night, and with the sky being clear, it was bright enough that I could easily see the quizzical look on John's face as he stood up, and I knew then that the death of the badger wasn't the only thing we were going to see that night. And I was right.

There was a large pool of blood on the hard dry earth next to the badger's open guts. John Redcorn began to explain to us that in ancient times his people would look into the blood of a badger and sometimes see the future. He invited us to try it if we wanted, and he said he'd go first. John positioned himself so he could see his reflection off the light of the moon in the blood. From where I was standing I could see his reflection as well. I didn't see the future or anything else and apparently neither did he. All I saw was John's reflection. But as he stood up I caught that quizzical look of his again, and I wondered if he saw more than I did . . .

Next went John Jr. He knelt over the blood, and what I saw was astounding. The reflection of John Jr. was him but as an old man! He must have seen the same thing as he gasped and moved away from the blood. Old John Redcorn had a huge grin on his face.

I went next but for some odd reason a cloud suddenly obscured the moon and I could see nothing in the blood. I asked John if we could wait for the cloud to pass but he said no, "we have seen what we were supposed to see tonight about life and death."

Old John Redcorn was right, and the blood had showed it. Old John died not six months later, looking exactly as he did in his reflection that night. And his nephew John is still alive and kicking at close to seventy years old and looks exactly like his reflection we saw in the badger's blood on that magical night.

COMMON PSI TERMINOLOGY

Today, the science of psi continues with the above formal associations and many others. The most common and researched phenomena currently include:

Telepathy. The ganzfeld experiment (*ganzfeld* is German for "whole field") is the most current and accepted technique used to test individuals for telepathy. In a typical ganzfeld experiment, the telepathic sender and receiver are isolated. The eyes of the receiver are covered, and he or she listens to white noise through a set of headphones. The ganzfeld technique uses a mild sensory field to quiet or mask sights and sounds from the outside world, putting the receiver in an altered state of consciousness. The sender is shown a video clip or still picture and asked to mentally send that image to the receiver. After scores of such experiments, presently totaling about seven hundred individual sessions conducted by about two dozen investigators worldwide, the results show that the target image is selected by the receiver (from a group of various images) 34 percent of the time on average. This is a highly significant result, suggesting that telepathy, at least as operationally defined in this experiment, exists.

Remote viewing. In this practice, the receiver seeks impressions about a distant or unseen target using subjective means, in particular extrasensory perception. Unlike the ganzfeld technique, the receiver is not placed in an altered state of consciousness and there is no sender: most modern remote-viewing experiments are investigating whether information can be gained without requiring a special mental state or sender. With remote viewing the experimental participants attempt to collect and then sketch information about remote photos, actual scenes, and events. Several thousand such trials have been conducted by dozens of investigators over the past twenty-five years, involving hundreds of participants, and the conclusion has been that remote viewing is something that can be perceived.

Psychokinesis on random number generators. Highly automated experiments studying the interaction between mind and matter have been developed with the rise in computer technologies. A random number generator (RNG), based on electronic or radioactive noise, produces a data stream that is recorded and analyzed by computer software. The subject attempts to mentally change the distribution of the random numbers. Dean Radin, Ph.D., chief scientist at the Institute of Noetic Sciences, cites the following data regarding RNG experiments:

> A meta-analysis of the database, published in 1989, examined 800 experiments by more than 60 researchers over the preceding 30 years. The effect size was found to be very small, but remarkably consistent, resulting in an overall statistical deviation of approxi-

mately 15 standard errors from a chance effect. The probability that the observed effect was actually zero (i.e., no psi) was less than one part in a trillion, verifying that human consciousness can indeed affect the behavior of a random physical system.[3]

Direct mental interactions with living systems. DMILS experiments study the psychophysiological effects of one person's intentions on a distant person. The advent of modern technologies such as EEG, biofeedback, and skin conductance response, also known as the electrodermal response, has provided an opportunity to discover whether biological systems may also be affected by intention in a manner similar to mind-matter interaction on RNGs. The cumulative database on DMILS experiments provides strong evidence that one person's attention directed toward a remote, isolated person can significantly activate or calm that person's nervous system.

Near-death experiences. A near-death experience (NDE) is a profound psychological event that may occur to a person close to death or, if not near death, in a situation of physical or emotional crisis. Because it includes transcendental and mystical elements, an NDE is a powerful event of consciousness; NDEs include one or more of the following experiences: a sense of being dead; an out-of-body experience; a sensation of floating above one's body and seeing the surrounding area; a sense of overwhelming love and peace; a sensation of moving upward through a tunnel or narrow passageway; meeting deceased relatives or spiritual figures; encountering a being of light or a light; experiencing a life review; reaching a border or boundary; and a feeling of being returned to the body, often accompanied by reluctance. The NDE belongs to a larger family of experiences that go beyond the usual limits of space and time and can transform a person's life and beliefs. They may be called spiritually transformative, conversional, mystical, religious, or transpersonal experiences.

According to the International Association for Near Death Studies, one-fourth of the 800 people who have submitted an account of their experience to the IANDS online NDE archives reported they were not close to death or clinically dead at the time. Instead, they were in emotionally intense situations, praying or meditating, sleeping, or in ordinary states of consciousness when this phenomenon occurred. IANDS refers to these as "near-death-like experiences" or NDLEs. Seventy-five percent of those who sent their accounts had a sense of being close to death, were in a life-threatening situation, or believed they were clinically dead."[4]

Psychiatrist Ian Stevenson, from the University of Virginia, conducted more than 2,500 case studies over a period of forty years and published twelve books. Jim Tucker, associate professor of psychiatry and neurobehavioral sciences at the University of Virginia School of Medicine, has expanded on Stevenson's work and is currently one of the most respected researchers on NDEs. His books on NDEs are both fascinating and informative.

4

Hyperspace, Holographic Fields, and Phase-Conjugate Mirrors

These three topics will be covered in depth in chapters 13 and 14 where I present the practice of shamanic viewing. For now, I will briefly describe them, as they will be part of the explanation for a few other practices before chapter 13. Many who study physics today agree that there are multiple dimensions beyond the four dimensions of space-time, but there is disagreement on how many there might be. Whatever the number (and the number may be infinite), these multiple dimensions constitute the hyperspace of our larger reality.

HYPERSPACE AND THE HOLOGRAPHIC FIELD

Hyperspace is defined scientifically as a space of more than four dimensions. This idea is now being seriously entertained by physicists attempting to unify the physical forces of electromagnetism, nuclear forces, and gravity. The unified theory of physics views all force fields and matter fields as existing in four dimensions. However, a fifth dimension explains hyperspace. A unified theory of mental and physical events becomes possible if the mental realm is a hyperspace that embeds physical hyperspace. Psi and paranormal phenomena seem to be outside our ordinary space-time reality but may be understood as normal events from the perspective of hyperspace. These events seem unusual simply because our ordinary view of four dimensional space-time gives us only a partial view of hyperspace.

Philosophically, this idea is at least as old as Plato and can be seen in his "Allegory of the Cave." Plato's allegory suggests that we usually identify ourselves with our three-dimensional shadows rather than with the higher dimensional beings we truly are. For shamanic cultures, what we term hyperspace, far from being a philosophical construct or theory in physics, is simply an unquestioned reality. Shamanism is based on the reality of hyperspace.

Embedded in the hyperspace are fields of consciousness. This is important for shamanic practices, especially shamanic viewing and healing, since our lifetime of experiences is not stored solely within the brain but in what can be called a holographic field in which our brain and body are embedded. This field has staggering storage capacity and resolves the puzzle of adequate information storage within the brain. During certain practices the shaman can access this holographic field of information.

Our holographic field is also entangled with other holographic fields. This can be tangibly verified in everyday life. How is it that a sleeping mother suddenly awakes to "know" her son has just been killed in Afghanistan? The quantum entanglement of holographic fields explains it. Another amazing example is Ludwig van Beethoven, who wrote Symphony No. 9 after he became completely deaf. This is an example of the awesome storage capacity of the holographic field.

Personal Story of the Holographic Field

One of my first experiences that confirmed for me the reality of the holographic field happened during a month-long visit with the Wirrarika tribe of Mexico. During that trip I went on a pilgrimage to Wirikuta with the Wirrarika, where I experienced death and rebirth. While lying on the ground of the high-altitude desert, I became immobilized from exhaustion.

I felt my whole being quickly disintegrate into millions of tiny multicolored specks. Some of the specks dropped to the ground, some mixed with the air, and some rose into the sky. Then everything went black, and my consciousness was gone. I'm not sure how long I lay there unconscious, but for all intents and purposes I was dead. The spirits of the hikuri *(peyote cactus) had killed me.*

I will be forever grateful that they did. When I felt my awareness return to my body, the first thing I noticed was that even though my eyes were closed I could "see" five vultures flying in circles above my body and I could somehow hear the air rushing through their wings. One of them swooped directly over my head, circled around, and landed beside me. In that moment I realized that the vultures thought I was dead, and they were anxious to feed. And then the foul odor of my body hit me. The hot sun was heating up body fluids that had percolated from my body onto the ground, creating nauseating fumes—which were attracting the vultures. I smelled like death.

And then the worst thing of all happened: I tried to open my eyes but couldn't. I tried to sit up, and I couldn't do that either. I realized that I was either paralyzed or dead—I wasn't sure which. A few things were certain: the effects of the plant medicine had subsided, I felt completely empty both physically and mentally—and I was terrified.

After a while I began to notice that my senses were incredibly acute, and even though I couldn't open my eyes, I could still see in a strange kind of way what was going on around me. I could also hear and feel, and the more I focused on each of my senses, the more I was able to perceive, until after a while I realized that the only limits to my perception were those that I imposed on myself. I slowly became aware that my holographic field was entangled with everything around me. And with that realization everything changed again. Once I let go of what I thought were my perceptual limits, the doors of the spirit world opened, and as I lay there helpless, I received a spiritual-energetic infusion from all the beings of the desert.

I could feel the individual energies of the plants, the butterflies, the rabbits, the birds, the mice, and even the soil, rocks, air, and sun—each pouring into me as if my body were an empty pitcher being filled with multicolored magical liquids. Even though my eyes were still closed, the sensations were acutely visual, and I could clearly see how each being had its own unique quality and color of light or luminous glow. As the glowing nature spirits filled my being, they also spoke to me about my life and my place in the world. I was given specific instructions about what to do. I wasn't told how I was to accomplish everything, but I knew clearly what the goals were.

From that moment on my spirit took control and guided me through the changes in my life that I couldn't make before the hikuri killed me and the spirits of nature refilled my being. Finally, I was able to sit up, and as I watched the vultures fly away without their meal, I regained control of my body. But I wasn't the same person. My rational mind wasn't in control any longer. It was still there in the background but in a way similar to how my spirit used to take a backseat to my ego.

The most important part of this story is how my spirit was totally repulsed by the life I had led with my ego in charge. I flew home to New York City and walked the streets, literally looking at the world with new eyes. I was completely overcome by the sheer magnitude of the human enterprise: the noise, the grime, the foul air, the crowds, and especially the lack of psychic connection to the natural world. I could barely hear any input from any other living beings. I became painfully aware that the humans had killed or scared away all the natural spirits. They had created a spiritual vacuum, an island of purely human concerns.

Surrounded by over seven million people, I never felt so alone in my life. My holographic field, now cleansed and refilled by the pure energies of nature, searched frantically for something to hook on to. It went from face to face, but no one's field would greet it. Everyone's field seemed to be locked away behind closed doors. I didn't know what to do, but I was sure that I didn't want to live that way. And then I felt a ray of light. Something beautiful and pure had touched my field. I turned around and it was a little girl. She was about three years old and holding her mother's hand while they waited to cross the street. She was staring right at me, and I knew instantly that she could "see" the glow of my spirit shining out from me. Her spirit still guided her. It hadn't yet succumbed to the ego-driven world. Unlike all the adults around her, I could see her field glowing as clearly as if she were a wild deer running across the plain or an owl silently watching from a tree. She smiled at me and then she was gone. But within that smile, I found hope and the realization that all these adults had learned to lock away their spirit, just as I had learned to do while growing up, but just like me they could all learn how to set it free again.

HOLOGRAPHIC FIELDS AND
P-C CONJUGATE MIRRORS

My experience reveals our capacity to see and feel the holographic field when we are in a proper state of mind. The term *sixth sense* has been used to describe similar experiences to those of quantum holographic entanglement. However, this old concept not only limits our understanding of all our senses, it also implies that there is a special sense organ somewhere in our body or brain that would account for psychic-type experiences. None has been found. Quantum entanglement of holographic fields explains the "sixth sense" experiences we have.

Another highly useful aspect of the holographic field is our mirrors of the mind. Experiments of the pioneers of holography constructed four phase-conjugate (p-c) mirrors from three lasers. Two lasers meet head on; when a third is aimed into this configuration, it reflects much like raindrops reflect sunlight to make a rainbow. Ordinary mirrors reflect light according to the angle the light strikes the mirror, but p-c mirrors "self-target"—the reflection retraces the path back to its source at any angle of incidence. The reflection merges spatial and temporal information from all three input beams so data from several sources can be combined and fed back to a specific location. Mirrors form and vanish instantly as the lasers go on and off. Here we see how this light apparatus might mirror actual brain function. Imagine millions of coherent packets of light traveling through white and gray matter, meeting in strategic places, creating millions of p-c mirrors that synthesize and reflect information automatically and accurately to meaningful sites.

Remarkably similar to the holographic laser experiments, in our brain we have four ventricles linked into a winged structure. The two lateral ventricles are centered in the cerebral hemispheres, the third between the two halves of the thalamus and hypothalamus, and the fourth between the cerebellum and the brain stem. The concept of the brain communicating with itself via phase-conjugate mirrors and that coherent light energy is involved with the process of translating information from hyperspace into sensory memory and then into awareness and the ability of expression is a proposal based on science. However, I bring it up here because during certain shamanic practices we can actually view our own p-c mirrors and those of others. Some shamanic cultures have known and used this information long before any modern scientific explanation.

In terms of advanced shamanism, throughout this book we will be exploring some of the psi phenomena listed above, as well as hyperspace, holographic fields, p-c mirrors of the mind, and many other practices inspired by shamanic cultures. These include shamanic work with Grandfather Fire, shamanic death and rebirth, shamanic levels of attention, acquiring and working with spirit animals and healing stones, shamanic dreaming techniques, autogenic training, shamanic viewing, and shamanic healing.

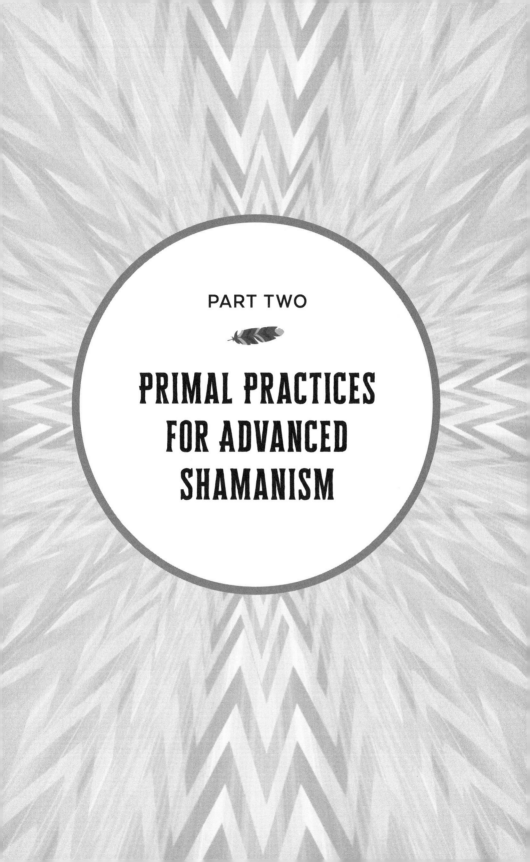

PART TWO

PRIMAL PRACTICES FOR ADVANCED SHAMANISM

5

Fundamental Practices: Part 1

This chapter and chapter 6 are devoted to six core practices that have the power to cultivate authentic shamanic experiences while fundamentally preparing you for the following practices. Most of these practices require long periods of time to fully complete, and I have intentionally placed them at the beginning of this book because you will need the experience and the tools of these practices for other advanced practices I will present. With few exceptions, authentic shamanic practices cannot be learned over a weekend or two. Almost all of the practices I will be presenting will take many months or years to fully accomplish.

During the course of the practices in this book, there are times when I will ask you to refer to another practice during the practice you are currently engaged in. Although the practices are organized and numbered linearly, you will at times be required to jump forward or back in the book during some practices. But please *do not* skip ahead and read the last practice of the book—The Five Points of Attention— until you are ready. If you do you will probably never accomplish this final practice. This will be explained in depth in practice 3. I can't urge you enough to be patient in order to fully experience the Five Points practice. Wait until the explanation of practice 3, and this will be made clear.

Practice 1

BRINGING FORTH THE SACRED FIRE WITH INTENTION

We begin the practices with a ritual of bringing forth Fire in a sacred way so that when working with Fire during certain other practices we have a time-tested shamanic method when engaging this powerful form of numinous energy. So important is this practice that I have laid it out in previous books. Here is the core explanation for those not yet familiar with it.

The rituals surrounding the preparation, ignition, and maintenance of the Sacred Fire vary greatly from one shamanic tradition to the next. I'm going to describe one way to go about these processes, a way that has evolved from many hundreds of experiences with indigenous shamans, work groups, and my own personal initiations and ceremonies with the Sacred Fire. I always encourage people to stay true to their own inner guidance in developing and employing rituals and ceremonies, especially when dealing with metaphysical powers in a shamanic setting; however, the way of relating to Fire that I am describing contains ancient and time-tested formulas that are successful at merging our human consciousness with Fire, and I invite you to try it this way whether or not you have previous experience with the fundamental energy of Fire.

The first step is to clear a small area where the Sacred Fire will lie. There is no need to make a giant fire. If you clear a circular area approximately thirty-six inches in diameter and make a bed for the fire eighteen inches in diameter, that should work nicely. Clearing the area implies removing all vegetative matter, and anything else that might be there, so that you have nothing but soil under and around the fire.

To make the bed for the fire, collect stones, preferably the size of your heart or fist, and place them in a circle on the area you have cleared. This formally delineates the space for the Sacred Fire to manifest and also solidifies the fact that you are ritually inviting and calling to the spirit of Fire to join you.

Next, you place the pillow for the Sacred Fire, a medium diameter log (six to ten inches in diameter), inside the stone circle and position it on the eastern side of the inside edge of the circle (the ends of the log will be facing north and south). Resting on this pillow will be the arrows of wood (usually thinner pieces of wood than the pillow) that will be the food of the Sacred Fire. The sticks used to feed Fire are called arrows because they point to a specific direction both physically and symbolically, and they are the vehicle of flight that delivers your messages to the spirit. If you placed your pillow in the east, all of the arrows rest on the pillow and point in the same direction toward the east and to the rising sun. Each time you give wood to Fire, you place the food in the same direction on the pillow, and in this way you are continually focusing your attention to the sun, which is the Fire that gives life to our planet. East is the default position; however, if you have a reason to point your arrows in a different direction, for example toward a trip you are taking or to a special place or person, simply position your pillow so your arrows point in the desired direction. The Huichol/Wirrarika shamans point their arrows to a pilgrimage site until they get there, and when they leave they reverse the pillow so their arrows point to home for the trip back.

How you actually ignite your fire will depend entirely on your skill and relationship with Fire. Since this is a sacred practice of working with Fire, and not a lesson in survival training, using matches or a lighter is fine. In all cases, whether experienced or not, remember that this Sacred Fire is fed exclusively with wood sticks placed only in one direction; placing them across one another would introduce opposing and distracting forces to the ritual. Making a quick and hot fire by crisscrossing sticks of wood can work well to maximize the efficiency of oxygen and fuel when making a fire for cooking or in a survival situation, but this is a Sacred Fire that is being induced into being for completely different reasons. The flame of the Sacred Fire is brought to life by a mixture of physical realities and metaphysical inputs. So please throw out all of your purely logical and scientific formulas and make the Fire with your heart and not your head.

Start by placing very dry and thin sticks as the first layer of arrows and then slowly add larger diameter sticks until the fire is established. If there are pine trees in the area you are working, dead, thin, lower branches are perfect for this. I usually carry a small supply of lower pine tree branches and resinous tinder with me. The tinder is friends with Fire, and it ignites very easily.

As soon as your Sacred Fire comes to life, start talking. You want to speak directly to the unique energetic phenomenon that is the flame. I refer to Fire as "Grandfather." I learned this from my Huichol shaman mentors. Although the visions Fire delivers aren't particularly male, as suggested by the name *grandfather,* I find it extremely useful to name Fire in this way as a form of both respect and personal human connection. In a world that is sometimes confusing, it is comforting and empowering to refer on a personal level to Mother Earth, Father Sun, Grandmother Growth, and Grandfather Fire, not just as a form of delineation but as a way to personally identify with the enormous powers that they imply.

To begin speaking with Grandfather Fire, it is proper to respectfully greet him and then briefly state your intention. If you are in a group, everyone can greet Grandfather at the same time. If you choose to have the group greet Grandfather Fire individually, then the person who lit the fire should speak first. The greeting goes like this, "Welcome Grandfather Fire, thank you for joining me (us) with your light, energy, and ancient wisdom. I am here before you tonight to [*briefly* describe what you intend to do with Fire; you will go into more specifics when you actually do your work]."

When you begin your work, it is proper to start by directly addressing Grandfather Fire by saying, "Grandfather Fire, in front of you, Grandmother Growth, and all my companions, I [clearly state the first item of your work with Grandfather Fire]." When we say "all my companions," we are not only referring to human companions but *all* the living entities and elements around you—animals, trees, wind, stars, and sky. This is the formal setup when working shamanically with

Grandfather Fire. From here you continue to feed sticks to Grandfather Fire (all sticks on the pillow in the same direction) when needed or place a stick arrow as an offering of intent while passing through the different phases of your work.

This is the general format for working with Grandfather Fire for any reason and for practices outlined in this book.

Practice 2
FIRE CEREMONY—RECLAIMING LOST ENERGY BY HEALING ENERGETIC DRAINS

This practice uses a powerful technique called recapitulation, which is performed while working with Grandfather Fire. Recapitulation begins with creating lists of people and events from your life that you want (actually need) to be energetically free from. Then one by one you cleanse them from your energy field through specific breathing techniques while psychically reliving the events. This intense and powerful practice can take years to fully perform; however, within a couple of weeks of doing it, the results both energetically and psychologically will be easy to feel.

I learned this highly effective technique of recapitulation from Mexican shamanic researcher Victor Sanchez, who developed it, inspired by the books of Carlos Castaneda. I spent many years learning about and teaching this technique with Victor in Mexico. On two occasions I participated in a two-week recapitulation workshop during which participants spent fourteen nights sitting inside wooden boxes to recapitulate their lives. I have also spent many years recapitulating on my own and have utilized this technique for probably close to two thousand hours, and it has changed my life for the better. Victor's specific technique is covered in his book *The Toltec Path of Recapitulation: Healing Your Past to Free Your Soul*. The technique I am presenting here is a condensed and modified version that I have adapted with the addition of the Sacred Fire as a numinous impartial teacher. In various moments during recapitulation, the Sacred Fire will act as a portal into both your consciousness and energetic body; in other moments, Fire will be a mirror in which we can see our actions.

For our first practice I want to start off by making sure we make a solid attempt to have as much available energy as you can upon entering into the other shamanic practices in the book. Energetic drains take real effort to deal with because they come in so many different varieties. For most of us, if we sit and think for a few moments, we can immediately come up with a number of situations in our life, both present and past, that are energy draining. These situtations would be the first ones to work on. But there are also events and situations that we don't want to admit to ourselves are energy draining. And of course we also have events from the past that we block out in an attempt to not be hurt by them any longer.

The good news is that once you begin to work on energetic drains that you are presently conscious of, the increase in available energy saved by healing those drains helps you to discover and deal with "undercover" drains that were previously hidden or that you were avoiding because you didn't have the energy to deal with them.

The basis behind recapitulation, as well as other techniques dealing with energy drains, is that you intentionally engage in healing them by identifying, patching, and then healing them. Patching involves actions that temporarily mend or stop an energy drain. To illustrate this, I'll run through a few examples using a technique adapted from teachings by my Wirrarika mentors.

In this technique Grandfather Fire is brought in to help inspire, facilitate, and purify. In all cases when working with Fire, I prefer to be outdoors with an actual wood fire made in a sacred way (see practice 1); however, with significant intention, a simple candle can be used effectively. I prefer five candles: a candle placed in each of the four directions plus one in the center.

The first stage is identifying energetic drains at mental, physical, environmental, and spiritual levels. Here is a list of some typical energetic drains:

Mental Drains

Negative thinking

Impatience

Superficial relationships

Repetitive thoughts or actions

Unresolved conflicts with people

Avoiding the forgiveness of others

Inability to ask for forgiveness

Trying to keep up with the neighbors

Physical Drains

Eating unhealthy foods

Misplacing emotional needs by treating your body poorly

Not getting sufficient rest

Not providing your body with exercise to keep it healthy

Paying too much attention to your physical appearance

Avoiding medical and dental issues

Spending day after day at a job that is physically unhealthy or overly
    sedentary

Environmental Drains

Stress about where you live, wanting to move

Transportation and household items in need of repair

Clutter and disorganization

Unreturned phone calls and e-mails

Missing being part of a supportive community

Lack of beauty or inspiring surroundings

Noise and too much television

Feeling overwhelmed by all the information you are bombarded
    with every day

Spiritual Drains

Missing quality friendships

Missing romantic partners

Being in a relationship that compromises your values

Not making the time to release and nurture your creative energy

Lack of activities that feed your spiritual nature

Clinging to outdated or intolerant spiritual beliefs

In reviewing the complexity of modern life, we can easily see that this is a short list of energy-draining possibilities. Having spent many years working with people in this technique with Fire, two broad categories are almost always present. The first is the energy-draining circumstance of tolerating dysfunction. This happens on physical and environmental levels: traffic, intense workload, loneliness in the media age, bad diet, inefficient processes, and wasteful activities. These things combined are energy killers. Our constant dysfunctional relationship with our environment and our hearts can result in a significant decrease in life force.

Another major energy draining circumstance happens when we take care of ourselves last. In other words, although providing for loved ones or fulfilling other types of obligations can feel satisfying and may be quite necessary, doing so also requires energy. If we continue to give our energy after we are already running low, not only do we risk health issues but also feelings of resentment and animosity may set in, which are major energy drainers and only make the situation worse. Taking the required time to take care of ourselves makes us more efficient when taking care of the things in our life.

Reclaiming energy in this technique begins by identifying the energy drainers I have listed above, as well as the others I have not, that are a part of your current life. Writing them down is the first step. You can list them in the manner I have done or group them into other categories such as:

- My Relationships
- My Body
- My Work

- My Money
- My Home
- My Thoughts
- My Spirit
- My Natural Environment

Once you have your list, sit or stand in front of the Sacred Fire and confess your energy draining actions to Fire.* Use your voice for this; don't try to use telepathy. Speaking clearly out loud will help you to project and move energy. If you have trustful companions to witness you do this, even better.

After the confession choose two or three energy draining actions that you feel confident you can heal. You want to make sure you have a good chance of healing these because once you do you will have more available energy for healing others. Don't go straight for the biggest ones. For example, if you are a longtime smoker and have tried to quit many times before, you probably don't have sufficient available energy to do it simply because of all the other smaller energy drains you have. By fixing the smaller ones first, you will then have the energy available for dealing with a major one like a long-term addiction. Healing energy drains has a snowball effect. The more you heal, the more momentum is gathered for continued healing.

Next, choose your first energy draining action: state it out loud, and while looking into the flames "see" yourself doing the action as if watching yourself in a movie. For example, if the situation you have chosen is your messy office, then visualize yourself in different moments when you have created the clutter.

Now, shift your perspective and relive moments in your messy office. Be there by seeing through your eyes and reliving how it feels in that space.

---

*This is nothing like confessing your "sins" as in the Catholic religion. Here we are dealing with energy drains, not morality.

After reliving this situation, shift your awareness back to being with Fire and make a commitment to resolving this issue and the time period it will take you. State it out loud.

In the flames visualize the outcome of your positive energy action. In this example you will see your office clean and organized.

The last step is to give your energy draining action to Fire and ask for help in completing your task. Typically, you give fuel to the Sacred Fire, so in this case you could write the energy draining situation down on a small piece of paper and feed it to Fire while asking for support. You can also feed a stick to Fire.

By completing these tasks, you will, however, have only patched the energy drain. Your continued vigilance will be needed to keep the patch on until you have fully healed. For example, just because you cleaned your office doesn't mean it will stay clean. Use the fire or a candle flame to stay connected with your energy draining commitments.

Obviously the above example is a simple problem compared to emotional trauma or physical abuse. But events of that kind can be dealt with in the same way. For example, if you have been feeling guilty for not making amends with a deceased loved one before he or she passed away, you would see yourself in the flames interacting with that person, and then you would relive your experiences with him or her and ask forgiveness or asked to be forgiven or whatever else needs to be said (do this out loud just as if the person were sitting with you). You then make a decision and a commitment with regard to this situation. For example, the patch would be to deal with a situation with a loved one that you have been avoiding. To fully heal, you commit with Fire from now on to say what needs to be said in the moment it needs saying.

To be truly effective with this technique you will need to use all your creativity and resources. Start small and begin healing the drains that are easier to accomplish. Once you do this you will feel an increase in available energy, and that energy will help you to conquer your more difficult energy draining thoughts and habitual actions.

Here are some tips and additional considerations that may help you when using this technique:

Practice reliving the past. Seeing yourself like a movie in your energy draining situation is fairly easy for most people, but shifting your awareness *into* the energy draining situation in order to relive it is tricky until you get the feel for it. To help, you can practice doing this with all kinds of positive situations as well. Consciously and energetically relive special moments in your life—beautiful places you have been, significant events you have attended—until you get a good feel for the process of reliving.

Make commitments. Coming up with commitments for patching energy drains will sometimes take a fair amount of creativity and may require more than one session with Fire. For example, if you constantly worry about money problems, a solution to this may not be readily apparent. First, ask the Sacred Fire and use the sacred flame to help you with insights and then be open to receive answers, especially answers that may not be the most comfortable to accept. If you still don't see a solution, work on other energy drains first. Once your available energy has increased, you will be able to work through any problem you face.

Make a plan of action. Moving from patching to truly healing a major energy drain requires sound strategy. You must come up with a legitimate plan of action that will keep you on a healthy energetic path. For example, patching an energetic drain caused by someone physically abusing you may include being able to forgive that person, reclaiming the energy you have lost to that situation, and helping other abused people. But truly healing from that event may mean intentionally creating healthy relationships with others or engaging in random acts of kindness with the people around you (even if they don't know you're doing something nice for them) so that you counteract the effects of the injury.

Forgive yourself if a patch comes off. Energetic healing can be a time-consuming and challenging process with both successes and failures. This is one of the main reasons to use the sacred flame. In moments of doubt and weakness, go to the Sacred Fire and feel the numinous energy throughout your whole being. Gain strength from this ancient energy, and then continue on your path.

This practice is obviously something you don't do on an everyday basis. It takes planning and preparation, and you may need to do it several times to accomplish your goal, but it's well worth it. With more of our energy available, we have a much better chance to fully experience the rest of the practices in this book.

Practice 3
THE THREE POINTS OF ATTENTION

This is an advanced practice taught to me by Huichol/Wirrarika shamans. The story of how I learned it is recounted in my book *Teachings of the Peyote Shamans: The Five Points of Attention.*

Once we have begun to heal our energetic drains and therefore have more available energy (practice 2), we can use this energy in various ways. One way to employ this energy is to both focus and expand our attention. Expansion in this practice is via splitting our attention—to consciously place our attention on first three and then five points. This splitting of attention is achieved without a reduction in any of the points.

For example, we will first split our attention into three points, but we will not be using only a third of our capacity on each. Each point will receive 100 percent of our attention. This situation is a shamanic paradox that is not easily achieved even with training and practice. Most modern people will never experience this integrative state of consciousness simply because they don't know it exists or that it's even possible. However, if you can experience the five points of attention, you open the door of shamanic consciousness to infinite possibilities in the realms of attention and perception. At this level all shamanic practices are more easily mastered. The added bonus of this practice is that in our everyday lives we become infinitely more aware, which fosters a calm and humble confidence during any situation. Grasping and then practicing this technique can take time. If you are patient and dedicated to learning it, in time it will become second nature, and you will wonder how you ever got through life without it!

Focusing on Two Points of Attention

In this part of the practice you will create a drawing that will serve as an instructional tool for learning about the five attentions.

1. Draw a circle with an even-sided cross inside the circle, using a stick on dirt or with pencil and paper. The four ends of the cross should intersect and stop at the circle.
2. In the center of the cross write the word *me*.
3. Where the right arm of the cross meets the circle write *object*.
4. Left of the center of the right arm draw an arrow pointing to *me*.
5. Right of center of the right arm put down an arrow pointing to *object*.

We can see the drawing has five points: four at the intersections of the cross and the circle and one in the middle. All the points are con-

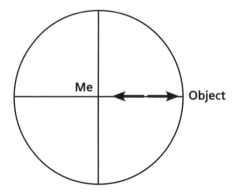

Fig. 5.1 Two Points of Attention

nected and illustrate the five points of attention. Right now, we have labeled two points: *me* (me, myself, I) and *object* (object, entity, thing, situation).

The arrow pointing to *me* illustrates your attention focusing on yourself. The arrow pointing to *object* illustrates the placement of attention on something other than you. As you can see, we now have two arrows, two points of attention. If you can place your attention on the object and still focus on yourself, then you have split your attention in two. This is not a normal state of consciousness for most people.

During most of the day attention is placed outward to what we are doing. In some moments we pay attention to our self, especially when we are being careful about what we say or when we are looking in the mirror or when we stub a toe. But we almost always are placing our awareness on one or the other. Rarely do we place our attention on both *at the same time*. When I explain this to my students, someone will often ask, "How is this different from multitasking?" Shaman Jesús provides an answer, excerpted from my book, *Teachings of the Peyote Shamans: The Five Points of Attention*:

Jesús looked at me quizzically. I wondered if I used the proper words in Spanish. So I added, "We call multitasking doing various things at the same time. Like many people drive their car, talk on their cell phone, read a map, and eat a bagel all at the same time. Isn't our attention split most of the time?"

Chuckling, Jesús replied, "The attention of the object can be used in a multitude of ways. But I am betting that the person driving that car is not paying attention to their essence, to their true being, while they are doing all those other things. That takes a special effort of concentration. And if they were to do that, I also bet that they would immediately stop talking and eating and pay closer attention on their driving. Or maybe they would give up driving altogether. In your other example, thinking about a situation, even one that has to do with yourself, is not the same as paying attention to your inner self. You are placing attention on the details of the situation."[1]

According to Jesús, we have three important aspects that make us who we are. We have our ego: I am this and I am that. We have our essence: our true being that we are born with. And we have our individual personality: our acquired characteristics.

Our essence is what lives inherently inside each one of us—it is our inner quality, our level of being, our innermost values. It asks us to seek questions: Who am I? Where did I come from? Where am I going? When people live their life centered in ego, they are imbalanced, in disharmony, like someone trapped on an island alone his whole life. There needs to be harmony among essence, personality, and ego. Harmony opens the door to true self-knowledge and the light of the divine.

Maintaining the first two points—simultaneously thinking of self and object—is the beginning of looking outward, beyond self. You place your attention internally in the direction toward your feelings and overall health, surveying yourself both physically and mentally, while also paying attention to the object, that which is outside yourself. However, once you have experienced enough times doing this, you will come to a point where the exercise becomes completely different because you will begin to touch your essence.

Focusing on Three Points of Attention

Now we come to another paradoxical shamanic situation: it is incredibly difficult to divide human attention in two, but it is actually easier to divide it into three and later five. These unexplainable situations are a big part of why I practice shamanism—the thrill of diving into the unknown, knowing sheer intellect will not reach the goal. It is only through experience that we learn about things that are true, even if we cannot explain it.

The third point of attention is *place*. This depicts where you are and why you are there. Now write *place* on your drawing at the point where the left arm meets the circle. In the same way as you did on the right arm, draw an arrow pointing to *me* and one pointing to *place*.

From now on focus on these three points of attention.

1. *Me.* Do not forget yourself. Always watch yourself. Pay attention at all times to your words, actions, gestures, habits, even your thoughts and emotions.
2. *Object.* Be thoroughly attentive to objects, entities, situations, anything outside you that you can interpret with your senses.
3. *Place.* Observe at all times where you are and be cognizant of why you are there.

It is most important to remember *not* to become infatuated with one point of attention. Whether it is yourself, an object, or a place, no matter how interesting, beautiful, horrible, entrancing, or atrocious something is, don't focus one point of attention to such an extent that the others are left out. If you do that you will miss the whole point. When attending to the three points at once becomes natural during your daily life, the challenge is then to keep that attention during special circumstances. The goal is to keep attentive to all three points, even during stressful moments.

My teacher had me experience the three attentions while crawling on the ground in the high-altitude desert where his tribe lives. I do this with students in my training classes in the Green Mountains: the woods are kinder on the knees but still very potent and appropriate. Placing yourself in a situation that is completely foreign to you makes splitting your attention from one to three easier because you are not as tempted to fall back on the habitual ways you use your attention. Without talking, having lots of people around, media distractions, upholding your ego and personality, and so on, breaking through and experiencing the three-way split of attention can unfold naturally and in accordance with your true essence.

The idea is simple. In a natural setting have a partner go approximately one to two hundred yards away from you. It's helpful for your partner to be ahead of you on a trail so you will know when you reach your destination (your partner). If you don't have a partner, you can use something to mark your destination. Wear whatever clothing you need to be safe, but avoid gloves if possible.

To begin, simply get down on your knees and focus on each of the three points of attention. Place attention on *yourself:* feel your body, and notice your feelings and emotions. Place attention on *objects:* notice all the different plants, rocks, colors, sounds, tastes, smells—everything that is outside your body and your head. Place attention on this *place:* keep cognizant of where you are in the *bigger picture,* beyond the ground you are crawling on. You are in the middle of a vast and magical place. These three states of attention are completely different from one another, although you will try to experience them all at the same time.

When you feel ready, begin to crawl toward your destination while keeping in mind that the physical destination is secondary to your real destination—simultaneous awareness of the three points of attention. The act of crawling in nature is a wonderful way to break down our feelings of superiority toward nature and allows us to place our attention outside the sphere of our merely human concerns.

In this setting the awareness of the three points of attention typically comes fairly easily. It is common when experiencing this to also feel a state of inner silence. Attending to the three points of attention while crawling in nature tends to quiet our inner voice of its incessant talking. When this happens paying attention to yourself won't be through words in your mind anymore. It will be more like a sort of pure knowing and feeling.

You will perceive everything purely through your senses, no filters, biases, or analysis: the feeling of the ground under your hands and knees, the sight of the shapes and colors of rocks, earth, plants, twigs, and insects, the taste of dust and sweat, the sounds of birds, the wind in the leaves, and your movement as you crawl along.

The attention of place can be bolstered a couple of ways—by raising your head and fully realizing where you are on a grand or planetary level and also feeling the energy of the place on an intimate level. How does the place feel? What season is it? What's going on right now in this place? This initial experience of splitting but being aware of the three attentions all at once is a remarkable achievement. While in this integrative state of consciousness your ego and personality are temporarily placed in the backseat, and your true essence shines through.

You may not have experienced your true essence since you were a very young child. For some of us, our true essence is only experienced during a dangerous or extremely special situation, such as a severe accident, the miracle of childbirth, or the death of a loved one. This practice opens the door to experiencing our essence on a daily basis without extreme circumstances being the catalyst.

When I asked the Huichol shaman about the practical use of the three attentions, he replied, "The experience you just had will only be truly practical when you employ it to other life situations. For example, when talking to people, working, writing, etc. If you can focus on your three points of attention during your ordinary life, you will see extraordinary results with regard to your quality of life. It is almost impossible to be living in your true essence and still have unhealthy feelings of anger, depression, arrogance, jealousy, selfishness. Your essence wants you to discover and live with your true talents and in states of happiness, kindness, cooperation, unity, and wonder. Also, once you have become proficient in living with the attention of the three points, you will then be able to raise your level to five points, which is a most magnificent and mature state of conscious living. People who live solely within their ego and personality cannot possibly comprehend this state of being."

When I teach this initial exercise of perceiving the three attentions at once, most people experience it on their first try. If you don't, simply try again right away or on another day. Don't pressure yourself. If you do feel you have accomplished this first step, be aware that you may feel tired or energetically drained. This is common for us modern people.

Our first attempt at reaching the three attentions tends to use up our current available energy. It takes great effort for modern people to make the breakthrough. This can be referred to as the "little death" because the dominating ego and personality are switched off. Your attention was split and pulled so far away from where it normally resides that when released from that far-off place, it snaps back and goes past its usual place. Kind of like the band of a slingshot.

The best thing to do right way is to do something nice for yourself (I'm talking about something healthy): take a walk, take a bath, go swimming, get a massage, eat a delicious meal. Also, I recommend not jumping straight back into everyday life. Give your energy some time to recharge. Through time and practice with this technique you will find that not only will you not use up your energy, you will gain available energy through living closer to your true essence.

Once you have initially experienced the three attentions, the practical use of this amazing ISC is the goal. At this stage of the training we attempt to cultivate the awareness of the three attentions during our everyday life. The most difficult aspect of this practice is learning how to experience the three attentions at will and hold onto this ISC over long periods or all the time, which is a tremendous achievement.

Because of the way we have been trained to think our whole lives, we easily slip back into one attention without even realizing it. When I first came back home after learning this technique, I would very naturally simply get sucked into whatever it was I was doing, which placed my attention squarely on the object. I would first have to intentionally realize what I was doing and then try to go back to the attention of three. It amazed me how well trained my awareness was to constantly remain on one attention. I could easily expand to three when I intended to, but in the beginning, without even realizing it, I would revert to one.

Eventually the more you practice, the easier it becomes to stay aware of where your attention is going. I developed a little trick that I used during my first six months of trying to master this technique (my teachers laughed when I told them about this trick, but it really works).

Get a timer; a sports timer works well. Set it for an hour or less (half an hour was best for me). During the beginning of your day, enter the awareness of the three attentions and try to stay there. If you are like me and most of my students when they started, you will quickly revert to one. When your timer goes off, check where your attention is. If not on three (which will probably be the case), reset your timer and refocus your attention to three and try to stay there as long as you can before your timer goes off. You will experience a wordless feeling of humble accomplishment when you finally hear your timer and you are still in the attention of three.

Master Three Attentions before Attempting More

My shaman teacher would not tell me about the other two attentions at all, nothing except that they exist, until I could prove mastery of the first three attentions. Once you know what the other two are, it's pretty much impossible not to try them, even if you haven't mastered three. But attempting to do the five attentions too soon can be devastating for your chances of learning the first three; if you don't learn the first three first, you won't make the ultimate goal of five. So please take this advice: don't ruin your chances of attaining the five attentions by reading the last practice in this book, practice 38 in chapter 15, until you have mastered this one. While you are engaged in mastering the first three attentions, I encourage you to practice anything else in this book except the practices in chapters 13 and 14, where you will learn how to cultivate the ISC of the five attentions for direct shamanic viewing and healing. As soon as you have mastered the three attentions, then go ahead and read, practice, and master the five attentions, no matter where you are in the other practices in this book.

6

Fundamental Practices:
Part 2

In the last chapter you learned how to prepare a Sacred Fire, how to gain more energy by freeing yourself from some of your energy drains, and how to focus on three points of attention simultaneously. All of these skills are fundamental to the practice of shamanism. In this chapter I present three more fundamental practices that go a little deeper into shifting your consciousness away from ordinary perception and toward shamanic union with the holographic field. Even if you are still working on mastering the skills presented in the last chapter—some of them may take years to perfect—you can continue to add to your basic shamanic toolbox by working on the practices presented here.

Practice 4
ACQUIRING SPIRIT ANIMAL GUIDES—
THE JICARA

Modern neoshamanic techniques employing guided imagery using animals have been shown to raise awareness of our relationship to the animal kingdoms. But though an animal that "comes to mind" may indeed have significance to someone's current life situation, classic shamanic practices that make tangible contact with the multidimensional realms rely much more on the shaman's knowledge of an actual animal than on what he imagines. The way to receive a visit from the spirit of an animal is to become part of the environment where the animal that contains the spirit dwells. The more you become part of that environment, and the more time you spend with and around the animal, the deeper the spirit of that animal will affect your holographic p-c mirrors and your hyperspace field. For example, a chance encounter with an animal while on vacation somewhere could certainly affect you, as the spirit of that animal makes contact with your holographic field and hyperspace, but living for a significant period of time in that environment and making contact on a daily basis with the spirit of that animal will place you into an interactive relationship with what animates that spirit. At this level you are becoming familiar with not only the spirit of that particular animal but also the living environment that sustains and nurtures it. By submerging your hyperspace and p-c mirrors into the living world of the animal, you are knocking on the front door of the house of the animal spirit and asking to come inside.

I realize that for many people interested in shamanism, the animals that are common to where we live are considered just that—common or ordinary—and so are often overlooked when it comes to tapping into their magic and mystery. As an experienced and professionally advanced Fire shaman for over twenty years, I have observed how animal spirits come to people as the people become open and ready to receive them. If you live in the city, the spirit of the city squirrel may be much more approachable for you to work with on a daily basis than the spirit of a deer living in a secluded place in the mountains. There is a reason you both live in the city, or the suburbs, or the country. By already sharing the everyday sights, sounds, and smells of the area where you live, you already have much in common with those beings that you share your neighborhood with. What you consider to be familiar can tell you a lot about who you are.

A powerful shamanic technique for employing the unique energy and essence of an animal spirit is to fashion a *jicara* that is infused by the spirit of the animal and by the living entities that support the animal.

The word *jicara,* in this context borrowed from the Wirrarika language, refers to a bowl used to hold sacred items. But in this case, even though the jicara exists in physical form, the objects being held by it come together to form something much more than the physical items themselves. The items contained by the jicara are the embodiment of something truly unspeakable. I'm going to call the unspeakable aspect of the jicara its spirit, simply because the word *spirit* is commonly used to refer to a type of invisible animating force.

Although the jicara has a physical appearance, it is not a static object, form of art, or some type of novelty item or trinket. On the contrary, when the jicara is fashioned from the living energies offered to you by a particular animal spirit, the jicara is alive with that spirit and can be worked with just as if the actual spirit of the live animal were with you.

Fashioning an animal spirit jicara begins with the bowl. The physical shape of the bowl helps create a spiraling vortex, which acts as a womb to hold the spirit of the animal. The bowl is usually a gourd or made of clay and should be fashioned by you or acquired from someone close to you who has a genuine love for the materials of the bowl. The jicara will not be fully activated until the bowl is consecrated with the blood of the animal in the presence of what I like to call the five life-giving energies: earth, water, air, fire, and spirit.

Consecrating the jicara with the blood of the animal means that you will need the physical body of the animal in your hands, most often found and already dead. Shamanic practice is fiercely opposed to any brutal force to find your spirit animal. Let me be clear that due to the catastrophic circumstances currently being faced by animal spirits throughout the globe, I do not condone the hunting of any predatory animal, and with prey animals I only suggest a form of "hunting" in which you don't actually hunt the animal but rather put yourself in a place to receive the animal if the spirit of the animal decides to grant you its flesh and blood. In all other cases, which compose the vast majority, you are rewarded with the body of an animal, by the animal spirit, because of your perseverance and commitment to that spirit. You will find this offering to you from the animal spirit *when you are ready* to receive it.

It can take time, even years, to find your true spirit animal. This is simply part of the process, and in the meantime you will begin to work with the animal spirit to establish your connection and initiate your relationship. This implies seeking out the physical manifestation of the animal and spending time with it—watching it, studying it, talking to it, and discovering everything you can about it. During this time you will be collecting experiences, which will play an important part in the formation of the jicara.

As you have more and more experiences with the animal, you can gradually begin to collect the essences for the jicara by obtaining specific items infused with the energies that support the animal. These items can include living energies from the animal's habitat, foods that it eats, items from other animals that are its ally or enemy—in short, anything that you deem significant to the animal through your actual experiences with it (not what you have read or been told about it) can potentially be used to form the jicara. The decision as to what or what not to use is purely personal; however, the more significant to the animal the items are, the more power the jicara will hold.

To illustrate what might be included in a jicara, here is a list of things that form my current jicara of the wild turkey spirit:

- One fully feathered wing from each of the last two wild turkeys that have given their life to me and that I've eaten. The feathered wings hold the key to the turkey's ability to mysteriously disappear, blend into its environment, and escape powerful entities that want to devour it.
- Drawings on the outside of the bowl depicting various significant events I've shared with the wild turkey spirit.
- Important foods that I've seen the wild turkey feeding on: acorns, crabapple, red cedar, blackberry, cricket, grasshopper.

- Items from the wild turkey's predators: red-tailed hawk feathers, red fox teeth, two bullet shell casings blessed with deer blood.
- Items that form the wild turkey nest: oak and tulip tree leaves, poison ivy and sumac vines.
- Miscellaneous items: I put soil from under a wild turkey nest into the bottom of the jicara to stick feathers into and to drip sacred blood into; apple tree twigs from the orchard I often find the turkeys in; a small piece of deer hide because for me the two animals are connected; a small Huichol yarn drawing of the sun to honor my Huichol shaman mentor's connection to the turkey, which is a bird of the sun; and small personal items from moments when the wild turkey spirit aided me in the course of my everyday life or during specific ceremonies and workshops.

This particular jicara is an active participant in my life, especially in the spring and fall when I renew the jicara with offerings and ask the turkey spirit to share its flesh with me once again. The items in the jicara sometimes change as my knowledge of this spirit evolves and grows and also when I add items from personal experiences that the wild turkey spirit has influenced in some way. These types of periodic additions keep the jicara alive and the relationship with it active. As you acquire new experiences associated with the spirit of a particular jicara, the power becomes cumulative, and the jicara grows from infancy to maturity as your relationship with the animal spirit deepens and intensifies.

The energy of the jicara can be used in many practical ways and is in no way imaginary. All of the energies and essences included in it are real and tangible, and most importantly they have been collected and honored by you through your hard work, time, and effort. All of the things that compose the jicara, and the countless individual moments you experienced while fashioning the jicara, make it a living extension of both the animal spirit and yourself. That is what gives the jicara the power to aid and support you. Each animal spirit, and therefore each jicara made to hold an animal spirit, has unique qualities pertaining to both the spirit of the animal and the person who fashioned the jicara. To continue with my example of the wild turkey jicara, here is a list of circumstances in which I have employed the wild turkey jicara or it has voluntarily helped me. Please be aware that your connection with this same spirit could be much different, and I'm including these personal examples simply to help illustrate the kind of circumstances in which an animal jicara can be employed.

Ceremonial use. Since for me the wild turkey is a bird of the sun, I use the feathers of the jicara during sunrise ceremonies and in moments during other ceremonies, rituals, or healings to infuse the light and energy of the sun into circumstances, objects, or living beings.

Renewal. I use the jicara to petition the spirit of the wild turkey to offer itself to me once or twice a year in the form of a live bird to consume and also to renew my jicara with fresh feathers and blood.

Merging. Since the wild turkey jicara is active in my shamanic work, I consult with it before and during many different kinds of situations. Sometimes this is done by talking directly to the jicara while it is sitting in its special place in my house and by merging my awareness and consciousness with the spirit of the jicara to receive its unique perspective.

The best way I have found to initiate this merging is by first activating memories of specific moments with the wild turkey, seeing the particular event like a movie in front of my eyes, and then reliving the event through connection in my hyperspace field. Through reconnecting with the energetic essences of the items that the jicara is holding, I infuse the energy of the wild turkey spirit into my conscious awareness. It is important to note that this technique is completely the opposite of imagination. By having a tangible connection at the most intimate level with all of the components of the jicara and to the wild turkey, all of their essences are available to me at all levels of my awareness—mind, body, environment, and spirit. I am in no way imagining my relationship to the wild turkey spirit; I have tangibly developed it over long periods of time.

Connection. I also use memory, not just mental but also bodily memory, to evoke the power of the jicara when I am not physically near it. Since I have such a tangible connection to the jicara, I can easily connect to it at any moment I need to. For example, sometimes when I am away from home writing, as I am in this moment, I connect with the jicara to obtain help with my writing. The energy of the jicara contains the grounding qualities of the earth and the patience of the hen that sits on her eggs for up to a month. Connecting to this energy of the jicara keeps me in my chair writing at times when I need help to keep seated and focused on what I'm writing.

The wild turkey spirit also does a lot of scratching and digging in the earth to find things, and when I connect to that movement of the turkey, it helps me to keep digging into the concepts and ideas I am trying to convey. When I connect to the wings of the jicara, sometimes I feel the light of the sun and that gives me inspiration. Other times I can feel the wind created by the forceful flapping of the wild turkey as it takes off from the ground in flight, and that invokes in me a state of mind where everything falls away except what I am doing with the words I am writing.

Protection. When traveling to places where I have a greater chance of being singled out and taken advantage of because of my looks or nationality, I ask the spirit of the wild turkey to help me blend in and walk unnoticed. Sometimes I will take an item or two from the jicara with me when traveling to especially dangerous places like the inner cities of third world countries where I could be easily singled out.

Group work. Since the wild turkey is a bird that lives in flocks, and I tend to be a solitary person, I sometimes use the spirit of the wild turkey jicara to help me when I work with groups of adults and children and also in my personal relationships.

The most important aspect to working with an animal spirit through a jicara is the collecting of the items and experiences connected with the animal spirit that you fashion the jicara from. Once the jicara is consecrated and fully awakened with the blood of the animal, you will be taught by the jicara itself how to use it. But getting to that point is the biggest challenge and implies a lot of work and commitment. The only way you can collect the essences and energies that sustain and nurture your animal spirit is if you spend significant time with it while learning all you can about it.

Some people are squeamish or even offended by the idea that the jicara has to be activated with the animal's blood. So let me just say that this absolutely necessary step should not be a source of preoccupation while you are collecting your experiences with the animal spirit and fashioning your jicara. When the animal spirit you are working with realizes a significant connection to *you* the *spirit will send you* the physical manifestation of its spirit in the form of a flesh and blood animal. I have found this to be true in every single case during my many initiations with animal, bird, fish, reptile, and insect spirits.

Even though with my example of the wild turkey I do personally take the life of the physical turkeys I use for my jicara, that is only my personal situation with that particular spirit. With the exception of the wild turkey, white-tailed deer, and a few species of fish, the rest of my many animal spirit jicaras are consecrated with the blood and body parts from animals that I find already dead in the moment and place appointed by the spirit of the animal. For example, the most recent jicara I made was for the red-headed woodpecker spirit. I would never think about taking the life of such a bird. But when both the spirit of the bird and I were ready, I found waiting for me the body of a red-headed woodpecker lying under its favorite dead tree—the same tree that I had sat under countless times while watching and listening to the woodpecker work. Again, the only way you will be able to collect this most important essence is if you are in intimate contact with the environment of the animal.

The hard truth is that if you can't work with the dead body of your animal spirit ally, then you have not yet accepted the organic reality of the world. In advanced shamanism we must relate to the spirit of the animal at a deep enough level that it is in the shamanic way. If you are a vegan, a vegetarian, or an animal rights activist, I want to make clear that this has nothing to do with eating meat or cruelty to animals. If we are naturally offered feathers, antlers, claws, or a tooth, it is paramount as shamans that we make use of them. Only when you look at the beautiful body of a dead animal and realize that the spirit of that animal gave this to you—a treasured gift to help you learn about the animal and take your knowledge to the next level—will you be able to thank the spirit by consecrating and activating the living spirit of your jicara with the flesh and blood of the animal it contains.

Since my wild turkey spirit was shy (all wild turkeys and most wild animals are shy), it did not want me to share a photo of its jicara. By contrast, my turkey vulture spirit is not shy in the least! Figure 6.1 is a photograph of my current turkey vulture jicara. It contains the following items:

Three large vulture feathers—two from the wing tips (on right and left side) and one from the tail (center).

A hawk feather (right side). Although the vulture and hawk aren't necessarily friends, they do share the thermals of the sky, and sometimes vultures will watch which tree a hawk lands in to feed after a kill, and it will eat the scraps on the ground that the hawk leaves.

A pea hen feather (left side). This is a rather rare and recent addition. On the farm where I live we have an adult peahen; surprisingly enough I have seen her "hanging out" and watching the turkey vultures spreading their wings in the morning sun, and they seem to be friends!

A small piece of branch from a dead tree this vulture and her tribe roost in. This item makes the spirit feel at home.

A deer antler. Deer meat made up a significant portion of this bird's diet via roadkill and during hunting season.

Two more smaller feathers from the same bird.

A stone from the cave where she was born. This also makes her feel at home.

Fig. 6.1 My turkey vulture jicara
(Photograph by Yuri Lev Studio)

Since the fashioning of an authentic jicara may take some time, I suggest you begin right away. You will need an animal spirit jicara for the advanced practice of shamanic dreaming (see practice 28 in chapter 12).

Practice 5
SHAMANIC DEATH AND REBIRTH

Cross-culturally, the theme and experience of the initiation of death and rebirth is an important element in the development of a shaman that is found in shamanic cultures throughout the world. This initiation typically includes:

1. An experience of suffering, followed by death, dismemberment, and rebirth.
2. An ascent to the sky and descent to the lower world, which is an out-of-body experience.
3. Conversations with spirits and souls.

In this rite of passage we intentionally pursue circumstances that bring out from within us the transformational power that is fostered through metaphorically dying and being reborn. But unlike other spiritual forms of this process where the metaphor is drawn up through words or commitments of being born again, in this ritual we actually dig our grave and submerge ourselves in it, thereby facing our mortality. This is about as close as you can get to the awareness of death without placing yourself in mortal danger or having an actual near-death experience. And in this ritual context you are totally submerged inside an organic field of energy (Mother Earth). Your hyperspace will mingle with Earth in such a way that you will be changed forever.

In his book *The Unfolding Self*, Ralph Metzner, Ph.D., an expert on transformative experience, gets right to the point with respect to the implications of the death-rebirth initiation:

Whereas in some Christian fundamentalist circles it is customary for people who have made a commitment to Christ to refer to themselves as "twice born," the original meaning of that concept goes much deeper than simply a profession of renewed faith, however sincere. It refers, actually, to the second part of a death-rebirth transformational process. The rebirth experience, to be authentic, must of necessity be preceded by an experience of metaphorically dying. This first, dying phase is inevitably anxiety provoking and problematical for most people. . . . In the mystery religions of ancient times and in many traditional cultures, "death-rebirth" was and is the name of an initiatory experience. Associated with it are the ritual practices such as entombment, profound isolation, or painful ordeal through which the initiate must pass. Afterward, the initiate customarily adopts a new name, perhaps a new garment, and sometimes a new role in society, all of which express the newly reborn being.[1]

In this practice of death and rebirth you will be digging your own shallow grave or tomb where you will spend an entire night or longer. The physical aspects of this rite of passage are just as important as the other activities. If you were to hire someone with a machine to come and dig the tomb for you, you would lose an incalculable amount of insights and lessons that come as a result of digging your own grave. The digging of the grave at many levels becomes a mirror reflecting the realities of birth, life, death, and rebirth.

Preparation

In the weeks prior to the ritual, you will prepare mentally and psychologically and also prepare the material items you will need. Internal preparation from the outside seems very simple but in itself can cause drastic shifts in consciousness and perception.

In your journal write down your unrealized bucket list—things you want to do before you die that you haven't done yet. Make a second list of all the people you want to say good-bye to before you die and what you would say to them. Write this list as though you were on your deathbed. Be succinct yet thorough. You will not be saying these things to the actual people but rather to the Sacred Fire before entering your tomb for the night.

Tell at least two trusted friends or family members where you are going (be specific). Make sure your "spot person" for this practice knows how to start a fire, how to keep a fire going, and the dangers of open flame and has all the tools needed to do his or her voluntary service for you. Also make sure your spot person has a working cell phone (if applicable), a detailed map of the area where you'll be doing the ceremony, and all instructions for the Shamanic Death and Rebirth practice. It's a long night! Remember to thank your friend or family member. Always honor the people who help you on your path, particularly those willing to feed your fire.

Personal items you will need include:

First-aid kit

Flashlight or headlamp with new batteries

Clothes and shoes appropriate for the season and for working outdoors (digging)

Change of clothes and shoes

Rain gear (in case of wet weather)

Hat for sun protection

Sunscreen

Bottle of water

Sleeping mat, camping pad, or extra blanket to lie on during the night

Sleeping bag or blanket for warmth

Pillow if you want one

Offerings and personal items (such as photos or sacred objects) to take into the tomb

You will need the following for building the fire and making your tomb:

Work gloves
Matches
Materials for starting a fire and enough wood to keep it burning
    all night
Shovel
Pick and adze, or combination pick adze (my favorite)
Branches or planks and cloth for the roof of the tomb

In addition to these items for making your tomb, you will also need:

Rope or cord (natural is best) long enough to run from the fire to
    inside the tomb
A piece of wood and a knife or some modeling clay for carving or
    molding a simple human figurine

Keep in mind that from the very first moment you decide to enter this rite of passage, the sacred time has begun. Everything you do from that moment until you come out of your tomb will affect your experience, so proceed with common sense, intention, and honesty. Many questions and fears are likely to be rolling around in your head. That's good. They are all part of the ritual. The more unsure you are about the perceived risks, the greater the possibility for growth and the more lasting the effects of the experience will be. Center your attention on steadily using your fears and insecurities to focus on your preparation.

In the hours or even days before this practice, I suggest you eat very little or fast and drink little water, especially in the hours right before entering the tomb. In over twenty years of employing this technique of the tomb with hundreds of people, I have never had a single participant leave her tomb until morning—even if she wet herself in the night.

Building the Tomb

Here are the basics of making the tomb:

1. The place where you will carry out the rite is extremely important because it is not just the physical location of the rite but also the co-creator of your experience. Optimally, it should be a place that is far enough from civilization that no noises from human activity are audible and where other people are not going to wander into during the rite. When choosing the site, keep in mind that you will be digging at least two feet deep into the ground so choose a location that has some type of topsoil or sand, not bare rock. You should test the site beforehand by digging a few pilot holes or even a full tomb to make sure the area will be suitable. Be sure to check the area thoroughly to avoid anthills, gopher or other animal holes, snake nests, and so on. Also, never perform the rite in an area near a cemetery or an archaeological site.

2. Once the site is chosen, you must decide exactly where the tombs will be located and positioned (if you are doing this ritual with others) and where the fire will be. If only one tomb is being dug, I suggest that it face east toward the rising sun. If there are multiple tombs being dug, consider placing the tombs in a circle around the central fire so the positioning of the tombs resembles rays of the sun coming out from the fire. The tomb or tombs should be approximately five paces from the fire; while lying in the tomb, the initiate's head should be positioned toward the fire. The tomb is rectangular in shape and slightly longer and wider than the person going into it. To set the dimensions of the tomb, simply lie on your back and have someone mark out the outline of the tomb on the surface of the ground using a stick, pick, or shovel. Mark out an area approximately four inches wider and longer than your body.

3. Now use whatever hand tools necessary to dig the tomb. I prefer a pick adze and sturdy shovel. While digging, place the soil away from the fire, not between the tomb and the fire. To measure the correct depth of the tomb, lie inside the tomb while on your side. Have a

friend place a board on the ground and over your shoulder that is facing up. The board should be very close to your shoulder but not touching it. This way you can either lie comfortably on your back during the night or on your side. Be sure to carefully check your tomb for size by actually lying in it. There should be two to four inches extra space all around your body but not more or you will lose some of the energetic qualities of the soil encapsulating you.

4. Once the digging is complete, construct the roof by placing branches or wood planks across the top of the tomb from side to side, *not* front to back. The roof will be completely covered with dirt and needs to hold the weight of the dirt and keep it from sifting into the tomb on top of you. Once the supports for the roof are in place, the easiest way to cover the roof so that dirt, when it is placed on top, doesn't sift into the tomb is to place a piece of cloth (hemp fabric or cotton bedsheets work fine) over the top of the tomb, making sure the cloth is large enough to extend at least six inches beyond the tomb on all sides.

   To complete the roof, shovel earth onto it to a depth of three inches. You can also use natural materials such as leaves, pine needles, field grass, and so on. Leave an opening at the head of the tomb (facing the fire) just large enough for you to enter the tomb. This open section will be covered with earth (except for an opening for air approximately four inches by four inches) by the Firekeeper after you are in the tomb.

   Once your tomb is complete, it is fine to take a shower or a swim and to relax if you have time before nightfall.

Working with the Sacred Fire

When darkness begins to fall, we begin to switch from the physically inspired processes to the more numinous levels of awareness as we prepare mentally, emotionally, energetically, and spiritually to enter the tomb for the night. Assisting us in this is the energy, light, heat, and music of the Sacred Fire. Fire watches over us throughout the night just as the sun did during the day. Thus Fire becomes our night sun.

In this ritual, as in most primal activities of this sort, Fire plays a significant role in the proceedings (review practice 1 for making a Sacred Fire). At least one person needs to stay up all night with the Sacred Fire while you are in the ground. This person is the Firekeeper and ensures a small fire is kept alive all night and that the person in the ground is okay. The Firekeeper should not talk to you during the night. If several people are tending the fire, they should not be talking; if absolutely necessary, they can briefly whisper.

The Firekeeper should also have a drum. At short intervals (about every thirty seconds) during the night, the Firekeeper will beat a slow but loud heartbeat rhythm—thump-thump, thump-thump, thump-thump. This is to awaken you should you fall asleep. Falling asleep is fine, but you don't want to just be asleep all night in your tomb. The best-case scenario is coming in and out of a sleep or partial sleep state numerous times during the night.

The Ritual

For simplicity I'm going to describe the ritual with one person going into the tomb (you) and another as the Firekeeper. Following this format, the ritual can also be completed by a group. When I lead this ritual as a Firekeeper, I usually have between five and twelve participants but have had groups as large as forty with multiple Fires and Firekeepers to assist.

Once the Sacred Fire is lit, here are the steps:

Step 1: Introduction to Grandfather Fire. We must formally introduce ourselves to Grandfather Fire. With respect, but for simplicity, I will now refer to Grandfather as simply Fire. Having traditions while working with Fire is a wonderful way to move into sacred time. One tradition to use here is that when you say, "Grandfather Fire, in front of you and all my companions," *all my companions* refers to *everything* around you, not just humans. After that statement you say what you need to say. In this case the Firekeeper introduces her- or himself to Fire and asks Fire for support in doing a good job helping you. This should be brief. For example: "Grandfather Fire, in front of you and all my companions, my name is Sasha, and I have come here tonight to support my friend James on his journey to death and rebirth. Please lend me your light, energy, and power to stay awake and keep feeding you, keeping an eye on his lifeline and periodically drumming."

At this point the Firekeeper will briefly introduce the drum with a few short words and then feed Fire with one small stick as an offering. From now on the Firekeeper does not talk to you when you are working with Fire.

In a similar way you now introduce yourself, asking for support on your journey. Explain that you are there to experience death and rebirth and end with a small stick placed on Fire.

Step 2: Express your unrealized desires or dreams. In this step it's important to not just read your list. The more powerful way is to silently read an item on the list and then to *say* the item out loud to Grandfather Fire. Take your time and realize the implications of each unfulfilled item. It's very common to become emotional at this step. It's perfectly natural to visualize places, people, situations, and so on, as you speak about them in front of Fire.

Step 3: Say good-bye. There is no perfect way to execute a last good-bye. Feelings of friendship, love, and familiarity are sometimes not easy to put into words. That's one reason we prepare beforehand for this moment. Read to yourself, then speak what you wrote to them through Grandfather Fire while putting the energy of your good-bye into Fire. In this moment many spontaneous things may come up as well. This is not the time to be shy or reserved. Use your voice to say good-bye to those on your list, recollecting the good times and bad, triumphs and failures. Speak to them as though you will never see them again.

Step 4: Set the line. Relieve your body functions one last time. Now the Firekeeper runs your line (cord or rope) between the fire and your tomb. Place the line under a rock of the bed of the fire (within the glow but not in the embers) and run it with enough line to reach the center of the tomb when you are inside. This line has nothing to do with physical safety (the ritual is not in the least dangerous physically); it is a symbolic connection between you and Grandfather Fire. Grandfather Fire will hold your line during the many situations that may happen while in the tomb and ensure you don't get lost. The Firekeeper should not touch the line after you go into the tomb.

Step 5: Entering the tomb. Just before entering the tomb, say good-bye to the Firekeeper. Get into the tomb, and when ready, the Firekeeper shovels the rest of the dirt onto the top of your tomb. This is one of the most surreal moments so far because now the ritual is becoming real in a physically tangible way. Once the tomb is covered, the Firekeeper pulls up a corner of the fabric of your roof so that you have an airhole about the size of a fist. The last thing the Firekeeper does is stick his or her arm through the hole, ensuring it is clear, and takes your hand one final time in good-bye.

Step 6: Inside the tomb. Once the Firekeeper's hand is gone, your journey truly begins. The journey, so unique and personal to each initiate, begins as the settling in process continues and the fears, anxieties, hopes, and dreams begin to increase and dissipate as the ritual unfolds. Each experience in the tomb is as unique as each individual, the lessons as profound as the mysteries of life and death. At this stage of the ritual, it is common to pass through a period of questioning or even rage or feelings of depression.

Once one passes through these initial phases of the ritual, sleep sometimes comes as you become more comfortable with the surroundings and with yourself. From this point you will probably pass through different levels between fully awake and fully asleep. In my experience this is usually the most productive way to spend the first night of this ritual because you get to experience many different levels and states of consciousness, which is also one reason for the periodic drumming throughout the night. The external sound of the beating drum facilitates the shift in states of consciousness. Although the experience of sleeping throughout the night in the tomb has its own benefits, shifting between being awake and asleep, and all the levels in between, has proven to be the most useful format for first-time initiates.

Once you have settled in I suggest that you perform a full session of standard autogenic training formulas (see pages 113 to 122 in chapter 9) to fully connect with your physical body. After doing that, throughout the night use any other formulas that you have learned: affirmation formulas, healing formulas, visualization formulas, and tunnel formulas.

After your autogenic training session there is really no way to predict what will happen while you are in your tomb; however, there are some experiences that seem to be common during the night. Below are a few:

- Feelings of disintegrating into the soil
- Feeling like a skeleton with no skin
- Leaving your body behind: out-of-body experiences such as hovering over the fire, looking down at your body, or flying off somewhere
- Life review, which is very common in near-death experiences
- Visiting with dead people, relatives, friends, guides, or even strangers, or visiting the land of the dead in the underworld
- Your consciousness flying up your life cord to the Sacred Fire and then beyond, the energy of Fire being your vehicle
- Dreaming with your spirit animal

Step 7: Resurrection. Shortly after dawn the Firekeeper drums for a few moments to ensure you are awake. Light will begin coming in through your airhole and with that light the knowledge that you have made it through the night still alive. The Firekeeper should give you at least fifteen minutes or more before taking you out. In that time it is good to reflect on your experience and think about what you will do in your life when you emerge.

When it is time the Firekeeper comes to you and asks if you are ready to emerge. Believe it or not, many if not most people want to stay longer. After spending the whole night in the tomb, it actually can become a very comfortable experience. Eventually, though, it will be time to emerge. Close your eyes as the Firekeeper shovels off enough dirt to lift the fabric of the roof so you can come out.

When you are out, lift your hands to the sky and shout, "Here I am for the first time!"—or something similar.

Step 8: Honoring your ritual death. Before filling in your tomb, symbolically honor the death of your old self—even though you didn't die you will never be the same after performing this ritual—by carving or molding a simple figurine of yourself to be buried in your tomb. Once your figurine is complete, uncover your tomb and place it inside the same way as you were lying in the night. Then bury your figurine by filling in your tomb while reflecting on the day that will someday come when it will really be you in the tomb.

Step 9: Reintegration. After this type of ritual it is best to reintegrate into society gradually. Hopefully you will have time to take a walk, go swimming, or simply sit quietly in nature. You are like a child again in the sense of being very impressionable and innocent. The ritual time has cleansed away a large portion of your normal defenses and left your true primal being to shine out ever more brightly. Now the trick is to remain shining. Keeping the awareness of death close to us in our everyday life is powerful and gives strength to our decisions and actions. By passing through this ritual, you are now ready to integrate all the practices in this book for your own well-being and the service of others. I have also found that those who have completed this ritual also become the most effective healers. In the following days, be kind to yourself and acknowledge the significant time and effort you have given to further your shamanic journey. You are now one of our tribe!

Practice 6
HEALING STONES—ACQUIRING TE'KA

The English language doesn't really have a proper name for the special stones we can work with and learn from. Many cultures, including the Wirrarika and Inka people with whom I have lived, do have names for these entities. Here I will borrow the Wirrarika name, which is *te'ka*. A te'ka is actually not likely to be your birthstone simply because in modern times the concept of birthstones has been turned into a marketing strategy for the jewelry industry, and these stones are minerals mined from the earth to be made into gems. The Burke Museum of Natural History and Culture in Seattle explains this nicely:

> Interestingly, there is no geological definition for the word gem, because a gem is a human creation. Minerals are formed by geologic processes in rocks in their natural environment. When we excavate precious or semiprecious stones, cut, and polish them into specific shapes, they become gems. When a gem is set into metal to be worn on the body it becomes a jewel.[2]

In terms of what we normally think about stones, te'kas are the opposite of gems. A te'ka is naturally found, not mined, and we do not shape or polish them—we *encounter* them naturally or they *call* to us. Encountering a te'ka most often happens when you least expect it. Those that go "hunting" for a te'ka rarely find an authentic one. Although I have heard stories of people encountering a te'ka indoors in such places as malls and rock shops, the vast majority of encounters happen when you get yourself out into nature and listen for the te'ka singing. Listening for a singing stone may seem like a strange notion, but I assure you it is happening all around you once you are open to perceiving it.

Not all stones will be te'kas for you, but all have the capacity. Think of it this way: not all the people you meet become your most important teachers, but each one of them *could*. That is the way to think about encountering a te'ka. It will be much easier to work with a te'ka that is put naturally in your path rather than to go searching for one. Whether you are simply taking a walk in nature near your home or have spent much time and energy to visit a special sacred site in a far-off land, it's okay to keep aware of the chance to meet a te'ka, but don't specifically go shopping for one like you would a new pair of shoes. Synchronistic events almost always accompany the encounter with a te'ka.

Many people like to collect special stones that catch their eye or evoke a certain unique feeling. Like me, you probably know of someone who has piles or even bags of special stones they have collected. So how do you know when you encounter a te'ka? The answer is simple: *you just know.* When you encounter a te'ka you will know. If you are not *sure,* then chances are you have not found one. They are that special.

Now that is not to say that you will immediately know what that te'ka is about: what its gifts are, if it would like to work with you, if it would like to be left alone, if it needs to be fed, and so on. It may take a good long while before those things are revealed. The largest te'ka in figure 6.2 has an interesting story. Well, they all do, but I'll share this one.

An Unmistakable Sign

I was walking along the creek bed in Oak Creek Canyon near my home in Sedona, Arizona, with my canine companion Sophie. The singing stones in that sacred canyon are amazing and everywhere. As we walked I came across a very unusual stone out of the millions that the canyon is home to. As you can see from the photo the stone has a naturally formed circle embedded in it. When I saw that I knew it was a very special stone, so Sophie and I sat with the stone for a while, but I didn't touch it or pick it up. After a while I decided to leave the stone where it was. I didn't hear it sing or call to me in any way to take it.

So we continued on our walk and later crossed the creek at a shallow spot. On the way back home, on the other side of the creek from where we encountered the stone with the circle, we ran into the stone again! Needless to say I couldn't believe my eyes, but for sure this was the same stone. Perplexed, and honestly a little spooked out, I once again sat with the stone, and after a while the stone told me it had something to show me and wanted me to pick it up, which I did. Now for another shock—I turned the stone over and on the opposite side it had another circle! Never in my life had I seen anything like this.

Obviously, I took the stone home with me; finding it in two different places in one afternoon was about as large a sign as you'll ever get from a te'ka! Throughout the years this te'ka has revealed itself as a healer, and I have employed it in hundreds of healing sessions with clients.

This photo of my te'kas was taken in 2007. I have other photos and now have more te'kas too, but this photo, taken by my friend and

Fig. 6.2 Some of my te'kas
(Photograph by Nancy Bartell)

professional photographer Nancy, is my favorite. It just seems to me that in this photo my te'kas are happy and all are getting along. Here is a list of te'kas you may encounter that can elevate your shamanic work, especially healing work, to deeper levels. They are also simply amazing entities to form a relationship with.

Balancing te'ka. This te'ka provides for stabilizing and balancing the holographic field and emotional and intellectual aspects of the phase-conjugate mirrors. It can create a stabilizing, calming effect and is a perfect tool for shamanic energy infusions, discussed in practice 36.

Guardian te'ka. The task of this te'ka is what its name implies. In some cases it is like a bodyguard that you keep with you for safety. Te'kas of this specialty often have the ability to intuitively warn you or give advice during the course of your day. Other types of guardian te'kas include those that look after your house and are often kept on a front porch or inside on a mantle or altar. Garden guardians keep the plants and soil safe, and I have even met guardian te'kas that keep pets safe and are often kept in or underneath a pet's bed. As compared with other types of te'kas that expend more energy, guardian te'kas typically require only periodic feedings of thanks and prayers of gratefulness from you. That is what they primarily feed on. They like to be told they are doing a good job and to know that they are appreciated. If at times they ask for something more, be sure to respond accordingly.

Physical healing te'ka. These te'kas are perfect for infusing energy into ailing glands and organs. They tend to have a large appetite for sunshine, rainwater, wind, earth, and fire. Unlike some te'kas that require little food, if this te'ka is not fed properly, its usefulness for healing will be negligible. When feeding it earth energy, simply bury it in the ground for a couple days.

Luminous te'ka. If you have a relationship with one of these te'kas, you are truly fortunate. While the te'ka of physical healing directly affects the physical body, the luminous te'ka collects luminous energy from sources such as the sun, fire, water, soil, wind, pollen, juice, blood, liqueur, sap, and saliva, and then transfers the energy of that life force to another living being, place, or space. If you or someone else requires an infusion of energy, this te'ka can help provide it. Especially when doing healing work, oftentimes a healer can't take a person (or other being) to a place where he or she can receive a direct energetic infusion from, for example, a sacred spring or Fire or mountaintop. In this case the luminous te'ka can be taken to the place, infused with energy, and then used by the healer to impart, or the individual themselves to receive, the luminous energy from the te'ka. Unless you have been trained by someone who knows how to do this, it is wise to first familiarize yourself with this process by working with it on yourself. Feed the te'ka with one source of luminous energy at a time. For example, feed the te'ka the light, heat, and flowing mystical properties of Fire, and then sometime later or the next day when you are not with the Fire any longer, ask the te'ka to release the Fire energy into your total human organism—mind, body, spirit— and learn firsthand the effects of that infusion. Then afterward listen to the te'ka for what it needs. Many times when working with Fire, the te'ka will then want water or some other form of liquid. Once you have worked with the te'ka during many different types of infusions, you will likely find the te'ka has more ability to transfer certain energies than others. It's common for some te'kas to work better with fire and sun, while others have keener talents for water or soil.

Courage te'ka. This is a powerful healing te'ka used in infusions for renewal after intensely painful events that leave one depleted, afraid, and confused. The courage te'ka is also helpful to consult *before* you enter a situation that you feel anxious about.

Transformation te'ka. Specializing in transforming a person from one mode of being to another, this te'ka is most helpful in those moments of life when we are in transition and need a "shove" to move us farther down a new path.

Shadow te'ka. I have noticed that many people involved in personal growth and spiritual awakening tend to focus on enlightenment by emphasizing "being in the light" and positive thoughts, prayers, and intentions—which is wonderful. However, negative thoughts and emotions, sickness, and darkness are just as much a part of our world and can't simply be ignored. Shadow te'kas have the ability to help us deal in a positive way with these shadow aspects of life. The best way I have found to work with a shadow te'ka is to bury the te'ka in the ground at least overnight. In this way the te'ka is cleansed by the enormous capacity of our Mother Earth to absorb and heal shadow energy. Then the te'ka can be taken to calm anger, pull out sickness, absorb depression, and generally help to restore balance between light and dark when the shadow has taken over. Many techniques exist for working with a shadow te'ka. Some include placing the te'ka on each chakra area of a client while making prayers of intention, placing the te'ka in a special little necklace bag that is worn for a full day and night, sleeping with the te'ka under your pillow, ritually confessing your energetic "drains" to the te'ka (see page 34), and taking the te'ka with you into the tomb during the death and rebirth practice (see page 60), among others. Once the te'ka has drawn the shadow energy into its body, the te'ka must be cleansed by either burying it in the soil overnight or placing it next to a very hot fire until it is hot and then into the youngest spring water available.

Dreaming te'ka. During periods of altered states of consciousness, a dreaming te'ka can help to focus the often random perceptions, images, and messages that we access. I have employed the help of a dreaming te'ka by simply holding the te'ka in my hands while speaking with Grandfather Fire, by placing the te'ka on the ground in front of me while sitting in meditation, having the te'ka with me during a sweat lodge ceremony and also while questing for vision on the land, and of course by having the te'ka next to me on my nightstand or under my pillow while sleeping. I have found that dreaming te'kas like to be fed and cared for in unusual ways. My dreaming te'ka has asked to be attached to my dog's collar when we go hiking; likes to watch educational programs on TV and listen to music; asks to sit in various places in nature, especially the nearby Oak Creek, for periods of time up to a full week; and likes to be placed and held in my mouth and the mouths of others (after being washed, of course), among others.

Nature te'ka. Although the name for this te'ka seems redundant, I have seen this te'ka work miracles for connecting or reconnecting people with nature. After working with this te'ka, I have had clients who live in the city and don't really enjoying being in nature suddenly plan a camping trip. One client who absolutely would not enter a natural body of water began to love to go for dips in a nearby stream. Something about the energy of this te'ka inspires one to realize that it's healthy to interact with nature. Even for me, sometimes when I find myself spending more time indoors than usual (mostly when I'm writing), one look at my nature te'ka and I'm out the door and into the woods and fields.

Tonic te'ka. As its name implies, this te'ka stimulates, strengthens, and rejuvenates. It is effective in helping to heal the intestinal track, heart, lungs, and spleen and to cure stomach ulcers and even a hangover. In addition, I have also seen it help with a bruised ego and for quenching the pride of a sore loser.

Magical te'ka. Although all te'kas have their own special sort of magic, there are some te'kas that are extremely fluid, adaptable, spontaneous in action, and unpredictable, although very disciplined, and that inspire you to fulfill tasks and dreams. These are the te'kas I refer to as magical or manifesting te'kas, and although they can be very helpful, you must be careful with them because you never know what will happen when you work with them. A magical te'ka does not care much about what you think of yourself or what you are doing with your life. A magical te'ka will show you who you really are and what to do in order to flow with creation, and many times this will be very different from what you expect. Magical te'kas are known for coyote teaching, which is very tricky. For example, if you employ a magical te'ka to help you learn how to heal people that have pain in their bodies, the magical te'ka may send you pain as a way of teaching you how to deal with it.

Mind te'ka. Working with this te'ka stimulates the intellect and enhances learning and analytical pursuits. In an integrative state of consciousness I have used the mind te'ka for memory enhancement, mathematical pursuits, and mental acuity for both myself and clients. Somehow this te'ka helps diminish limiting thoughts and concepts, allowing us grow in aspects of the mind we never thought we could.

Seeing te'ka. This te'ka is pretty much the opposite of the mind te'ka. Its specialty is to help see or view events of the past, present, or future, especially when using it in conjunction with a Sacred Fire or candles. Unlike most other te'kas, which are never one particular kind of rock, seeing te'kas are almost always a type of lava stone, such as basalt or obsidian.

Traveler's te'ka. In a similar way to the guardian te'ka, this te'ka provides protection from the hazards of travel. It accomplishes that by elevating your intuition during situations where more than one logical course of action is available. I often use my travel te'ka when booking flights or deciding on which days to travel when I'm not sure.

Maternity te'ka. This is one of my newest te'kas; I only found out it existed last year. I was out walking with a small group of friends in the hills of west central Vermont. One of my friends was five months pregnant. While walking through a patch of boulders, she stopped and said, "Hey, can you guys hear that?" We all stopped but heard nothing out of the ordinary. She sat down for a few minutes while we all remained silent and then walked a short distance carrying back with her a stone that was a little smaller than a football and of similar shape. She claimed it was quietly singing to her (which really didn't surprise me). She and I worked with the stone many times during her pregnancy, and during that time she rarely went anywhere without it, claiming that it had a remarkable effect on her and when she wasn't near it or holding it she would have increased back pain and goofy or even scary thoughts. During her delivery she claimed it helped to keep her calm. She later gave it to her sister when she became pregnant, and she reported the same healing effects. Obviously, I never tried it, but I could see the effect it had on both of them.

Happy te'kas. These te'kas are often found in groups. They have a similar feeling as the luminous te'kas, but the difference is that unlike the true luminous te'ka, which likes and even needs to work, the happy te'kas accomplish their task by simply making you feel happy. Infusing the energy of a happy te'ka during shamanic healing almost always produces immediate results.

Encountering, working with, and caring for te'kas is a remarkable and rewarding aspect of shamanism. The better you get to know these companion helpers, the more you will be able to use them in many ways. Probably the most powerful way will be described in practice 36 as we employ te'kas for shamanic healing. Since you will need the tools of the te'ka for that practice, I suggest from now on that you be open to finding and hopefully collecting te'kas.

PART THREE

THE SHAMANIC DREAMSCAPE

7

Lucid Dreaming

To begin this section on shamanic dreaming, I will first explain the modern term and experience of lucid dreaming. For us modern folks lucid dreaming and shamanic dreaming will share consistencies in the beginning stages simply because the initial goal of both is simply to become aware you are dreaming while you are dreaming. Learning to do this in the culture of my dreaming teachers—the Wirrarika—is very natural and nothing like what we modern people must go through. Unlike our culture, dream recall is simply a part of everyday life for the Wirrarika. From a very early age, every morning a Wirrarika child is asked by her mom or grandfather, by the shaman or even many people: "What did you dream last night?" This Wirrarika custom of asking about and recounting dreams continues throughout life.

This dream recollection is key to beginning to learn lucid dreaming. Moving from intentionally remembering dreams in high detail to realizing you are dreaming while you are dreaming is a natural progression. For Westerners the best way to learn the highly advanced techniques of shamanic dreaming is to first become proficient at lucid dreaming. We are going to dive into this most important subject soon.

Most modern dream researchers agree on a simple definition for lucid dreaming: in a lucid dream the dreamer knows that he is dreaming while he is dreaming. For those of you proficient in lucid dreaming, you could skip this section and continue on to shamanic dreaming in chapter 11, but I suggest you stick around anyway because you might learn something new.

A BRIEF HISTORY OF DREAMING

We all have dreams that upon our wakening startle us with their clarity: the dream felt so real that while we were dreaming it didn't feel or seem like a dream at all. Many, if not all of us, have also experienced a lucid dream (LD) in which we somehow knew we were dreaming while we were dreaming it, and upon awakening we remember that we knew we were dreaming while dreaming. Recent polls conducted by dream researchers suggest that around 80 percent of people have three to five lucid dreams per year. That's a really small percentage—1 to 2 percent of dreams for a whole year. After people participate in a weeklong class on how to induce LD, the percentage rises to 10 to 40 percent. After many months of practice inducing LD, many participants report 80 percent frequency, and there are highly experienced oneironauts (lucid dreamers) who, after many years of practice, report 100 percent frequency when they intend to lucid dream.

Lucid dreaming and shamanic dreaming share many themes and processes, but shamanic dreaming takes lucid dreaming to another whole level. So now you may be wondering why we should practice LD. Good question. The easiest answer is also the simplest: because we spend around a third of our lives asleep, why wouldn't we want to have access to that part of our life instead of being in a state that resembles a coma? Below are some of the potentials lucid dreaming offers. Later, I'll get into the whys of shamanic dreaming.

Gain control. Explore your dream world with total clarity, and direct and manipulate dream themes, settings, and plots at will.

Get inspired. Collect ideas and creative motivation for the waking world from your subconscious.

Fulfill fantasies. During LD you can do whatever you want.

Therapy. While lucid dreaming you can face your fears, phobias, anxieties, past traumas, and even nightmares.

Gain energy and power. Lucid dreamers have shown that proficiency in lucid dreaming carries over many positive changes in the waking world.

WHAT IS AND WHAT IS NOT LUCID DREAMING

There are two states of consciousness before and after sleep that are often confused with lucid dreaming. The hypnagogic state and the hypnopompic state are terms used to describe the borderline state between wakefulness and falling asleep and being asleep and waking up, respectively. Both states may tap into the subconscious mind in a similar way and sometimes in an even more powerful way to normal dreams, although hypnagogia (falling asleep) is usually more pronounced than hypnopompia (waking up). Common experiences during hypnagogia include visualizations such as phosphenes (colored specks of light), geometric patterns, kaleidoscopic imagery, and flashing dream scenes similar to an ongoing dream. Since we are still partially awake, we often consciously decide to hold a scene or image or to let it go and pass to another. Personally, I find it quite enjoyable and peaceful to see phosphenes and to be able to control their movements while transitioning to sleep and have found this to be very conducive to evoking lucid dreaming once asleep.

Hypnagogia and lucid dreaming share some qualities, but they are not the same state of consciousness. During the hypnagogic state I can to a certain extent direct the images that I see, in a similar way to lucid dreaming, but I am not asleep yet. Being aware of the hypnagogic state can be very valuable to entering lucid dreaming. It is an effective technique to "carry over" an image or scene into a lucid dream. More about that later.

A second state of consciousness often confused with lucid dreaming is the prelucid dream state. Although we can at times move from hypnagogia to lucid dreaming, especially with training and practice, normally we pass into normal sleep and then through a prelucid dream state first. The prelucid state is in most cases a very important bridge to becoming fully lucid. While in a prelucid state our dream seems utterly real, and many times we are astonished at the clarity. It's quite common in this state to say to oneself, "This can't be a dream." Or to ask, "Am I really dreaming?" If you are making statements or asking questions to yourself about your dream, you have arrived at a state of consciousness where you could easily cross the bridge to lucid dreaming; however, this is not always the case. Often we stay in this dream state, it fades away, or we wake up without experiencing lucidity.

While dreaming we can often feel, or actually be, in charge of what is going on in our dream without being aware we are dreaming. Our unconscious is a tricky animal and is basically in charge of what we are dreaming. If you are in some form connected to your subconscious, it may seem like you are consciously in charge of your dream when actually you are not. Many times, especially for novices, this also occurs even when you are fully aware you are dreaming (LD). For the vast majority of people, it takes a lot of practice to be consciously in charge of your dream even when you know you are dreaming.

Strictly speaking, being in charge or having the ability in some way to control your dream is not a necessary component of lucid dreaming. Being fully aware that you are dreaming is the only requisite. You can be fully lucid in your dream with your unconscious mind still in charge. In this common circumstance you are simply consciously "going for a ride" in your dream. These experiences of being lucid while your unconscious is in charge can be supremely enlightening! You can lucidly experience fulfilling fantasies and facing fears, phobias, anxieties, past traumas, and even nightmares, with your unconscious mind in charge of the dream.

Letting your unconscious mind be in charge during lucid dreaming also opens up the possibilities of discovering and experiencing circumstances your conscious mind is not capable of due to many factors, the most important being the controlling aspects of our ego. During lucid dreaming, you are you but you are also not you. You are not encumbered by societal pressures, family, or work. No one expects you to behave a certain way or "get things done" while you are sleeping! Because of this, lucid dreamers tend to have a plethora of mystical, divine, and numinous experiences. They also tend to experience intense pleasure and even states of ecstasy, sexual ecstasy included. The occurrence of lucid dreamers reaching orgasm while lucid dreaming is well documented in dream study laboratories. Oftentimes lucid dreamers have such powerful experiences that they are incapable of putting them into words upon waking, and these feelings of awe continue for days, weeks, or years.

However, through many years of lucid dreaming, and listening to descriptions of lucid dreams from lots of people, I can also tell you that most lucid dreams are not overly inspiring, stimulating, or therapeutic. Sometimes they can be downright dull. Knowing you are dreaming doesn't automatically make dreaming more exhilarating or enlightening. In most cases lucid dreaming with the unconscious mind "feels" the same as ordinary dreaming, which is actually a good thing. Some people resist lucid dreaming because they're afraid they'll lose the spontaneity and unpredictability of normal dreaming. But that is not necessarily the case. As already stated you can be fully lucid but not be in charge. However, there are many times I want to be in charge of my dream time, and learning how to do that is a remarkable asset in one's life.

One of the most positive benefits of learning to be in charge of your lucid dreams, and later to actually control them (this may seem to be the same but it's not and will be explained more later), is that during lucid dreaming we generally feel supremely confident! We are aware we are dreaming, so anything is possible. I can be in charge of whatever I want to be; I can submit and be humble if I want to. I can change my attitude to circumstances in my life that I might be struggling with for years in a blink of an eye. I can transcend negativity and pessimism and overcome my fears during my lucid dreams and carry the awareness back to the physical plane.

Lucid dreaming also tends to cultivate a unity of consciousness and the cosmos. Lucid dreamers regularly display a shift in their normal awareness toward a more holistic view of the world. Through lucid dreaming they discover a supremely expanded view of life, objects, nature, and other human beings. Through seeing objects, places, and life-forms, including people, as fields of energy while lucid dreaming, the lucid dreamer learns to obtain the same sort of information on the physical plane. This awareness allows the lucid dreamer to see and read other people's energy patterns more easily, sense more clearly others' moods and thoughts, and react more effectively and creatively.

To summarize, the learned ability to be consciously aware we are dreaming while we are dreaming is such a powerful enhancement of life that when it happens we are changed forever for the better. Lucid dreaming is in my mind one of the cutting-edge modalities that can lead humanity away from our anthropocentric lifestyles and toward a holistic reality. Once we master lucid dreaming, we open the door to the powerful tool of shamanic dreaming.

Practice 7
CLEANSING YOUR DAY
IN PREPARATION FOR LUCID DREAMING

Anything we do consistently during the day will inevitably show up in our dreams. Our dreams are largely filled with subconscious impressions from our day. We all know that previous events and people from our past can also show up in our dreams. Not only that, energetically draining events from our past or from the day before can negatively affect both our current waking life and our dream time.

In addition to reclaiming lost energy by healing energetic drains from the past (practice 2), it's important to prepare for your journey into the dream world at night if you want to be successful. If we can clear ourselves of stress, tension, deep emotions, random thoughts, and all the various situations of the day, we can fully focus attention on the intention to first remember dreams and then achieve the goal of becoming aware we are dreaming while dreaming. To do this we can perform a simple ritual that can become a wonderful habit. I wouldn't consider this a shamanic ritual but rather one that can augment and support our attempts at shamanic dreaming.

1. Sit down in a comfortable position before going to bed. It's best to sit on your bed, or somewhere close to where you will sleep that night.
2. Simply sit for a minute and notice where your thoughts are. When ready, close your eyes and begin to visualize the events of your day.
3. You can visualize events as if looking at a movie screen in your mind, or you can take the visual perspective of looking at the scene from the outside or above. Take one event at a time, and breathe it in through your nose while reliving it. If it is an event you want to energetically discharge, then forcefully breathe it out through your mouth as you visualize the energy leaving you and dissipating. If it is a pleasant event, simply exhale through your nose and notice how the event made you feel. Reviewing energetically positive events is a great way to fortify positivity before dreaming; however, it is important to clear the energy-draining events before dreaming. Do as many events as you feel necessary. If you had an easy day, this process could be very quick; if you had a hard day, it will obviously take longer. In any case don't rush, take your time, and get your energy moving to be in a clear and positive state.
4. When you feel finished, stand up, take one more deep breath, and while exhaling sweep your energy field clean by placing your hands on the top of your head and sweeping down over your chest, abdomen, genitals, legs, and feet. When you get to your feet, swish your hands out away from your body. The sweeping can be done slowly or rapidly, whatever feels right to you in the moment. Do this once or many times. I usually do it a few times just because it tends to feel really good and refreshing. I often find myself smiling after this, which is perfect for what comes next!

Practice 8
IMPORTANCE OF A DREAM JOURNAL

I am making this simple task an "official" practice for our work because of how important it is. In the past decade or so the activity of journaling has become extremely popular. Now there are books, workshops, and even conferences on journaling. Journaling enthusiasts typically use the activity for problem solving and stress reduction, and I'm told it can also be very enjoyable. It's been proven to improve mental and physical health and can lead to increased self-esteem.

I have to admit I personally am not big on journaling for myself, but I have more than a few friends who love doing it and have been doing it for many years. I spend so much time writing, I can't even think about keeping a daily journal about my life and thoughts. However, my *dream journal* is something I have kept up on and off for close to thirty years because it is so important to cultivating lucid and shamanic dreaming for modern people. Unlike the Wirrarika, we typically don't have someone who will ask us every morning what we dreamt the night before. If you do have someone like that—awesome! But the dream journal is still pretty much indispensable for modern people in setting up lucid dreaming for many reasons. Every lucid dream researcher and teacher will tell you the same thing.

Why? Stephen LaBerge, Ph.D., known as the godfather of modern lucid dreaming due to his pioneering work at Stanford University and founding of the Lucidity Institute in 1987, puts it this way:

> Your lucid dream training will start with keeping a dream journal and improving your dream recall. Your journal will help you discover what your dreams are like. . . . Learning to remember your dreams is necessary if you want to learn to dream lucidly. Until you have excellent dream recall, you won't stand much of a chance of having lucid dreams. There are two reasons for this. First, without recall, even if you do have a lucid dream you won't remember it. Indeed, we all have probably lost numerous lucid dreams among the

many thousands of dreams we have forgotten in the normal course of our lives. Second, good dream recall is crucial because to become lucid you have to recognize that your dream is a dream while it is happening. Since they are your dreams that you are trying to recognize you have to become familiar with what they are like. . . . You can accomplish this by collecting your dreams and analyzing them for dreamlike elements. . . . Before it will be worth your time to work on lucid dream induction methods you should be able to recall at least one dream every night.[1]

I suggest you buy a special dedicated journal with a lock to record both goals, intentions, and detailed recollections of your nightly dreams. It's important that others don't handle or especially don't look in your journal, thus the lock. If you care to share your dreams with others, especially other lucid dreamers, that's fine and can be very helpful, but this work is extremely private and shouldn't be shared without your knowledge. Also, having a special pen to write with makes the experience more special, even sacred.

We're going to get into when and what to write in your journal shortly. But here I also want to mention a helpful tip from my experience. Often when waking from a dream in the night and not ready yet to wake up for the day, I don't want to become fully awake because I know in my still half asleep (or more) state, I can easily slip right back into dreaming. Waking up to the point of turning on the light and writing might, or would, detract from going back to dreaming. But if I didn't make some effort to immediately record the dream, I would almost always forget it. Waking up in the morning, I would know, on the periphery of my consciousness, that I had dreamt but wouldn't be able to remember the dream. I think we all experience this.

The solution I came up with is to hang a small whiteboard on the wall next to my bed with a marker attached to it. When I briefly wake up and remember my dream, I scribble a few key words on the board so I can remember the dream when I'm fully awake. When I'm awake I take cues from the scribbled notes and write out the details of the dream in my journal. As stated earlier, dream recall is a vital step to lucid dreaming. The little tricks and techniques we use and come up with to polish our dream recall all help in our goal to become lucid.

Practice 9
CREATING LUCID GOALS

In 2007, David R. Hamilton, Ph.D., conducted research at the Dominican University of California involving 149 people aged from twenty-three to seventy-two years old, from many different backgrounds and cultures. The purpose of the research was to compare different techniques and strategies used to achieve our goals. Participants were divided into five groups.

Group 1 was asked to think about goals they'd like to accomplish over the next four weeks and reflect on the importance of those goals.

Group 2 was asked to write down their goals and reflect on their importance, as group 1 had done.

Group 3 went a little further. Not only were they to write down their goals, but they were also asked to write down some actions they could take.

Group 4 went further still: they wrote their goals down, reflected on their importance, and wrote some action steps, but they also sent these action commitments to a supportive friend.

Group 5 did all that group 4 did, but they also made weekly progress reports to their supportive friend.

As you might have guessed, Group 5 achieved the most and Group 1 the least. Group 5, in fact, achieved 78 percent more than Group 1 did.[2]

Writing out your dreaming goals will absolutely help with:

- **Clarification.** Being clear and prepared for any adventure increases the probability of success. For example, if you are going on a trip with a specific destination in mind, you can clarify what to pack, how you will get there, and knowing when you have arrived. The same goes with lucid dreaming. Writing down your goals forces you to select something specific and decide what you want.
- **Motivation.** Writing down your goals and clarifying them is just the beginning of the journey. When going on a trip you have to prepare, get on the road or plane, and actually arrive. Writing down the goals and reviewing them spurs the motivation toward the actual actions.
- **Keeping on track.** So many circumstances pull us this way and that every day. Writing down goals helps us filter out what are the most important actions to take.
- **Evaluation.** Written goals are like mile markers on a highway. They enable you to see how far you have come and how far you need to go. They also provide an opportunity for celebration when you attain them!

So the first items to write in your journal refer to why you want to lucid dream. Clarify your motivation. Examples:

I want to explore consciousness.
I want to fly around in my dreams.
I want to learn shamanic dreaming.
I want to heal myself.
I want to heal others.
I want to improve my self-confidence.
I want to overcome . . .

I like to make a title page as the first page of my journal. Then at the top of the second page goes the date and the heading "Motivation," followed by why I want to lucid dream.

Next, I'll write some affirmations and truths about what I'm doing. Examples:

> I will do my best to prepare for dreaming so I will be successful in becoming lucid.
> I will try not to be frustrated when not successful.
> The process of learning lucid dreaming takes time; I will go at my own speed.
> My dream journal is a magical item of my subconscious and dream world.
> I am clear on my motivation to do this and have written it down in my journal.
> I will be successful in lucid dreaming!

Now don't forget at any moment to write down feelings, emotions, thoughts, affirmations, doubts—whatever. It's really interesting to see what we wrote in the beginning of the lucid dream journey months and years later.

After this initial section in your journal, skip at least ten pages for future goals, affirmations, and notes. On the first page of the actual journal you will record the dreams you have on your first night; put the date at the top and the two most important six- and seven-word phrases for this stage:

> I will remember my dreams tonight.
> I will write down my dreams tonight.

Place a bookmark at that page so you can easily find it when you awaken during the night. I'm going to give detailed instructions about writing down dreams in the next chapter. But first let's look at induction techniques—techniques for inducing lucid dreams.

Practice 10

ENHANCING PROSPECTIVE MEMORY— REALITY CHECKS

The reason for writing out the above phrases before going to sleep is to stimulate what psychologists refer to as prospective memory. Prospective memory means remembering to perform intended actions in the future or, simply, remembering to remember. Examples of prospective memory include remembering to take medicine at night before going to bed, remembering to deliver a message to a friend, and remembering to pick up certain items while shopping. Making lists, using sticky notes, and writing on a calendar, among other physical cues, can help us remember what we want or need to do in the future.

I am notorious for making a shopping list and then getting distracted and leaving it at home. I did just that yesterday when I went to the grocery store. But though I didn't remember all the items on the list, the act of writing the list enabled me to remember the important ones. It seems that importance is key to prospective memory. Leaving on time to catch a plane will usually outweigh insignificant items on a grocery list. Remembering your spouse's birthday will probably outweigh taking out the trash. If the task is very important your prospective memory will remain active to the goal and keep checking if it's time to do it until you actually do it. Much of what we intend to do in our everyday lives, whether at home or at work, involves habitual tasks repeated over time. When it comes to these kinds of habitual tasks, our intentions may not be explicit. We don't write down or form an explicit intention to insert the key in our front door to open it when we get home. We just do it. Forgetting to pick an item up at the store may be no big deal; however, prospective memory failures can sometimes be devastating. For example, aircraft pilots must remember to perform several actions sequentially prior to takeoff and landing, and failure to remember to perform any of these actions may result in injury or death.

For lucid dreaming, we can effectively use a concrete prospective memory cue: right before you go to bed, write down in your journal and say to yourself that you will remember your dreams that night—and really believe it! But we are also going to want to perform certain tasks during the dream, the most important being the awareness that we are dreaming. Since we can't take our journal or a list with us to remember, we need to remember without these tools. *Learning to remember better in our waking life* can greatly help us to remember while dreaming. As already discussed the importance of an event or task helps motivate us to remember. It's the same with lucid dreaming: the more we desire to become lucid the more motivated we will be to remember.

The following technique has two aspects with regard to lucid dreaming. The first is to exercise our prospective memory and the second is to perform reality checks while exercising prospective memory. Anything we do consistently during the day will inevitably show up in our dreams. To learn lucid dreaming, you must be able to spot the difference between a dream and waking reality. During normal dreams you accept it as real life. It's only when you wake up that you realize you were dreaming. By integrating reality checks into your waking life, you will soon do them in your dreams. This will snap your conscious mind to realizing: "I'm dreaming!"

Reality checks are very easy to perform; however, the more passion and energy you put into them, the more effective they will be when carried over into your dream time. To be truly effective, reality checks should be performed many times during your day—twenty times is a good number. Basically the reality check has a physical component along with asking a simple question, "Am I dreaming?"

Some teachers of lucid dreaming suggest setting an alarm on your phone or watch to remember to do your reality check. In my experience it is far better to combine intentional prospective memory with the reality check by doing your reality check when you see a predetermined item(s) during your day or you do something specific during your day.

The first step is to write down a list of twenty-one targets, things that are likely to happen during a normal week. Once you have your list, break it down into three items for each day of the upcoming week and write this schedule down in your journal. You will not be taking your journal with you, nor a list of the three targets. This is an exercise to strengthen your prospective memory without using lists or sticky notes or alarms. Here we are exercising our mental power of recall. Examples:

I will do a reality check whenever I:

Buy something
Write something down
Hear someone say my name
Handle cash
See a yellow car
Hear someone laugh
Turn on a TV
Turn on a computer
Throw something away
Read something
Check the time
Hang up the phone
Put a key in a lock
See a bird
See an advertisement
Open a door
Eat anything
Flush a toilet
See the stars
Smoke a cigarette
Turn on a light

This is just a sample list; you must make your own. Obviously, if you are an editor you would choose something else besides reading as a target, or if you are a telemarketer, something besides hanging up the phone. We want the targets to be things we will do a few times a day (like flushing a toilet), not all day long.

When you hit a target, it's time for a reality check. A reality check can be lots of things:

Touching. What happens when you touch something solid?
Breathing. Can you hold both your nose and mouth shut and breathe?
Jumping. When you jump, do you come right back down or do you float down?
Reading. Can you read a sentence twice without its changing?
Mirrors. Does your reflection look normal in the mirror?
Math. Can you add up two numbers for a correct answer?

Each of these reality checks can be useful. My preference is holding my nose and mouth shut and the palm test, which is not on the above list. To do the palm test, open one hand and then forcefully tap the index, middle, and ring fingers of your other hand on the palm of the open hand. I prefer this test over the others because seeing (finding) your hands in a dream is one of the main techniques of becoming lucid, which we will discuss later.

The more often you do a reality check in waking life, the more likely it is that you will do the same reality check in any given dream to test if you are aware that you are dreaming. The key to reality checks is to do them mindfully and frequently while at the same time asking yourself, "Am I dreaming?" "Am I awake?"—or some other variation of this question. If you are not asking yourself the question in waking life, then chances are you won't ask yourself the question in the dream. It is the question, not the action itself, that will make lucid dreaming successful.

Your brain creates neural constructs based on experiential learning: patterns of thinking based on your real-life experiences. For example, we know about the laws of gravity: we know that in the waking world we can't just jump off the ground and fly away. There's no question about it, just as there's no question that 71 percent of Earth's surface is currently water, Earth is in the Milky Way Galaxy, and the Browns won't win the Super Bowl this year. Consequently, most of us continue through life without ever questioning the world around us. We become so accustomed to our reality, we forget to question it. And this applies in the dream world too.

However, when we question our reality on a regular basis, we open ourselves to actually experiencing alternate realities. When this becomes second nature in waking life, it will become second nature in dreams too. This is the bridge we are looking for to the world of lucid dreams. The other benefit of doing frequent reality checks throughout the day is that it ensures that you are constantly thinking about lucid dreaming. The more you focus on something, the more likely it is to occur, especially in the case of lucid dreaming. A perfect example of this is my current situation with writing this lucid dreaming portion of the book. Since I started writing it and have been focusing on it all day for many days, the number of my dreams has increased and my recall has been outstanding. Remember: whatever we do in the waking world naturally affects our dream world. By constantly thinking of lucid dreaming while awake, we enhance our chances of becoming lucid while we are dreaming. Reality checks, reading and researching about lucid dreaming, and other techniques I will present shortly all combine to help us with our goal.

Summary of reality check technique:

1. Make a list of targets. Choose twenty targets that you know you will hit during a one-week period, multiple times a day. Group them into three targets for each day, and write them in your journal. Below are examples of daily targets for the first two weekdays.

Monday
Open a door
Eat anything
Flush a toilet

Tuesday

Hang up the phone

Put a key in a lock

See a bird

2. Memorize the day's targets. When you get up in the morning, after you write in your journal about your dreams of the night, read and memorize your reality check targets for that day. Don't read ahead; read only the targets for that particular day.

3. Remember to perform your reality check while doing your targets during the day If one of your targets is putting a key in a lock, while you insert a key, you will have to use your prospective memory to do your reality check. While doing your physical reality check, sincerely ask yourself, "Am I dreaming?" At this point I would suggest doing another different reality check because sometimes in dreams one is not enough to convince ourselves. In the waking world the answer to your question will more than likely be, "No, I'm not dreaming." Remember, *the action of questioning your reality* and state of consciousness in your waking state while increasing your prospective memory is the point of the exercise. Soon you will be doing this while dreaming. The more you do it while awake, the easier it will be to do while dreaming. Keep track of your targets hit during the day with a small notebook or just a piece of paper. Also write down the targets you missed. Many times I have had the "put a key in a lock" target on my list, but often when I get to work in the morning and turn off my car, I realize I've missed my very first reality check when I started the car. That was a failure of my prospective memory, which needs improvement.

4. Tally up your hits and failures. At the end of the day write a tally of your hits and failures in your journal so you can mark your progress. This technique has a definite snowball effect. The more you practice, the better you get. Congratulate yourself when you see improvement, and smile knowing you are intentionally raising your awareness and developing your memory. If you realize you are missing a lot of your

targets, continue with the process and try not to be discouraged. Keep trying your best, and you will get it. Remember, hitting your target is only a portion of the technique related to prospective memory. Just as important is actually performing the reality check in a conscientious and high-level manner and sincerely questioning reality. If you fail to do either, hitting the target becomes somewhat trivial.

8

Mastering Dream Cycles
for Lucid Dreaming

Lucid dreams happen during sleep. So it's important to have a basic understanding about sleep, and from there we can take that understanding and apply it practically to help induce lucid dreaming. One of the most prevalent misconceptions about sleep is that sleep is just a matter of our bodies and minds "turning off" for several hours, followed by our bodies and minds "turning back on" when we awake. In short, most of us think of sleep as a passive and relatively constant and unchanging process. In fact, sleep is a very active state. During sleep our brain activity is even more varied than it is during the normal waking state, and our bodies move frequently, as we roll about during the night. All of this has been measured for decades by sleep researchers. Here is a brief overview of tools used to measure sleep:

There are three fundamental measures used by scientists that define the stages of sleep we go through during the night.

1. Brain wave activity is measured by an electroencephalogram (EEG). This machine provides the summary of electrical activity from one area of the brain.
2. Muscle tone is measured with an electromyogram (EMG) machine.
3. Eye movement is recorded via an electrooculogram (EOG).

The EEG reading is the most important measure in differentiating between the stages, while the EMG and EOG are most important in differentiating rapid eye movement (REM) sleep from the other stages. When awake, most people exhibit brain wave (EEG) patterns that can be classified into two types of waves: beta and alpha.

Beta waves are those associated with day-to-day wakefulness. These waves are the highest in frequency and lowest in amplitude and also more desynchronous than other waves; that is, the waves are not very consistent in their pattern. This desynchrony makes sense, given that day-to-day mental activity consists of many cognitive, sensory, and motor activities and experiences, and thus when awake, we are mentally desynchronous as well.

Alpha waves occur during periods of relaxation while we are still awake. In an alpha state our brain waves become slower, increase in amplitude, and become more synchronous. Meditating, autogenic training, biofeedback, and other relaxation techniques are associated with producing alpha wave activity, which has been shown to have positive health benefits.

The first stage of sleep is characterized by theta waves, which are even slower in frequency and greater in amplitude than alpha waves. The difference between relaxation and stage 1 sleep is gradual and subtle. As the sleeper moves to stage 2 sleep, theta wave activity continues, interspersed with two unusual wave phenomena. These phenomena, which occur periodically every minute or so and are the defining characteristics of stage 2 sleep, are termed sleep spindles and K complexes. The former is a sudden increase in wave frequency, and the latter is a sudden increase in wave amplitude. Stages 1 and 2 are relatively light stages of sleep. In fact, if someone is awoken during one of these stages, he or she will often report not being asleep at all.

During a normal night's sleep, a sleeper passes from the theta waves of stages 1 and 2 to the delta waves of stages 3 and 4. Delta waves are the slowest and highest amplitude brain waves. There is no real division between stages 3 and 4 except that, typically, stage 3 is considered delta sleep, in which less than 50 percent of the waves are delta waves, and in stage 4 more than 50 percent of the waves are delta waves. Delta sleep is our deepest sleep, the point when our brain waves are least like waking. Consequently, it is the most difficult stage in which to wake sleepers, and when they are awakened, they are usually sleepy and disoriented. Interestingly, sleep walking and talking are most likely to occur in delta sleep.

Besides these four basic stages of sleep, another, unique stage of sleep exists—REM. This stage gets its name from the darting eye movements that accompany it (rapid eye movement), as indicated by the EOG. Interestingly, it is also characterized by a sudden and dramatic loss of muscle tone, which is measured by the EMG. In fact, the skeletal muscles of a person during REM sleep are effectively paralyzed. This stage is also associated with a unique brain wave pattern. During REM sleep a sleeper's brain waves demonstrate characteristics that are similar to hypnagogic or hypnopompic states, being a combination of alpha, beta, and desynchronous waves.

Most importantly to psychologists, this is the stage of sleep most associated with dreaming. When a sleeper in a research lab begins to exhibit the physiological indices of REM sleep and he is awakened, the great majority of the time the sleeper will report that he was having a vivid, story-like dream. During other stages, on the other hand, the sleeper normally does not report dreaming.

William C. Dement, M.D., Ph.D., is one of the world's leading authorities on sleep, sleep disorders, and the dangers of sleep deprivation. He is the director and founder of the Stanford University Sleep Disorders Clinic and Research Center. "The vivid recall that could be elicited in the middle of the night when a subject was awakened while his eyes were moving rapidly was nothing short of miraculous. It [seemed to open] . . . an exciting new world to the subjects whose only previous dream memories had been the vague morning-after recall. Now, instead of perhaps some fleeting glimpse into the dream world each night, the subjects could be tuned into the middle of as many as ten or twelve dreams every night."[1]

In a normal night's sleep, a sleeper begins in stage 1, moves down through the stages to stage 4, then back up through the stages, with the exception that stage 1 is replaced by REM; then the sleeper goes back down through the stages again. One cycle, from stage 1 to REM takes approximately ninety minutes. This cycle is repeated throughout the night, with the length of REM periods increasing and the length of delta sleep decreasing, until during the last few cycles there is no delta sleep at all.[2] There are many scientific charts available that illustrate our stages of sleep. I have found this one to be concise and easy to understand:

STAGES OF SLEEP

WAKING	REM SLEEP	NREM SLEEP			
		Light Sleep		Deep Sleep	
Stage 0	Stage R	Stage 1	Stage 2	Stage 3	Stage 4
Eyes open, responsive to external stimuli, can hold intelligible conversation	Brain waves similar to waking. Most vivid dreams happen in this stage. Body does not move.	Transition between waking and sleep. If awakened, person will claim was never asleep.	Main body of light sleep. Memory consolidation. Synaptic pruning.	Slow waves on EEG readings.	Slow waves on EEG readings.
16 to 18 hours per day	90 to 120 minutes per night	4 to 7 hours per night			

Practice 11
WAKING DURING DREAMING

From the above information, we know that dreams occur almost entirely in REM sleep and that REM sleep takes place at the end of a sleep cycle. Each sleep cycle lasts about 90 to 110 minutes. If you sleep for eight hours, you are sleeping through about 5 cycles of sleep.

The REM portion of the sleep cycle is small in the first 2 to 3 cycles and gradually becomes longer during the later cycles toward the end of our typical sleep time. Our most memorable dreams happen at the end of our sleep cycles, the longest being cycles 4 and 5, or 6 if you sleep nine hours.

The goal of this practice is to figure out your personal sleep cycle to determine when you are mostly likely to be dreaming. Even though we don't have EEG, EMG, or EOG machines like dream scientists, for most people it's easier than it may sound. Through a few nights of trial and error, we can find out enough to start with. Since 80 percent of all dream recall is associated with waking up during REM sleep, we can significantly increase our recall with a strategy for waking. Before I knew about this practice I had already discovered years before that when I woke during the night and remembered a dream(s) and then went back to sleep, I almost always landed in the same or another dream automatically. This still happens to me to this day. However, many times if we awake during the night, it is not at the end or during a dream, so training in dream recall is vitally enhanced if we intentionally awake during a dream. We can do this with a simple alarm clock. Since our goal is to wake briefly and then go back to sleep, I suggest using a different, maybe not so loud or obnoxious alarm—setting your cell phone alarm on vibrate, which won't wake you all the way up like an audio alarm might.

Sleep cycles are different for everyone and can even be different from night to night, but if you are a typically scheduled sleeper like most people, you can easily determine patterns. Science very clearly shows us that our typical cycles are 90 to 110 minutes, so let's start with 100 minutes. We also know that REM is longest during cycles 4, 5, and 6. For your first night try targeting close to the end of your fifth cycle, let's say a half hour before then, which is a perfect time to be dreaming. If we use 100-minute cycles that would be 470 minutes divided by 60 equals 7.8 hours. So for this first trial I would set the alarm for 7.5 to 7.75 hours after falling asleep. If you have to wake up to start your day in 8 hours, then go with the 7.5-hour alarm time. To hit near to the end of the fourth cycle, go with 6.1 (370 divided by 60 equals 6.2): set your alarm for 6 hours after sleep.

When you wake up do a quick inventory. Were you having a dream? How do you feel? If you feel rested, awake, and dreamless, you probably didn't wake up during REM but in a light sleep. If you did wake up in the middle of a dream—success! You hit REM right on target, and you can map out your typical sleep cycles. If you didn't hit your target on this first try—no problem. Simply adjust ten to fifteen minutes either way for the next couple of nights till you hit it. Our sleep cycles are not exactly the same every night, but we can discover patterns during this trial-and-error technique that can significantly raise our level of dream recall and increase our chances for lucid dreaming when we go back to sleep.

While practicing this technique also be sure to take notes in your journal about times you wake up during the night. This will also help you in targeting REM/dream times. For example, I know that my first cycle is shorter than the others (I think for most people that's the case), but I almost *always* wake up three hours after going to sleep no matter what time I start. Nearly every night it's the same: three hours after I go to sleep I wake up and then go back to sleep. Sometimes I take a drink of water, sometimes I urinate, and sometimes I just look at the clock and fall right back to sleep.

So even though my first cycle is shorter, by the end of my second cycle, I am almost exactly at 3 hours or 90 minutes a cycle. At the end of this second cycle, I hardly ever remember a dream. This is because REM sleep is short in duration during the first and second sleep cycles. Through practicing the alarm clock technique, I also know that my other cycles are almost always 90 minutes, with REM or dream sleep occurring much more in the later cycles. The times I have the most dreams are between 6 and 6.5 hours of sleep, between 7 and 8, and between 8 and 9. It may take you many nights to learn your own patterns; however, don't forget that for pretty much everyone the later and especially last cycle of the night includes the most REM sleep. It's not only something that any lucid dreamer will tell you (including me), it's a scientific fact.

Another benefit of mastering your sleep cycles is that you can time when it's the best for you to wake up and start your day. If you are forcing yourself out of REM sleep to get out of bed, you will feel groggy and tired. If you time your awakening to when you are in light sleep (the beginning of a new cycle), you will feel refreshed and ready to go.

Practice 12
URINATION-INDUCED LUCID DREAMING

Practice 12 is a technique that many lucid dreamers call a WBTB (wake back to bed) induction technique. Some versions of WBTB techniques suggest that when you awake, either naturally or with a cue (like the alarm in practice 11), you intentionally stay awake for an hour or more before going back to sleep. For some people this technique works, but I never found it helpful for me. Intentionally or naturally waking, yes, absolutely, especially waking in the early morning during the later sleep cycles is most effective for dream recall and inducing lucid dreams. But I have found it better to either go right back to sleep, or scribble some dream notes and then go back to sleep without waking up completely. This way I go right back to dreamland.

However, as I expressed before, I almost always wake up after three hours' sleep, even if for just thirty seconds. I look at the clock, roll over, maybe write some notes on my whiteboard (it's mounted to the wall next to my bed, and I can write on it without getting up), or take a sip of water and go right back to dream sleep. The other habit I have is having to pee (usually just once) during the night. Believe it or not, and you can shake your head and laugh all you want, this circumstance has invaluably helped me and others with dream recall and lucid dreaming.

Here's why. Have you ever had to pee really bad while sleeping and actually dreamed that you did go and pee? Then when you wake up a short time later and you still have to pee, you realize you were dreaming. Peeing in a dream, when you really do have to pee, is an especially vivid and real dream experience. This usually happens when you know you have to pee, but you don't want to get up, so you fall back asleep for a while until the urge is too great and you get up.

While learning to lucid dream this would happen to me frequently, especially when I lived in a house that only had a woodstove for heat in the winter. Many times in the middle of the night I had to go pee, but the house was really cold and I didn't want to get out of bed. I knew eventually I would have no choice but to get up, but I'd wait just a few more minutes . . . I would then fall back to sleep and have the most vivid dreams—mainly about going to the bathroom, either in my actual house or somewhere else. The physiological need of having to urinate affected my subconscious and dreams and made them feel like some of the most real dreams I have ever had. Upon awaking again and still having to go, I was beyond surprise that I hadn't already gone—that's how real the dreams were (and still are at times).

You likely know the way to your closest bathroom from your bedroom so well that you could probably get there blindfolded without much difficulty. So getting up and going and then getting back in bed to sleep is something you can easily accomplish without actually waking completely up. This waking up and then going right back to sleep is a natural form of the last practice and is awesome for dream recall and getting right back into a remembered dream.

Having to pee in the night later became a valuable lucid dreaming technique when I started to experience intentional lucid dreaming. The sheer urgency of my bladder needing release at one moment turned a vivid dream experience into a lucid dream experience. Really needing to pee super badly, and my subconscious knowing that and expressing that in my dream, created the bridge to knowing I was dreaming and the need to wake up. I didn't *just* wake up, *I told myself in my dream to wake up.* Big difference.

For those of you that already get up and go on a nightly basis like

I do, I would simply use this WBTB experience in a positive way by recalling any dreams you just had before going to pee, and using this break in sleep to enter back into any dreams you've had or plant the intention to dream as you fall back to sleep.

If you don't normally wake to pee during the night, you can use this technique:

1. Make going to the bathroom one of your targets during the day. It's one of the things you are sure to do multiple times. Repeatedly reality checking when you go to the bathroom will train your subconscious to do it while dreaming.

2. Drink a lot of water or tea before bed, enough that for sure you will need to go during the night. This is an effective and safe way to intentionally trigger a dream (of going to the bathroom) and doing a reality check in your dream. This reality check could induce lucid dreaming right then or when you come back to bed after going.

3. After you come back to bed, write whatever you need to in your journal or just go back to sleep with the intention of being aware you are dreaming in your dreams.

4. Alternatively, if you're hard core, you can load up on water again before you go back to sleep. This will almost ensure that you dream about going again because you will have to, and that affords you yet another chance for a reality check while dreaming and becoming lucid right then or when you get back to bed.

Much more than being a joke or something gross, the physical need for urination while asleep is a potent psychophysiological occurrence that can be very productive to lucid dreaming.

Practice 13
THE SLEEP RHYTHM ADJUSTMENT TECHNIQUE

This is an effective technique especially for beginners. We know we have definite sleep cycles and that we also have a biological circadian rhythm based on our twenty-four-hour circadian clock. Our circadian rhythm can be adjusted (entrained) to the local environment by external cues that include light and temperature. We also have learned rhythms. Depending on our daily schedule, we decide what time is best to go to sleep and wake up. After some time on the same schedule, our subconscious somehow learns what time it is. For many years I needed to get up for work five to seven days a week at 5 a.m. no matter what time I went to sleep. When I no longer had to wake at that time, for many months I still did, no matter what time I went to sleep. Most of us have experienced this.

We can actually use this phenomenon in our quest for lucid dreaming with this easy but effective technique. As the name implies we are going to temporarily adjust our sleep rhythm. This is accomplished by simply getting up ninety minutes earlier than your standard time for one week, basically taking out one sleep cycle. For this week get up when the alarm goes off (ninety minutes earlier than usual) even if you don't want to. (It's only for one week!) On the second week you will see the results. After your early week is complete, begin getting up ninety minutes early on every other day. Your subconscious and your body now expect to get up earlier. This means that on the days you're sleeping in later, your brain will be more active ninety minutes before you wake up, which makes it much easier to become lucid while having early morning dreams.

For this sleep rhythm adjustment technique to work, it's really important that you don't go back to sleep on your early mornings. Get up and do something. Anything! It's perfectly normal to wake up early on your sleep-in days. This is actually a good thing because if you awake knowing you can sleep in for another ninety minutes, you can plant the intention to dream in your mind, or go back into the dream you just had or one from earlier in the night, as you fall back to sleep.

9

Autogenic Training and Lucid Dreaming

The last technique to perform before going to sleep involves placing ourselves in an attentive state of relaxation. This can be facilitated in a few different ways. Some teachers of lucid dreaming suggest meditation practices, while others prefer intentionally relaxing the various muscle groups in the body. However, a few practitioners believe we should not attend to the body at all—that by focusing on the body we become distracted because it has nothing to do with dreaming. In my opinion we should not neglect to attend to our body; quite the opposite. Through passively connecting our mind and body, we can not only attain a deep state of relaxation but also set up a state of consciousness of passive concentration that is very beneficial to dream recall and lucid dreaming while we fall asleep.

The important practice of cleansing our day has helped to clear ourselves of distracting thoughts. Now before sleep we will go even further by intentionally relaxing our total psychophysiological organism—mind and body—and enter the state of passive concentration or passive volition. Please review the previous overview of passive volition on pages 7–9.

The technique I found to be the most useful to practice just before sleep is autogenic training (AT). I have written a complete guide to AT, *Advanced Autogenic Training and Primal Awareness,* and suggest you read it and engage in the practices. The scope of AT practices in that book is much broader than what we need for lucid dreaming, but the complete range of AT practices combined with primal mind awareness provides a perfect complement of activities for lucid dreaming that are performed while we are awake.

Although AT is performed while awake, the recommended practice of the seven "classic" techniques is three times a day, spread out in your daily schedule. The last practice of the day is usually right before sleep, and after the last practice you usually do fall asleep, which is perfect for what we are doing here. Below is a basic outline of the seven classic AT practices. Each training typically takes a month or so to master. Almost anyone can master AT if they take the time and have the desire. Studies of AT students and teachers have shown that students report having an 80 to 90 percent success rate. Whether this is just wishful thinking I don't know, but those numbers seem accurate for my students. I am including this very condensed guide here simply because even if you haven't mastered it, the practice of AT is still beneficial for setting up dreaming.

Autogenic training can be done in many different positions, as described in my AT book, but here we are setting up dreaming so the practices described in this book are all done in the same position, as follows. As you get into bed lie on your back with your legs outstretched and slightly apart with your feet falling slightly outward, arms lying by your sides, palms facing downward. Alternatively, you can rest your down-turned hands on your pelvis. The main thing is to be comfortable. A pillow under your head and under your knees may be helpful. Keep your head and neck straight. It is not advisable when learning AT to roll on your side, as you would when going to sleep.

Before I begin explaining the AT practices, it is important to introduce what is called the cancellation. Please pay careful attention to this. We will be using this in every AT session. When you are finished with an AT exercise, it is best to end your session in a way that will return you to your normal state, awake and alert. You may in time come up with your own way. Here's the recommended way to start:

1. Close your eyes.
2. Open your fingers wide. Bend your elbows so your forearms form a right angle with your chest, palms facing.
3. Take a deep breath while at the same time bringing your hands together in a prayer position with the sides of your thumbs firmly touching your chest.
4. Exhale deeply while gently throwing your arms out in front of you and allowing your hands to separate.
5. Open your eyes.

This can be done once or as many times as needed until you feel fully alert. In most cases throwing your arms is done very gently at the end of a series or session. But if, for whatever reason, you need to stop immediately during a session, you can cancel more forcefully by throwing your arms out strongly and exhaling powerfully.

Practice 14
THE "I BREATHE ME" EXPERIENCE

The first training is so simple that from the outside it might even seem silly, but as you get inside and go deeper, you will understand how important it is to the whole series. The importance of the first training with our breath sets the stage for passive volition—the cornerstone of autogenic training.

There are many relaxation, healing, and meditative techniques that employ altering the breath as part of their process and are quite effective. But in AT we do just the opposite. In this training we try to do nothing at all with our breathing!

Breathing is an autonomous activity of the body that we know we can control, so it is the perfect activity for the body to begin learning AT but more importantly passive volition. During AT the muscular and vascular systems, including the heart, naturally integrate with our breathing. During AT it is not desirable to alter our breathing intentionally since we want to self-regulate our body through passive volition and not active adjustment.

In this training we try to do nothing at all with our breathing, and so we use the passive sounding phrase, "I breathe me." The statement, "I breathe me" makes it clear that regulation of the breath will come naturally and spontaneously during the training. We use this phrase while concentrating not on our chest but on the air that comes in and out of our noses and mouth. In a comfortable AT position and focusing on our breath without trying to alter it, we can enter deep states of relaxation and ready ourselves for the other trainings by entering the state of passive volition.

Keep the following points in mind whenever you practice autogenic training.

- Practice alone in a setting that is warm, quiet, and dimly lit. You want to be comfortable and in a place with as little possibility for interruption as possible.
- Wear comfy clothes and no shoes.
- Keep your eyes closed while practicing. If you need to make notes for yourself or remember the material, it's okay to open your eyes to read the instructions; just close your eyes again while you practice.
- It can help the initial training to lie flat on your back on a hard, carpeted floor or rug. This will enhance your ability to feel the heaviness of your arms and legs. If that is not practical for you, a bed, couch, or exercise or yoga mat will do fine. After you have mastered the complete training sequence you can use your autogenic formulas under any other circumstances you like, whether sitting, standing, walking, or lying down.
- Make sure your bladder and bowels are empty.
- It's best to practice before meals.

- Avoid intoxicants and smoking beforehand.
- If you fall asleep during a session, repeat that routine in your next session.
- If you practice in bed at night, you could fall asleep before you complete your cycle. Therefore, if you practice at night, in bed, consider this to be in addition to your basic practice.

It's recommended to do this training many times during your first day. It will be the first step to all the other trainings, so it's important to take your time and get used to it.

1. Get into a comfortable AT position.
2. Concentrate on the breath coming in and out of your nose and mouth without trying to regulate it.
3. For a minimum of two minutes or for as long as you want, just let the breath flow in and out while slowly repeating the phrase, "I breathe me."
4. Do not vocalize the phrase; simply hear the words in your mind. It is not necessary to say the phrase to yourself on each breath because that becomes too repetitious. I usually say it on each breath for the first few and then maybe after every three or four. Do whatever feels comfortable and natural for you.

Practice 15
THE HEAVINESS EXPERIENCE

The second training is based on the neuromuscular system because it tends to be the second easiest system influenced by conscious efforts, and it also provides a concrete set of practices that stimulates deep levels of relaxation. There are many ways to relax muscles. Two of my favorites are hot springs and massage. However, the goal here is to self-generate muscular relaxation.

When we are active our muscles are quite naturally in a state of tension to accomplish whatever it is we are doing. When the neuromuscular system is in a relaxed state, we usually have a feeling of heaviness in the extremities. It's quite common to be aware of this feeling just before or after sleeping. In this training we will focus on heaviness in our arms and legs and our neck and back muscles. It's easier to focus on the arms and legs, so first we'll work on those body parts.

First, spend two minutes passively breathing and repeating, "I breathe me," as in practice 14. Then, beginning with your dominant arm (if you are left-handed, begin with the left arm), passively focus on each area and internally repeat the following phrases:

- Repeat to yourself six times the phrase, "My right arm is heavy."
- Repeat to yourself six times the phrase, "My left arm is heavy."
- Repeat to yourself three times the phrase, "My arms are heavy."
- Repeat to yourself six times the phrase, "My right leg is heavy."
- Repeat to yourself six times the phrase, "My left leg is heavy."
- Repeat to yourself three times the phrase, "My legs are heavy."
- Repeat to yourself three times the phrase, "Both my arms and legs are heavy."
- Turn your attention away from your arms and legs and say to yourself, "I am very quiet."
- Remain relaxed for a minute or two.
- Cancel the practice as recommended earlier (hands in prayer position at the chest and then thrown gently outward).

Now we incorporate the neck and back muscles. Getting in touch with these muscles is a little more difficult than with the arms and legs, which we are used to seeing when we use them, but with patience you will be able to do it. The phrase we use in this training is as simple as the others: "My neck and back are heavy."

Repeat the previous sequence—relaxing both arms and legs—and then add the following step before finishing with, "I am very quiet."

- Repeat to yourself six times the phrase, "My neck and back are heavy."

- Turn your attention away from your neck and back, and say to yourself, "I am very quiet."
- Remain relaxed for a minute or two.
- Cancel the practice.

Practice 16
VASCULAR DILATION

Similarly to how electrophysiological devices can measure muscular relaxation of the AT heaviness trainings, we can also measure an observable change in warmth during this AT training. Findings have shown a six- to eight-degree increase in tissue warmth during the "my arms are warm" section of this training when a person is well trained. This practice affects the entire peripheral cardiovascular system— arteries, capillaries, and blood flow through muscles and skin. Begin, as in practice 15, with two minutes of passive breathing, slowly repeating, "I breathe me." Then passively focus on each body area at a time, beginning with the dominant side first (whether the left or the right arm), while saying the following:

- Repeat to yourself three times the phrase, "My right arm is warm."
- Repeat to yourself three times the phrase, "My left arm is warm."
- Repeat to yourself three times the phrase, "My arms are warm."
- Repeat to yourself three times the phrase, "My right leg is warm."
- Repeat to yourself three times the phrase, "My left leg is warm."
- Repeat to yourself three times the phrase, "My legs are warm."
- Repeat to yourself six times the phrase, "My arms and legs are warm."
- Repeat to yourself six times the phrase, "My neck and back are warm."
- Turn your attention away from your neck and back and say to yourself, "I am very quiet."
- Remain relaxed for a minute or two.
- Cancel the practice.

Practice 17
REGULATION OF THE HEART

The phrase we use for this training is, "My heartbeat is calm and strong." When we say the phrase to ourselves, we take our mind to the area of our body where our heart is. Your heart is about the size of your fist and is located behind and to the left of your breastbone or sternum. During the training we can also pay passive attention to any place in our body where we feel our pulse. This could be a hand, a foot, your temple, your neck, or any other place. I have had multiple injuries to muscles around my left rib cage, so I often feel my pulse there, especially during AT.

During AT we have learned the experience of warmth by passively connecting with our peripheral cardiovascular system and experiencing vascular dilation. We've experienced muscular relaxation through passively concentrating on heaviness and our breath. The next step is to combine the heaviness and warmth experience and add the heart. As before, adopt a comfortable AT position in a quiet setting and spend two minutes in passive breathing, slowly repeating, "I breathe me." Passively focus on each area at a time, beginning with the dominant side.

- Repeat to yourself three times the phrase, "My right arm is heavy."
- Repeat to yourself three times the phrase, "My left arm is heavy."
- Repeat to yourself six times the phrase, "My arms and legs are heavy."
- Concentrate on your heartbeat, and repeat to yourself six times the phrase, "My heartbeat is calm and strong."
- While still aware of your heartbeat say to yourself, "I am very quiet."
- Remain relaxed for a minute or two.
- Cancel the practice.

Practice 18

WARMTH IN THE ABDOMEN

The celiac plexus, also known as the solar plexus because of its radiating nerve fibers, is a complex network of nerves (a plexus) located in the abdomen, where the celiac trunk, superior mesenteric artery, and renal arteries branch from the abdominal aorta. You can locate this area by looking down at your belly and putting a finger halfway between your navel and the lower end of your sternum (where your rib cage comes together just below your chest): that's the center of the solar plexus.

The solar plexus is the center of the autonomic nervous system. In AT we desire to connect with this area of our body because through many interconnected nerves, such as the vagus nerve, it serves as a relay station directly from our organs to our brain. In a nutshell the solar plexus gives our brain the information it needs to regulate the functioning of our body, so by getting in touch with it we can passively affect brain function. The solar plexus training can bring about deep states of altered consciousness if and when you connect to this central point of your nervous system.

During this training it is common for me to hear from clients feelings of weightlessness, floating, and even out-of-body experiences where they see themselves from outside their body, usually from above. The solar plexus is the second-most difficult area to connect with, exceeded only by training the brain, and may take much more time to learn than the previous trainings. Unlike our arms or legs, we never see our solar plexus, and we never feel it, unlike our breath or heartbeat, which makes it difficult to focus our attention on it. But with patience and practice it is possible to passively focus on this very important area.

Spend two minutes passively breathing, slowly repeating, "I breathe me." Then passively focus on the following areas (beginning with the dominant side):

- Repeat to yourself three times the phrase, "My right arm is heavy."
- Repeat to yourself three times the phrase, "My left arm is heavy."
- Repeat to yourself three times the phrase, "My arms and legs are heavy and warm."
- Repeat to yourself three times the phrase, "My heartbeat is calm and strong."
- Repeat to yourself six times the phrase, "My solar plexus is warm."
- While still aware of the area of your solar plexus say to yourself, "I am very quiet."
- Remain relaxed for a minute or two.
- Cancel the practice.

Practice 19
COOLING THE FOREHEAD FOR ADVANCED PRACTICE

Our brain has four distinct regions called lobes: frontal lobe, temporal lobe, parietal lobe, and occipital lobe. Our frontal lobe is the largest region of our brain, sitting just behind our forehead. This highly complex and specialized region helps to control many different and important skills, which include:

Organization
Concept formation
Mental flexibility
Personality
Execution of behavior (the frontal lobe is also called the executive system)
Abstract reasoning
Problem solving
Planning
Judgment
Ethical behavior
Inhibition

Expressive language

Affect

Attention

Passively getting in touch with this part of the brain through AT has many benefits in terms of relaxation, peace, and well-being. However, this training is by far the most challenging to accomplish. Unlike the other practices, which produce an 80 to 90 percent success rate, studies show only a 40 percent success rate for the forehead cooling training. For those that feel the cooling, it usually takes seven to fourteen days to learn. The feeling will not be cold but closer to the feeling of blowing on the back of your hand or the relaxing effect of a cool (not cold) cloth on the forehead. But it doesn't really matter if it happens for you or not. Even if you don't feel your forehead cool, that won't take anything away from the relaxation, peace, body connection, and health benefits that practicing any part of AT produces.

As before, adopt a comfortable AT position in a quiet setting and spend two minutes passively breathing, slowly repeating, "I breathe me." Passively focus on each area at a time, beginning with your dominant side:

- Repeat to yourself three times the phrase, "My right arm is heavy."
- Repeat to yourself three times the phrase, "My left arm is heavy."
- Repeat to yourself three times the phrase, "My arms and legs are heavy and warm."
- Repeat to yourself three times the phrase, "My heartbeat is calm and strong."
- Repeat to yourself three times the phrase, "My solar plexus is warm."
- Repeat to yourself six times the phrase, "My forehead is pleasantly cool."

- Repeat to yourself three times the phrase, "My neck and back are warm."
- While still aware of the areas of your neck and back, say to yourself, "I am very quiet."
- Remain relaxed for a minute or two.
- Cancel the practice.

10

Visualization for Advanced Lucid Dreaming

Visualization has historically been a key practice in most if not all Eastern mystical traditions and more recently has been adopted by many Westerners due to its effectiveness. Over the centuries thousands of volumes of literature concerning both the esoteric and psychological processes of visualization methods have been produced throughout the globe.

With our standard AT formulas we plant the seed and simply let it grow. If I try really hard to feel my dominant arm get heavy, it won't. Neither will I feel warmth in my solar plexus if I concentrate with all my might to do so. The same is true for autogenic visualization. We must plant the seed and simply let it grow. It is true that autogenic visualization is much more dynamic than the standard formulas, and you have the ability to "control" what to visualize. But the more passively you can accomplish your visualizations, the more successful you will be.

To set up AT visualization, after a good standard AT session and with eyes closed, we rotate the eyeballs upward and inward looking at the center of the forehead. This is very similar to the third eye meditation in yogic practice and corresponds to the agya chakra. The technique is as follows:

1. Close your eyes.

2. Relax and breathe normally for a few moments until you feel still and quiet.

3. Now concentrate on the middle of your forehead for a few moments but keep your eyes straight.

4. After a few moments of concentrating your attention on the center of your forehead, move your eyes up and in (or in and up) so they are pointed to the area between and about one inch above the space between your eyebrows.

Practice 20
THE SPONTANEOUS EVOCATION OF COLORS

Once you feel comfortable with adopting and holding the third eye position, it's time for the first training, which has to do with visualizing colors. Begin by completing a good session of standard formulas, but don't cancel at the end. Simply remain in your AT state. During the session or near the end, you may already have seen or are still seeing colors or lights as if projected on your closed eyelids like a movie screen. This is quite common for people in the later stages of learning the standard formulas and those that have mastered them. If you are not already seeing colors, simply remain relaxed, and they may appear in five minutes or half an hour. It may take a few days for some people; we are all different in that way. Just be patient and passive, and have good standard AT sessions, which are the core of this whole process.

Spontaneous colors and lights come in many forms. In this first training simply passively watch them and don't try to control them. I have seen lots of different color schemes. The most commonly reported by my clients are static dots of different colors or a single color, slowly moving dots, colored dots moving together in a formation, multicolored or single colored swirls, random diluted colors that are hazy or smoky. It may be that you see none of this and instead see your own version.

At some point, no one knows when, if you are integrating passively, you will probably see a merging of what you normally see into one single color. We can call this your base color. During your regular AT or when you are very relaxed, it's common to see this color. Remember, this process could take days or weeks, but once you get the hang of it, your color will appear very rapidly, sometimes even unexpectedly during your AT.

Summary:
1. Perform a good standard AT session, but don't cancel at the end.
2. Concentrate on the middle of your forehead for a few moments, and then gently move your eyes in and then up to your third eye.
3. Maintain your passive AT state for twenty to thirty minutes or until colors begin.
4. Passively observe whatever colors or formations arise for ten to fifteen minutes.
5. Cancel.

Practice 21
COLORS ON DEMAND

Now it's time to use passive volition to evoke your base color and other colors. Some colors, such as purple, yellow, and orange, usually produce a feeling of warmth. With red, be careful. If you see red and are still comfortably relaxed, then fine. If you start to feel agitated or aggressive, cancel immediately. Blue and green are known to have a cooling effect similar to the coolness of the forehead formula.

From here it is perfectly natural and advisable to visualize colors in formations such as hazes, clouds, or something that resembles colored "shadows" slowly moving across your visual field. In time you can visualize geometric patterns, which often morph into a kaleidoscope of colors, shapes, fractals, patterns, spirals, checkerboards, grids, webs, and funnels, either static or drifting. If what you are seeing is static, try experimenting with movement, such as making your vision bigger or smaller or turning, curving, or rotating. Some researchers claim that similar processes to the ones described here happen spontaneously while we are awake and when asleep, although we do not consciously acknowledge them due to our normally active psychological functioning. It is only through passive volition that we consciously tune in to these processes.

Summary:
1. Perform a good standard AT session, but don't cancel at the end.
2. Now concentrate on the middle of your forehead for a few moments, and then gently move your eyes in, then up (third eye).
3. Maintain your passive AT state for twenty to thirty minutes or until colors begin to appear.
4. Bring to mind specific colors, and observe how they manifest. Visualize colors taking shape and having movement. There is no set time limit; however, I have found that for most people forty-five minutes to an hour is an average period of time for the entire session.
5. Cancel.

Practice 22
DEVELOPING A LUCID DREAMING PRACTICE—
A TWO-WEEK INTENSIVE

Now, it's time to actually embark on this magnificent journey!

I suggest you stick to this practice regimen for at least two weeks, maybe longer, until you consistently recall (and record) at least one or more dreams each night. Hopefully you have completed or are working on practice 2 and so have increased your available energy. If you haven't already, you need to get a special dream journal and pen. I have made this very clear in practice 8: keeping your journal of goals, reality checks, and recalling dreams is vital to this stage. Before beginning your two-week regimen, make sure you have clearly defined your initial goals in your journal (practice 9), and you have a full week of reality checks listed (practice 10).

Your first night of officially beginning your journey should be very exciting. Even though we will be practicing passive volition, there is no substitute for determination in actually sticking to the daily and nightly schedule. Here is a numbered checklist for the first two weeks beginning just before going to sleep on your first night. Do whatever you normally do for getting ready for bed and then:

Step 1. Place your dream journal (complete with goals and reality checks) next to your bed. Also, if you decided to hang (or just have) a whiteboard next to your bed, make sure that is set to go.

Step 2. Perform practice 7 (Cleansing Your Day).

Step 3. Review practice 12 (Urination-Induced Lucid Dreaming) and practice 14 (The "I Breath Me" Experience).

Step 4. Review visualization and autogenic training and practice 20 (The Spontaneous Evocation of Colors).

Step 5. Start the first page of the dream recall section of your journal. Write the date and your intention: "I will remember my dream(s) tonight."

Step 6. Get in bed, turn out the lights, and lie comfortably on your back. Close your eyes and begin, "I breath me"—passive, uncontrolled autonomic breathing that naturally takes you into a relaxed state.

Step 7. When ready, perform whichever AT session you feel most comfortable with in that moment.

Step 8. After your AT session begin practice 20 (The Spontaneous Evocation of Colors).

Step 9. As you begin to feel sleepy, drop your eye position from the third eye to normal. If you saw colors or other kinds of images, keep them with you as you fall asleep. If you didn't see anything, that's fine; as you get closer and closer to sleep, hypnogogic images may appear anyway. The more you practice these techniques, the easier they become. The seeing of colors and other hypnogogic images will simply become natural as you fall asleep.

If you wake up during the night and you recall a dream, write it down in your journal or erase board. If not, that's fine. When you wake up in the morning, stay perfectly still for a few moments (or minutes) and recall any dreams and write them down. Make sure to have the date and your location (for future reference). You may find it helpful to jot a quick list of key words or phrases as an outline so you won't forget things while writing. Write as much of your night's dreams as you can recall, including details. I find it helpful to write in the present tense. If you don't recall anything simply write down any feelings, thoughts, emotions, affirmations, and so on that come to you.

After writing in your journal, review and memorize your reality checks for the day. Don't even look at the checks for the other days; concentrate solely on today. If you need to, review practice 10 on reality checks. Go about your day, and remember to do your checks very well! At the end of your day, write in your journal about your checks. Did you do them? Were you successful? Remember, if you can't remember to do things in your waking world, you have basically no chance of remembering while in the dream world.

During this first two-week-or-so period, do not use practices 11, 12, or 13 related to intentional waking and altering sleep rhythms. These techniques are more advanced, are not very useful until developing good dream recall, and are used to help induce lucid dreaming. Right now we are only concerned with prospective memory reality checks and dream recall. If you do wake up naturally during the night for whatever reason, that's great. Usually, especially at the end of your sleep cycles, you will more easily remember dreams. But let's not intentionally induce awakening yet. One step at a time.

The regimen for your second and successive nights will follow the same steps, with these slight changes: When you first get into bed, begin practice 14 (The "I Breathe Me" Experience) for step 6. On the second night, perform practice 15 (The Heaviness Experience) in step 7 and for the following two nights. Starting on the fifth night, perform practice 17 for step 7 for three nights and so on for practices 18 and 19, doing each for three consecutive nights. Practice 20 is really difficult and may take months or years of diligent practice to experience; some people never do. If you didn't experience practice 19 in the three days allotted, don't worry; it's really difficult too. I suggest spending however long it takes to experience practice 19 before moving to practice 20. The chart below clarifies the days and practices for step 7. We will also be changing step 8 during the two-week period, but this change is totally up to you and how your visualization practice is evolving. We only want to change step 8 and move on to the next visualization techniques after we have fully experienced the current one.

	DAY 1	DAY 2	DAY 3	DAY 4	DAY 5	DAY 6	DAY 7
Step 7	AT session of choice	Practice 15	Practice 15	Practice 15	Practice 17	Practice 17	Practice 17
Step 8	Practice 20	Practice 21 or 22	Practice 21 or 22	Practice 21 or 22	Practice 21 or 22	Practice 21 or 22	Practice 21 or 22
	DAY 8	DAY 9	DAY 10	DAY 11	DAY 12	DAY 13	DAY 14
Step 7	Practice 18	Practice 18	Practice 18	Practice 19	Practice 19	Practice 19	Practice 20
Step 8	Practice 21 or 22	Practice 21 or 22	Practice 21 or 22	Practice 21 or 22	Practice 21 or 22	Practice 21 or 22	Practice 21 or 22

For example, on night one our visualization technique is the spontaneous evocation of colors. If this didn't happen for you, simply apply the technique again on night two of step 8. Each of the standard AT techniques and advanced visualization techniques may take many days, weeks, or months to experience. I suggest trying each of the classic techniques for three nights (per the chart) to simply try them all out. At the end of this first two-week training, I suggest you keep practicing them and also begin practicing the many other techniques in my autogenic training book. However, with the two visualization techniques, they have even more of a snowball effect than the standard formulas. You will find it much more productive not trying to go to practice 22 until you accomplish and vividly experience practice 21.

Once you have completed this two-week training, you have laid a wonderful foundation for the next steps of lucid and shamanic dreaming. If you have been diligent in your practice, you may have already induced some lucid dreams during this period or experienced one or more spontaneous lucid dreams. Simply by diligently practicing AT, dream recall, prospective memory, and visualization, you have intentionally prepared your psychophysiological organism to bridge the paradox of consciousness in dreaming.

11
Three Bridges
to Shamanic Dreaming

As discussed, a lucid dream is a dream in which the dreamer knows that he is dreaming while he is dreaming. This type of dream has been employed by shamans throughout the world for ages. Although an exceptional accomplishment, knowing you are dreaming while dreaming (lucid dreaming) and recalling the dream are only the setup for shamanic dreaming, where the goals are much larger. Consciousness while dreaming, self-awareness, and the ability to passively control the dream are key factors of shamanic dreaming. Lucid dreaming is not the same as dream control. We can have lucid awareness without control, and we can manipulate the dream without any awareness that we're dreaming.

To make the passage from lucid to shamanic dreaming, we first must metaphorically cross three bridges of dream states. First, we need to experience the ability to reenter a dream. Then we need to find in our dream something we intended to find while awake, and from there we learn the techniques for changing a dream. Once we cross these three bridges, we will be able to start interacting with sentient beings in the dream landscape—one of the most difficult and respected forms of shamanism.

Practice 23
FIRST BRIDGE—DREAM REENTRY

Now that you have accomplished the preparation for lucid dreaming, it's time for the next task and the most challenging one yet: crossing the bridge from skillful dream recall and becoming aware you are dreaming while in your dream to reentering your dreams. We are going to go straight to the most effective technique I know, which was explained in practice 11. (Review chapter 8 and practice 11 on page 104.)

Steps 1 through 9 in this stage will be the same as the previous, which you are now very familiar with, except you are going to add setting your alarm for step 6. The key points to remember are:

REM is longest during cycles 4, 5, and 6. So for your first night, try targeting close to the end of your fifth cycle. Let's say a half hour before then, which is a perfect time to be dreaming. If we use 100-minute cycles, that would be 470 minutes divided by 60 equals 7.8 hours. So for this trial I would set the alarm for 7.5.

Step 10. When your alarm goes off, try to turn it off with your eyes closed and with as little movement as possible. Keep your eyes closed and recall if you were dreaming. If so, try to remember every detail you can about the dream and then quickly write your notes about it.

Step 11. As you drift back to sleep, keep the memory and feeling of the dream you woke up with and passively use the affirmation, "I'm going back to my dream, and I will be aware when I get there."

Step 12. Upon reentering your dream, be aware that you are dreaming. Do not consciously try to change or control anything; simply and passively go with the flow of your dream while knowing that you are dreaming.

Step 13. When you wake up in the morning, stay perfectly still for a few moments (or minutes), recall any dreams, and then write them down. If you were able to reenter your dream aware that you were dreaming, congratulations! Write as much of your night's dreams as you can recall, including details.

If you did not awake while dreaming when your alarm went off, then simply adjust your wake cycle in 10-minute increments. I would start with earlier awakening, but if that is not successful, try staging your alarm a little later than your first try. You can also try hitting the end of the fourth cycle—370 divided by 60 equals 6.2. Set your alarm for 6 hours after sleep.

Once you have found and can consistently awake during your dream cycle, keep practicing reentering your last dream, or you can reenter any other dream you remember from the night. It is totally possible and very common to reenter a dream but not be aware you are dreaming. In this case you simply wake up while dreaming and then go back to sleep and back to the same dream. Upon awakening you may remember that you woke up during the night and went back to the same dream. I do this all the time if I wake up from a dream I really liked, or one that was intriguing, or somehow special. Sometimes I'll wake up and say to myself, "Darn! I want to go back!" So this will occur intentionally by my willing it to, or I'll just drift back to sleep and find myself back. This can occur whether you are aware of dreaming or not.

In this stage if you are aware you are dreaming either before your alarm awakes you or after you go back to sleep, simply enjoy being aware you are dreaming and see where your dreams take you. This is a favorite activity of mine and probably will be for you too. However, I'm going to add a word of caution here. Most schools of psychotherapy follow Freud's ideas that the unconscious mind while dreaming will present the dreamer with some kind of problem to be solved. Don't get stuck in this place of trying to figure your dreams out. Many dreams that happen while we are aware we are dreaming don't arise out of problems; on the contrary, they seem to come from other realms of consciousness, such as creativity and joy. I truly believe that our culture's strong urge to interpret dreams is so ingrained in us that many will need to make a major shift in attitude to fully enter this stage of dreaming. In this stage dreams may very well provide messages, but it's not our task to analyze them.

Another thing to mention at this point is that it's common while being aware that you are dreaming to sort of fall back into normal dreaming whether you realize it or not. Sometimes we can tell that our awareness that we are dreaming is not there anymore, but many times we don't realize what happened until we wake up. This situation is completely normal at this stage. It's sort of like learning to ride a bike. When you learned to ride a bike, you likely fell down frequently but kept getting up and trying again until you learned to balance. Continuing the analogy: before going fast, popping wheelies, or riding with no hands, you first learned to ride without training wheels. For this stage of shamanic dreaming, you first must learn to balance—to not fall back into normal sleep. This is why I suggest passively going for a gentle ride while aware you are dreaming. Eventually, through much practice and many falls, you will acquire the balance to go farther and faster.

Continue practicing this technique until you become proficient (not perfect) at reentering your dream in a state of being aware you are dreaming. At that point proceed to the next practice. Also continue performing reality checks during the course of your waking day, especially the check of tapping the fingers of one hand onto the palm of the other.

Practice 24
SECOND BRIDGE—DREAMING REALITY CHECK

The only sure way to know you are aware that you are dreaming is to perform a reality check while dreaming. During the previous practice, we intentionally avoided doing anything except to simply remain in the state of knowing we are dreaming. Now that we can do that, we will intentionally perform the reality check in step 12 of our dreaming practice. In attempting this, we will alter our goal in steps 1 and 11 to, "I will see my hands in my dream."

Right now as you are reading this, put the book down and place both hands in front of you so you can see them clearly. This is what you are going to try to do in this reality check. Seeing your palms is usually what happens, if it happens. Seeing your hands in your dreams is not easy. However, as opposed to many that have attempted lucid dreaming and failed at this task, if you have been diligently preparing by following the previous practices, I have every confidence that you will be successful. It may take time, maybe a long time, but you can do it.

A lot of situations may arise during this reality check. Some include:

Your hands may appear translucent or fuzzy.
You may have too many or not enough fingers.
Your hands may look like something else, such as claws or mittens.
Your hand may change from one thing to the next.

In my experience and those of my students, the very act of being able to raise your hands in front of your face while dreaming is the most important aspect of this practice. No matter what they look like, you have intentionally performed a reality check in your dream. Of course, it's possible that you just randomly saw your hands during a normal dream. However, if you have done your extensive dreaming preparation, this is highly unlikely. At this point in your training, if you passively intend to see your hands in your dream and you do, no matter what they look like, you have crossed the second bridge. I suggest you keep practicing this technique, intending to see your hands just as they appear in physical reality. But even if you saw your hands in another form, by succeeding in your intention to see them, you can now move on to practicing the third bridge.

Practice 25
THIRD BRIDGE—CHANGING THE DREAM

At this point we are not merely spectators of our dreams, unless we choose to be. If we desire we can intentionally manipulate our dreams while fully aware that we are doing so. Or can we? There could be a lot of debate on this subject as there is so much going on in the dream that we are clearly not consciously intending but is nonetheless under some level of our control. We could speculate that what we don't consciously control may in fact be under the control of the subconscious mind. The theory here is that because the dream is constructed by our subconscious, everything we negotiate in the dream is, in effect, a construct of the subconscious mind, including what we meet in the dream.

My position is that of course the dream is initially constructed by our subconscious mind when we dream during REM sleep. However, REM sleep is very close to waking consciousness, as opposed to non-rapid eye movement (NREM) light and deep sleep. Our subconscious knows our waking consciousness very well and makes presumptions *until we decide otherwise*. Once we are aware we are dreaming, everything changes. Is our subconscious creating the dream? Well, I'm asleep, so yes. Can I somehow consciously and intentionally manipulate the dream my subconscious has created? With training and practice—absolutely!

Through experiences of my conscious mind, my unconscious mind knows that my conscious mind thinks that I am a man, planet Earth is round, water is wet, fire is hot, gravity holds us down, and so on. However, when I'm conscious inside my subconscious dream, the normal rules don't apply. If I want to walk through a wall, breathe underwater, or fly to the top of a mountain, no problem. When we dream normally, we are basically spectators of our subconscious creations. When we are aware we are dreaming, we can choose to be spectators or not. For most people this truth is fairly easy to accept or, at the least, seems like it could be plausible.

What is usually not considered is that through manipulating the dreams that we are aware we are having, we can gain knowledge of what is happening or will happen in the waking world. At the most basic level of this phenomena are the very common precognitive dreams. Anyone who has had one can attest to their validity. It's all interconnected; all we need are the tools to plug in.

In this practice and from now on you have the experience to know what you need to set up your dreaming. However, after almost thirty years of experience in this form of shamanism, I still suggest you keep a journal, do reality checks throughout the day, and practice AT.

For me, my dreaming alarm simply became a part of my life, so I continued using it for years. At some point I stopped using it and found that I would almost always wake up after my fourth sleep cycle, which still happens more than 90 percent of the time. Whether you keep using your dream alarm, which I suggest you do, it's always productive to try practice 12 (Urination-Induced Lucid Dreaming) and practice 13 (Sleep Rhythm Adjustment Technique). The dream cycle waking techniques are still helpful even for experienced dreamers.

This third bridge is vital to the work of a shaman. I would consider crossing this bridge the biggest accomplishment in shamanic dreaming. Although supremely difficult, anyone with sufficient diligence and practice can cross the third bridge. Crossing the third dreaming bridge entails purposely changing your dream. The training you've been doing with prospective memory (reality checks) is vital to crossing this bridge because the best way I have found in learning how to do it is to use a very special object of your choosing.

While over the second bridge, we explored our dream without focusing on any one item in the dream. The task was simply to be fluid because, while we are learning to consciously navigate a dream, stopping often causes us to wake up. The third bridge is a test of how well we have learned to both navigate and stay in our dream. Focusing on an item that we place in the dream without waking up allows us to cross into a new dream. This probably seems hard to understand, but stay with me and it will become clearer.

The first thing to do is select three to five personal items. This should be super easy but is extremely important. These items should be ones that you see or use every day and that you have a deep personal attachment to. My dreaming items almost always come from my manifestation altar. Since they sit on my altar in my bedroom, I see them every day, and many of them I use frequently. For example:

- **Healing te'ka.** Extremely special rock, about the size of a cantaloupe, that I found in the Oak Creek Canyon in Sedona near my house there. I have had this rock for many years and use it to do healing work. It has traveled far and wide with me and sits prominently visible at all times, usually in my bedroom. This healing te'ka is much more like a buddy than a rock!

- **Red machete.** I got this sacred item in Mexico to harvest peyote with the Huichol in Wirikuta. It has been blessed by several shamans and by sacred springs, deer blood, and peyote. When making a Sacred Fire I will often use it to slice thin pieces of wood.
- *Takwatsi.* This is the reed case that houses the sacred items I carry with me on pilgrimages or to ceremonies.
- **My father's watch.** My father passed many years ago when I was fourteen. This is one of the few things I have of his.
- **Any of my books.** Because of the time and effort in creating a book, I obviously have a deep personal attachment to my published work.

If I were to see any one of these items in my dream, there would be absolutely no question of what they are. These items are more than just objects: they are sacred entities with the power to easily alter my consciousness. You don't need many items—quality, not quantity, is the key. Although I have used each of these items in my dreaming practices, unless I have a special reason to use one, I tend to use my healing te'ka or other special te'ka for dreaming. This is simply because they are not in any way created by man. Also I can "clean" them very easily and thoroughly. Whenever I use my healing te'ka as part of a healing ceremony, I will always clean it afterward by using sun, fire, running water, or wind, or burying it in the ground. This way it is free from human intentions and energies. My indigenous dreaming teachers are actually very careful not to let others even see their dream item(s).

Once you have chosen your items, put them together somewhere close to where you sleep. The second thing to do is add them to your prospective memory training. While performing reality checks during the day, visualize one of your sacred items. For example, if one of your targets for that day is to reality-check after flushing a toilet, while you reality-check with your hands, close your eyes and visualize one of your sacred items. If you are legitimately attached to the item, it should not be difficult to visualize it in your mind. Simply hold the image for thirty to sixty seconds. If you are going to visualize more than one, see them one at a time.

What we are doing here is intentionally training ourselves to visualize our sacred items in the waking world when remembering specific cues (targets) so we will be able to easily "find" or see them while dreaming. We have been training our prospective memory since we began learning conscious dreaming; now we are simply taking it to the next level. It is extremely important to visualize your sacred item many times during the day via a memory target.

After your nightly preparations and before going to bed, write in your dream journal your goal to find your sacred item. When doing your visualizations before sleep, visualize your sacred item and plant the seed again with an intentional sentence such as, "I will find you," "I will see you in my dream," or something similar. While you are in your dream and aware you are dreaming, visualize your sacred item or expect to simply see it there with you in the dream. You already have your eyes closed while dreaming, so visualization is different in that you can visualize your item wherever you want to see it in your dream.

As with all of these advanced shamanic dreaming practices we are now learning, this one can take a great deal of time and patience. When you eventually do find your sacred item, how will you know you are not simply randomly seeing it in an ordinary dream?

Here's what to do: focus your attention on it the same way you would if you were staring at it in the waking world or visualizing it during the day. If you are having a normal dream, you won't be able to continue focusing on the item. Once you are aware that you are dreaming the item, it can take you anywhere you want to go. I know that sounds strange, but it's actually not. Your sacred item is a *nierika,* a portal in the dream world. The other way to look at it is that the sacred item is a beacon showing you where the portal is.

Remember, even though you are aware you are dreaming, you're still dreaming. Your sacred item isn't "really" there at all. It is a conscious manifestation of your waking world inside your dream world. This conscious manifestation is merely a representation of the level you have attained at being aware you are dreaming. Now that you have attained this level of mastery, you can use your portal to direct and, even more importantly, change your dream.

While focusing on your sacred item (portal), plant the seed of changing the dream using passive volition. This is one of the main reasons for learning autogenic training and doing it before sleep. When you know how to passively manipulate autonomic functions of your body, the same technique can be applied to manipulate autonomic functions of the subconscious.

"Changing the dream" can be experienced in different ways. Sometimes the portal changes from what looks like my sacred item into a spiraling vortex that I get sucked into and then "land" in another dream. Some people experience the portal as a door or window. Depending on how aware I am (there are still various levels at this stage), the view out the door or window can be manipulated so that I can see where the portal will take me. I have also experienced the sacred item or portal simply dissolve or dissipate along with the whole dream, and when the dream comes back, it is a different dream. This can seem like falling asleep in a dream and waking up in another dream.

It is important to note that in the beginning it's quite normal to have the dream simply fade away, or you wake up when you plant the seed of changing the dream through the portal. It can be frustrating when this happens because you feel so close to actually doing it, and then it doesn't happen. For this reason I want to reiterate what I said at the very beginning: dealing with your energetic drains and reclaiming lost energy is vital to proficiency in dreaming. When you get stuck or feel you are not moving ahead in your dreaming practices, go back to practice 2 and work with the Sacred Fire to get clear. Also, don't forget to cleanse your day before dreaming. This should be a habit for you at this point. I can tell you from personal experience and from the experiences of others, you will not cross the third dreaming bridge if you are in an energetically poor condition.

Crossing the third bridge is a monumental task for most modern people. Once you are able to find the portal (your sacred item) and manipulate it to change your dream, you can move to the next practice.

12

Sentient Beings in
the Dreamscape

The art of meeting sentient beings in your dreamscape has four steps, and it is imperative to learn them in the order I have laid out. Trying to jump ahead in the practices will yield diminished results. First is getting a feel for the dreamscape. This is extremely important as it is the foundation for the next steps. Once you are comfortable navigating in the dreamscape, you open to new worlds that include all types of sentient beings.

Meeting with sentient beings in your dreamscape has many advantages as a shamanic practitioner. They deliver important messages, give advice on personal matters or specific remedies for healing clients, and can even become good friends.

Practice 26
FEELING THE DREAM LANDSCAPE

Changing or directing your dream by finding the portal and going through it is exceptional. But now you need to know what to do and what not to do. The first suggestion is called feeling the dream landscape or dreamscape.* This includes feeling everything *except* sentient

---

*For simplicity, from now on dreaming experiences that happen after crossing the third bridge of dreaming I will refer to as happening in the dreamscape.

beings. The notion of sentience is a big and debatable subject that we're not going to get into here.

For our shamanic work here, there are the four categories of sentient beings that I will refer to as the complex beings that to *begin* with we *do not* want to interact with at any level while consciously navigating the dreamscape: humans, animals, divinities, and tormented spirits. Personally, I place trees, flowers, and even rocks and water, not to mention Fire, in a category of sentience. However, they resonate much differently from the four complex categories I suggest to stay away from.

We are going to deal with some of those four categories soon but not yet. As I said, crossing the third bridge is a true accomplishment, but we are still babies at this point and need to be extremely careful. Opening to feelings, energies, and desires of humans, animals, divinities, and spirits can be truly dangerous until we become experienced navigating the dreamscape without their interference. And trust me, they will interfere!

So first it's best to practice in places of nature, or really any place devoid of the four complex sentient categories. Before you find and open your portal to the dreamscape, you can plant a seed of passive concentration regarding where you want to go or what you want to see in the dreamscape. What we are looking for here is to place our dreaming consciousness in a location, position, or situation of experiencing or feeling positive energy. We want to "exercise" our dreaming awareness so it becomes even more clear and resilient.

There are basically two different views for both the object (what you are seeing, feeling, experiencing) and the subject (you). In the macroscopic (grand) view, you are literally looking at the dreamscape from a place that has a grand view! This could be on top of a mountain, looking out over the ocean, watching a sunrise or sunset, flying through the clouds, and so on. On the other hand a more intimate view is always stimulating—viewing a single flower, a rock, a whirlpool, a flame, a grain of sand.

There are two views for the way this happens. The first way is that you see the scene as an observer, as you would by looking at it through your own eyes. And you feel the scene and experience the emotions it stimulates as if you were actually there. The second way is that you see yourself from the outside, acting in the scene as if you were watching a movie or looking at a picture or photograph. During this second way it is common to not actually see yourself clearly, but somehow you know that it's you. While dreaming, notice and remember feelings, emotions, intuitions, and messages so you can clearly write about your dream in your journal. I suggest a minimum of twenty to thirty authentic dreamscape experiences *and* feeling absolutely confident you can wake up at any moment from the dreamscape that you choose before moving to the next practice.

Practice 27
ANIMAL TOTEMS

Meeting and interacting at various levels with animals in the dreamscape affords us countless opportunities to learn, help, and be helped. It's staggering to realize how many animals we physically and psychically share the planet with. Before getting into the whys and hows of dreaming with animals, let's just be sure what we are talking about with the word *animal*.

A generally accepted description of animals is multicellular, eukaryotic organisms of the kingdom Animalia. All animals are motile, meaning they can move spontaneously and independently at some point in their lives. Their body plan eventually becomes fixed as they develop, although some undergo a process of metamorphosis later on in their lives. All animals are heterotrophs: they must ingest other organisms or their products for sustenance. Animals are divided into various subgroups. Two main groups are vertebrates, such as birds, mammals, amphibians, reptiles, and fish, and invertebrates, among them mollusks (clams, oysters, octopuses, squid, snails), arthropods (millipedes, centipedes, insects, spiders, scorpions, crabs, lobsters, shrimp), and annelids (earthworms, leeches).

No one knows how many animal species inhabit Earth. The latest scientific estimate places animals at 7.77 million species, of which only 953,434 have been described and catalogued! This means that more than 80 percent of animal species on the planet are unknown to us. The reason I bring this up will be made clear shortly. However, realize this right now: close to 8 million *species* of animals means there are *many trillions* of individual animals. Right now there are an estimated 7.3 billion people (one species) on the planet. *One trillion animals is a thousand billion.*

Okay, so it's safe to say we share the planet with an astounding number of other animals, and we always have. Throughout millennia our ancestors developed many ways of relating to the animals we shared the planet with and that were key to our survival. I'll get straight to the point with regard to shamanism. Ancient shamans as well as authentic shamanic cultures today relate to animals on both the physical and spiritual level. The various techniques employed by shamanic cultures to connect with the spirits of animals are used for many reasons, some of which are:

To petition for success in hunting

To acquire the spirit of an animal to increase personal knowledge and power

To petition for the animal spirit's protection (either personally or for the tribe)

To temporarily borrow the unique perception of the animal to see in enhanced ways, to spy on enemies, or to obtain spiritual visions

To honor and celebrate the relationship between the tribe and the animal kin-doms

To connect with the spirits of deceased ancestors who have taken animal form

To ask advice in the area of expertise of a particular animal

Now the question of whether initiation with animals and their spirits is an activity that would have benefit to people of modern society is an interesting topic and one that I have been exploring for many years. My current point of view is that the answer lies squarely in your personal intention and level of openness to discovering your true potentials. If you enter into shamanic initiations with animals with preconceived and romantic notions, the only thing you are likely to gain is the fulfilling of those notions. On the other hand, an open and honest meeting without preconceived notions is likely to gain you experiences and insights you never dreamed possible.

Relating to animals beyond the merely physical requires an expansion into altered ways of thinking and feeling. There are primarily two ways of understanding this. Animal totems and animal spirits. A totem will be a manifested representation that includes all the characteristics of an animal species. An animal spirit is an energetic replica of a specific individual animal. So a totem is like an emissary representing a species, and a spirit is an individual of that species.

For example, if I were to list all of the characteristics of the animal species lying at my feet right now—a German shepherd dog—this would be a generic list that includes all that we know about the species. However, if I wrote a list of characteristics about *my* German shepherd (Sophie), the list would be specific to her. As a breed, German shepherds are known to be very loyal. Is Sophie loyal? If loyal means following me around everywhere, making sure where I am and what I'm doing, giving me a kiss five minutes after being disciplined—then yeah, she's very loyal. But if loyal means being overprotective and biting people that she feels are threatening to me but aren't (which German shepherds have been known to do), then no, she is not that loyal. She's never bitten a person, and I doubt she ever will unless someone physically attacks me and she is there. German shepherds also vary in their responses to water. I have had male German shepherds that didn't like to swim: they would go in up to their bellies, and typically that's about it for them. But Sophie and other German shepherds I've had, both male and female, love any body of water and will dive in and swim even if it's freezing cold.

Same goes for undomesticated animals. The idea, which I'm sure you get by now, is that all lions, seagulls, and dolphins share a similar amount of species-specific traits, but each individual lion, seagull, and dolphin is unique. An individual animal spirit will be a unique expression of the animal totem. Both spirits and totems can be approached very intimately in the dreamscape, but it's important to realize the difference.

I'm going to begin talking about animal spirits simply to recognize the importance of these relationships. However, for this section on animals relating to the dreamscape, we will be primarily working with animal totems and not spirits. For those of you familiar with my work, in particular the material in my book *Ecoshamanism*, you will already know I have strong opinions with regard to relating to specific animal spirits and how many neoshamanic practices miss the whole point. For those not familiar with my point of view on acquiring animal spirit allies, it will become clear if you keep reading, but in the meantime, the importance of dreamscape encounters with animal *totems* is significant, and these encounters are extremely valuable. We will talk more about animal spirits later.

In many ways relating with and creating relationships with both animal totems and spirits have similarities, the most common topic being the simplest one: What animals can be totems and why? If you look at most modern books on totemism written by people of Western culture, they tend heavily toward what can be called the BINABM—big impressive North American birds and mammals. Some of this has to do with the aforementioned tendency to equate totemism with native North American cultures and therefore North American animals. And because we tend to be anthropocentric, we favor animals more like us, which makes mammals the most popular, followed by birds, then other vertebrates, and finally the often-ignored invertebrate kingdom. Finally, we like what are known as charismatic megafauna—basically, big animals that we think are really, really cool. You're going to see a lot about wolf, deer, bear, eagle, hawk, and cougar. Unless you get a totem animal dictionary written by someone trying to include more animals than anyone else, you're not likely to run across entries for platypus, sea slug, or rotifer. Oddly enough, very few people work with primate totems of any sort.[1]

Totems such as domestic cow and domestic chicken don't get nearly as much attention as they ought to because they aren't flashy or impressive, and many people think of them as stupid or dirty. Why have cow as a totem when you can have elk? And yet cow is so much more relevant to our experience, not only as provider of food but also as a reflection of what our culture has become through technology and apathy.[2]

We can have relationships with animal totems, and they with us, in many different ways. These complex relationships can be compared to the multifaceted relationships we have with people during our lives. Here are a few examples:

- Primary totems are what most people think of as totems. They're your life totems, the ones who are around for most, if not all, of your life.
- Secondary totems come into your life of their own volition, either to teach you a particular lesson, to ask for your help with something difficult, or simply to be with you during a particular stage of your life.
- Tertiary totems are ones you go to for help with specific situations, such as help with a spell or ritual, and the relationship rarely goes beyond that.

Here is an overview for the shamanic dreaming steps with animal totems. This is obviously a very complex and personal practice that only you can experience; the best I can do is provide a format to guide you. In reality only you will truly know what to do once you are there.

1. After your sleep preparations, write in your journal that you will find your portal and then one of the three animal totems, depending on your current situation.

2. Once you know you are dreaming and have found the portal, change the dreamscape.

3. In the new dreamscape your animal totem may be waiting for you; if not you will have to find it. In some cases, if your intent was strong before entering sleep, the animal totem that you need or that was sent to you will already be there. Other times the animal totem will be purposefully elusive as part of its teaching process with you, and you will have to search in the dreamscape. On some occasions I have had to change the dreamscape many times in this search. Here's an example: the first dreamscape I changed to was a high-altitude desert. But after searching and not finding the animal totem I found my portal and changed the dreamscape to a beach by the ocean. There I found my portal again, and the dreamscape became a farm in the country. There I found a tertiary animal totem in the form of a baby lamb.

4. When you have encountered the animal totem, whether it was waiting for you or after searching, there are many things that can happen. Here are some examples:

   • Energetic sharing and communication. Without thought or speech you feel the unique energy and intent of the animal totem that you take with you back to the waking world. This often occurs while the animal totem is also feeling your energy.

   • One-way communication. Without intentionally sharing any-thing (that you know of) with the animal totem, it "speaks" to you a message either verbally or energetically. Sometimes this message is very clear; other times it seems to be vague, and you need to figure out the meaning upon waking. Or you try to talk or express yourself to the animal totem. Sometimes you can tell it is listening, and other times it seems like you are not getting through. The totem may simply leave, as in the next example.

   • Communication through action. Without any viable interaction, the animal totem flies, runs, or swims away. In some cases, the animal totem simply disappears. These situations are far from uncommon. If you have the feeling the animal totem wants you to follow for some reason or to try to catch it, go for it! I have had experiences (especially with tertiary totems) where following them or chasing them was the main lesson. This can happen in the same dreamscape where you encountered the animal totem, or the animal totem may travel through other dreamscapes as part of the lesson. I have had this latter situation happen many times. Instead of communicating any kind of thoughts, the animal totems had me follow or chase them through many dreamscapes to show me what I needed to know. I will talk more about this when we get to the shamanic healing section of the book.

- Two-way communication. You have a dialogue with the totem. Unfortunately, this seems to be the rarest form of encounter. It would be nice to just simply have a nice conversation with the animal totem, which can happen, but this usually only occurs with a primary totem that you know well. Except for rare occasions a true dialogue with an animal totem only happens after many years or even decades interacting with the animal totem in the dreamscape.

5. All of the above situations are amazing experiences no matter if you are a beginner or highly seasoned shamanic dreamer. Now you must be sure to remember your dream. No matter what part of your sleep cycle you are in, you must wake up fully and record every detail of your dream. Here are some suggestions of what to record, but you may think of others too:
- Describe the dreamscape.
- If you were in multiple dreamscapes, describe them all sequentially.
- Do you recognize the animal totem? If so, is this an animal species you have encountered physically in the past or only in pictures or other forms of media?

- Do you know which of the three types of animal totems you just encountered?
- Which of the above four situations happened? Describe what happened.
- Describe the energetic feeling or overall intent of the animal totem.
- Did you receive a direct or indirect message or lesson? If so, describe it.
- If you received a message or lesson, do you understand it or do you need to try to figure it out?
- If the animal totem simply left and you did not find it again, do you have a feeling why or know why that happened? (This is common so don't look at it as negative; many times it's simply part of the process.)
- How do you feel about the encounter?
- Do you feel you will encounter this animal totem again in a dreamscape in the future? Describe why or why not.

The above text is primarily for use by beginning shamanic dreamers. For most people it can take many years or even a lifetime to passively intend to shamanic dream with an animal totem, but I also know people who have flown right into it after mastering lucid dreaming. In any case, once you are able to encounter animal totems in your dreams, the next step is set up the intent of "why" before you sleep. Shamans always have an intent for what they are doing. In the above practice the intent was to encounter an animal totem. Now it's time to develop a relationship with the totem on whatever level that may be. There could be many reasons for interacting with an animal totem. Some include:

Experiencing the sheer awe and joy of it (yes, this is a valid reason)
Feeling the energetic qualities of the animal totem to fortify, strengthen, and guide your waking life
Gaining the wisdom of the animal totem

Petitioning the animal totem for an answer to a specific question

Petitioning the animal totem for protection—for yourself, someone else, or even places

Petitioning the animal totem for help and support in shamanic healing (more about this soon)

Asking the animal totem if there is something you can do for its species (or a specific animal) in waking reality

Only you can decide how and when to interact with an animal totem: the level of connection you have to the animal totem will determine that interaction. You may have an instant connection to the animal totem and interact in all the situations listed above right away. In most cases petitioning the animal totem for something only happens after you are both extremely comfortable with each other. In any case, interacting with animal totems in the dreamscape is a remarkable experience and can evolve into a valuable tool both for you and them.

Practice 28
INTERACTING WITH SPIRIT ANIMALS

A spirit animal, or animal spirit, is an energetic replica of a specific individual animal that you can work with while shamanic dreaming. This animal spirit will have the overall energetic qualities of the animal totem but will also have individual traits, tendencies, habits, and so on. As in the previous description of my German shepherd companion: Sophie likes to swim; other shepherds don't, but all of them are still German shepherds. Some hawks fly higher than others; some cats prefer sleeping to hunting. Some deer live to a ripe old age while others aren't as smart and are killed young. But even with their individual traits and quirks, they are still part of their species.

The same goes for animal spirits. I have provided instructions on encountering and obtaining animal spirits in practice 5, so hopefully you already have one or more animal spirit jicaras. There are no shortcuts in these advanced practices. Unless you are one of the very few people who already have the requisite experience and items neces-sary to fashion an animal spirit jicara, it will probably take you many months or even years to obtain your jicara. If you don't have a jicara, return here when you do in order to learn to shamanic dream with your animal spirit.

Now that you have your jicara, you are no doubt thoroughly famil-iar with the energy of the animal spirit. Congratulations! This is a great accomplishment. The next step is dreaming with the individual spirit of the animal infused in your jicara. Two different situations can occur at this stage. You may be certain that the animal spirit infused in your jicara is an animal that you knew well when it was alive. Or you may know the animal totem very well but either are certain you didn't know the exact animal infused in the jicara when it was alive or aren't cer-tain if you did. To clarify, here are two examples from my many animal jicaras: a turkey vulture and a doe.

I first discovered turkey vulture eggs while hiking the rocky ridge of Spring Mountain with Sophie. Even though they are most awesome when soaring the thermals, turkey vultures lay their eggs on the ground. That is one of many reasons they are so valuable as spirit guides to shamans—they have the energy of both earth and sky. We found the eggs in a small cave and visited the birds as they grew and eventually learned to fly. By the time they learned to fly, they knew us and had no fear of landing near us when we visited. Over the next few years I watched other broods hatch in the same cave and grow up. I visited and learned with generations of these vultures that lived on the mountain; at least twenty knew me and were my friends. I had known all of them and their parents their whole lives.

One day an adult male, one of the parents of the eggs I originally found and a good friend of mine, swooped down and landed in the tree next to me. I could swear he was giving me a stare I had never seen before, and it kind of creeped me out. After a while he took off. The next day, hiking up the mountain, I found his dead body near the top. Needless to say, I was very sad but also happy because he left his body where he knew I would find it. This is an example of knowing the spirit of the exact animal infused in the jicara.

Similar to the vultures, I knew many generations of a particular small herd of deer (generally ten to fourteen depending on the year) near where I lived, and most of them, with the exception of the older bucks, weren't scared of me, which is unusual with wild whitetailed deer. I spent a lot of time with them in their energetic space, mostly while in my tree stand. For a couple of years I wanted to make a jicara of a deer spirit with one of these amazing beings, especially after I fell asleep one day under a tree and woke to find one of the young does licking my face and another sniffing my boots. But I had given up hunting, and a spirit had not yet offered its *iyari* (spirit) to me—until one day I climbed my tree stand and immediately saw a dead adult doe not far from my tree.

Upon reaching her I found she had been shot, probably the day before, but the hunter hadn't found her. When I touched her I knew instantly that she had run to my spot on purpose after she was shot. She wanted me to find her. I have her animal spirit infused in a jicara. However, even though I have been, and still am, extremely close to this herd and many of the individuals, I honestly didn't know which exact doe this was, as she and her sisters looked so much alike. This is an example of knowing intimately an animal totem and having an animal spirit jicara but initially you don't know if you knew the exact animal until you dream with it.

The main difference between working with animal totems and an animal spirit during shamanic dreaming is that interactions with your spirit animal will be infinitely more personal. As stated before, animal totems encountered during shamanic dreaming are emissaries of that species. Even though they can be quite valuable, they are kind of like an all-purpose version of a given species that only appears in the dreamscape. The spirit animal infused in your jicara will be much different and considerably more potent and powerful in its dealings with you. This animal came to you in the *waking world* and left its energy for you when it died so you could find its spirit in the dreamscape.

With that said, many of the reasons for interacting with your spirit animal are the *same* as for animal totems, so I won't list them again. The *difference* lies in the familiarity, understanding, and mutual bond that is developed through the countless experiences you will share with your spirit animal. You will become intimately connected to your spirit animal, and it to you. This is a sacred union that defies explanation with words. At the highest levels your spirit animal becomes an extension of you, and you become an extension of it.

Although this comparison is not completely correct because you will never own your animal spirit, the analogy of your spirit animal being similar to a loyal pet (especially a canine like my German shepherd) is valid for many reasons. If you treat your animal spirit with respect, it will show you unconditional love and support no matter what you do. If you leave it for long periods of time, it will probably be mad at you, and just like my Sophie it will pretend to ignore you for a while until it forgives you. If you don't feed it, it will starve. Your animal spirit will want to "go outside and play." It will want to protect you. It will want a job to do to feel wanted. It will want to be praised for a job well done. In a nutshell, having an animal spirit in your life is about the most serious relationship you can have. This relationship transcends physical reality, time, and space. For a shaman this relationship is just as important as, or for some even more important than, that of family and friends.

Your Spirit Animal and You in the Dreamscape

At this point in your development as a shamanic dreamer, you have come a long way, so it's difficult to say exactly what will happen next with regard to shamanic dreaming with your spirit animal. However, through my own experiences and those of my mentors, colleagues, and students, there are some specific and general situations that seem to be common and that can be discussed, listed, and taught.

I'm going to provide a list of helpful suggestions to guide you, but for now let's just say you have your animal spirit jicara next to where you are going to sleep; you have intended to passively find your spirit animal in the dreamscape; and you are ready to use all of your experience and knowledge to travel into the mystery and complete the first task. The first task is simply to encounter your spirit animal in the dreamscape. I suggest you use your jicara as your portal. The first time you attempt to shamanic dream with your spirit animal, or maybe several times, or even every time, one of three situations is likely to occur:

1. You are in the dreamscape aware that you are dreaming, and without even seeing your jicara you encounter your spirit animal. This is very rare but is known to happen. The power of your jicara being near to you while dreaming is very potent.
2. You are in the dreamscape aware that you are dreaming, and you find your jicara. You use the jicara as your portal to change the dream, and in that dream you encounter your spirit animal. This is the most common situation that occurs at this level.
3. You are in the dreamscape aware that you are dreaming, and you don't see your jicara. If this happens, you will need to find another one of your portals. When you do, change the dream. Do this as many times as needed to find either your jicara or your spirit animal, whichever comes first. If you find your jicara first, use it to change the dream, and you will almost always encounter your spirit animal in that dream.

If the situation arises that you don't see your jicara so you use another portal to change the dream multiple times and still can't find your jicara, don't worry. Simply try again the next night. If on multiple occasions the same thing happens, don't get discouraged; you will do it. Take a break from trying for a few nights, and instead use your other portals to hone your dreaming skills.

Encountering your spirit animal in the dreamscape for the first time is an intense experience no matter what happens. It's so intense that you might even just get thrown out of the dream and wake up. If you don't wake up, what do you do next? I'll answer that in a moment, but first let's answer a question many shamanic dreamers also ask at this juncture: How do I know this is my spirit animal and not a totem emissary or phantom apparition?

The answer is simple. If you found your jicara and used it as a portal to change the dream, and in that dream your spirit animal was waiting, you can be sure it's your spirit animal. When you use your spirit animal jicara as your portal to change the dream, it can and will only take you to one place—the dream where your spirit animal is. Even the most malevolent entities in the dreamscape can't change the destination of a jicara portal. Now once you get to the dream where your spirit animal is, anything can happen. If you don't find your jicara and use another portal, you can be tricked but not with the jicara. It has one place it takes you—to your spirit animal. Period.

Now, if you encountered your spirit animal right away without even the need for the jicara portal, you can be almost certain this is your authentic animal spirit. Malevolent tricksters in the dreamscape don't know in what dream or where you will enter the dreamscape, but your spirit animal, through your physical jicara, surely did because here it is! I have never experienced or heard of any other shamanic dreamer at this level experience anything but the spirit animal when it appears right away once the dreamscape is entered.

Back to the original question—what to do once you encounter your spirit animal in the dreamscape. This will largely depend on your spirit animal and your previous relationship when it was alive in your waking reality. If you had a healthy and mutual relationship with this animal before it died, this initial encounter will most likely be a happy reunion. Your animal spirit will probably be surprised and overjoyed to see you. Throughout the years, I have had animal spirits almost freak out when they first encountered me in the dreamscape.

My first shepherd Aragorn barked and howled and kissed my face until I was soaked. My deer ran around in circles. My turtle was hilarious—he poked his head out to see me and then went back in like he was thinking about it and then would pop his head back out. He did this many times until he was sure it was me and then started bobbing his head up and down in joy. In these situations the next step is easy: you and your animal spirit simply continue on and develop your relationship by traveling around and exploring the dreamscape. The relationship will continue to grow and deepen. As a dream shaman you will no doubt have work to do in the dreamscape, and your spirit animal will want to help you.

If you are not sure—or you are sure that you don't know this particular spirit—it is probably because the animal emissaries of that species sent you this spirit. In this case you must have a strong connection to this species in the waking world and with the totem in the dreamscape. Now that you have the jicara of a specific animal of that species, it is time to develop a relationship with it in the dreamscape. This is a very exciting situation: because of your familiarity with the species in the waking world, getting to know it in the dreamscape will come very naturally.

In both cases—whether you know this particular spirit animal or not—it doesn't really matter who takes the lead. Unless there is something pressing that you and the spirit animal need to do together right away, usually you both travel to where you first met the species in the waking world. In some cases, you may travel to the dream where you first found your spirit animal. Otherwise, you usually spend time together in a dreamscape that resembles or is identical to the place in the waking world where you developed your relationship with the animal or its species. For my animal spirit vulture, it was the rocky terrain near the top of Spring Mountain. For my doe, it was the oak forest. For my turtle, it was the pond near the back of my old house.

At this level of shamanic dreaming, it is important to remember that anything is possible in the dreamscape. As we have learned by advancing this far, in the dreamscape we are not encumbered by gravity, physicality, temperature, or any other laws of nature or governmental laws. We are completely free to do *whatever* we want. While traveling and also performing shamanic work in the dreamscape, I do suggest that you keep up high moral standards as you would in your waking life because what you do in the dreamscape can and will have repercussions in your waking life both positive and negative. Your animal spirit has no human agenda other than being with you and helping you if it can.

With all that said, the sky is not the limit anymore! In the dreamscape you can do whatever your spirit animal can and more. You can fly with your hawk, run as fast as your deer, swim to the depths with your whale. The main point here, which is utterly amazing, is that now you have a companion in the dreamscape. And not simply some random companion. Your spirit animal either was your friend, mentor, or teacher in the waking world or the emissaries sent this spirit to you. In either case this was no accident. You were meant to be together.

For this simple reason it is imperative that you experience and learn as much as you can with your spirit animal. Otherwise, what's the point? As a shamanic dreamer with a spirit animal you have reached a level of proficiency that few modern people will ever attain or even think to attain. Sure, it is fine to explore and have fun with your animal spirit in the dreamscape; I do it all the time—it's healthy. But don't miss this opportunity for continued growth and for helping others by stopping here.

After a period of time, usually a few weeks of dreaming with your spirit animal, getting your particular process down of how you find it in the dreamscape, traveling around and exploring, the time will come for the next step—melding of perception. This is one of the amazing rewards you will realize for all of your work and perseverance reaching this level of shamanic dreaming.

As stated above and throughout this book so far, anything is possible in the dreamscape. However, until now you were still limited whether you realize it or not. You were limited by your own perception. Sure you can fly with your hawk or run like your deer, no problem. But you can't perceive as a hawk or a deer. How could you—you aren't one of those species. Well, in the dreamscape with your spirit animal *now you can.*

Why is this important? Because this is an opportunity for growth with epic possibilities. Yes, it is possible to meld our perception with animals in the waking world. But from my experience these occurrences are very rare. For many years I have been teaching students and clients how to merge their perception with the elements of fire, water, wind, and earth. My specialty is fire; also the merging of perception with trees and plants. These are potent experiences that can empower your life and your work with clients if you are a healer. But merging perception with the complexity of an animal in the waking world is very difficult and pretty much impossible for modern people, except for those who have mastered this level of shamanic dreaming. What's important here is that once your relationship with your spirit animal is consummated through time and experiences together, merging of perception is simply a natural progression and is not difficult at all in the dreamscape.

How does this happen? In the beginning the merging of perception is easiest when you and your spirit animal are *active*. After learning how it feels to do it, you can merge while standing still or right when you first meet in the dreamscape. When you are flying, running, swimming, or jumping with your spirit animal in the dreamscape, you can more easily merge or meld perception because you are actively *doing* the same basic thing.

The merging can happen in two ways. Let's use flying as an example.

1. While flying with your spirit animal, you ask its permission to passively merge with it. Your dreaming body (which is essentially energy) joins with your spirit animal. You are now the bird, and the bird is now you. You are looking through the eyes of the bird. If you look to where you just were, you are not there anymore because now you are the bird.
2. While flying with your animal spirit, your animal spirit through intuitive communication senses you want to merge, and the animal spirit's energy body joins with yours. You are seeing with

your own eyes but with the added perception of the bird. The bird is now you, and you are the bird. If you look to where the bird just was, it isn't there anymore because the energy body of the bird is now joined with yours.

In either case this is a remarkable and marvelous experience. You now have the opportunity to see, feel, and sense in ways you never have before. In terms of perception this is one of the most profound experiences you can ever know. It's easy to *imagine* doing something like this, but when you actually do it, the experience is beyond words. The information, understanding, and knowledge you can acquire during these moments is staggering.

My first experience of merging with my animal spirit in the dreamscape was with my turkey vulture companion and teacher. Turkey vultures are usually considered gross to modern people. They are considered ugly compared to most birds, and they typically eat rotten carrion, which people consider disgusting. However, the truth is they are amazing birds that fill an important niche in nature. First of all, they are the cleaners and cleansers—a very important job. They are amazing at flying on thermals. Except when taking off, you will almost never see a turkey vulture flap its wings while flying. Since they are born on the ground and then learn to fly, they have dual vision. They are infused with the energy of Earth when they are chicks, and then they are infused with the energy of wind and sky. They can see thermal energy and ride it.

My first time merging with my turkey vulture spirit animal in the dreamscape was one of the most profound experiences of my life: To be able to see and ride the thermals in giant spirals higher and higher. To see with pinpoint accuracy everything below me. To fly with my brothers and sisters and roost together in the trees at night (they are very social birds) and then spread my wings to dry them in the rays of the rising sun in the morning. To actually see, feel, think, and sense how he does is indescribable.

One of the key benefits of these kinds of experiences is that they foster a peaceful inner knowing, a humble but powerful confidence and calmness in the waking world. You have experienced something so tangible yet elusive, impossible yet possible, mysterious yet real that ordinary concerns shrink and are more easily dealt with, compared to the sheer awe and expansion of consciousness during these moments.

Interacting in the dreamscape with your animal spirit, whether merging or not, also provides us with a healthy respite from the hectic daily world of modern life and the often chaotic and confusing dreams we have during ordinary sleep. Nothing quite compares to falling asleep knowing you are going to consciously travel to another realm of reality and experience wondrous activities and situations.

However, here I will add a word of caution. I know full well, and am supremely confident, that if you have attained this level, you are a committed, sensible, and probably highly intelligent person. Less committed people, addicts, and those that can't or simply don't follow through with their plans never make it here. For this reason, this word of caution usually doesn't apply but still needs to be said because I have known a few amazingly gifted and skilled shamanic dreamers that have gone this way and needed to get dragged back. *The dreamscape is not a substitute for waking reality.* It is a complement that can be employed in various ways to improve daily life. Don't fall into the trap of wanting to be there more than you want to be here. Use the power of the dreamscape to enhance your life, not hide from it.

One last item here about spirit animals in the dreamscape. During the course of nearly thirty years, I have had the good fortune to realize many intimate relationships with animals and then their animal spirits. I currently have seven jicaras that I dream with. Usually not all at once, only on special occasions. So obviously it's possible to have more than one. I'm going to say this even though I probably don't have to: when or if you make a second or more jicaras, the animal spirit and jicara you infuse with it must be acquired and made in the same painstaking way as you made your first. There are no shortcuts, and you can't hurry it. It is amazing to share experiences and travel the dreamscape with more than one spirit animal. When or if the time comes, I'm sure you'll know it.

Practice 29
HUMAN SPIRIT GUIDES

Experiences with your animal spirit(s) in the dreamscape are almost always positive. You have intentionally fostered this special relationship through hard work, perseverance, and time. Encountering human spirits is a whole different ball game that should be greatly considered before being entered into. This is a vast subject that would need many volumes to fully explore. The best I can do here is offer some insight and suggestions from a shamanic perspective in the space allowed.

In the shaman's world the existence of spirits in "this" world—including humans and spirits residing in nature, along with spirits occupying other realms, such as an afterlife or an in-between existence after death and before a new incarnation—is simply an undisputable fact. Spirits and souls are at the very core of shamanic practices; this view guides shamans in all cultures. It is how particular shamans interact and relate to the spirits that separate them both culturally and pragmatically. Spirit guides exist cross-culturally, in all shamanic traditions. These guides are accessed in different ways, including trance states and shamanic dreaming.

Most shamanic cultures view spirit guides as having various levels of knowledge and power, similar to how shamans have various degrees of experience and wisdom. The easiest way to relate to this is to place spirits at three levels in a similar way to how the shamanic cosmology divides the levels of transpersonal consciousness into the lower, middle, and upper worlds.

The concept that spirit guides have various levels of knowledge can be looked at in two ways. The first way is that the particular spirit learned and accumulated knowledge pertinent to its last or only life. The second and more popular way in the shamanic world is that a particular spirit has undergone multiple incarnate lives on Earth (reincarnation), and the level of knowledge is directly proportional to the advancement of the spirit during those lifetimes. In this case the more lifetimes a spirit has undergone the better chance that it will have advanced in knowledge. So an elder spirit will probably be a more knowledgeable guide than a younger spirit, although it seems that all levels have their place in the pantheon, and age is certainly not the only criteria, as we will see.

The question of how particular spirits are matched with particular shamans remains a mystery. It could be that in the spirit world an orderly pairing of the needs and wants of a shaman with the specialties of a particular spirit happens. In this case a beginner shaman would be helped by a younger spirit who has had similar past-life issues, or an experienced shaman would be aided by an advanced spirit who relates to knowledge at a deeper level. We see a similar method in our educational system: college students are taught by professors with advanced degrees.

According to the Population Reference Bureau and the *CIA World Factbook,* throughout the world an estimated 360,000 babies will be born per day and 151,600 people will die per day in 2011: 250 births per minute and 105 deaths![3] That's a lot of spirits or souls continually coming and going. Since there are more coming than going, where do the new spirits come from? From the shamanic perspective, we are all part of a great oversoul or giant field of consciousness energy that splits off and divides to create individual spirits. Once a spirit is created, it will come back at death and join the collective. It is generally thought that it can then be born again.

The being-born-again part is very mysterious in that once the spirit is again part of the collective, the energy, memories, and consciousness of that spirit combine with the greater whole. What and how much of the previous self is remembered inside of or after being in the collective is often associated with the level of advancement of the spirit. That people also sometimes remember not only past lives but also past lives of other people then becomes completely possible as a spirit being born can share in the collective memory of the oversoul. This may explain why multiple people at any one time may think they are the reincarnation of, say, Mother Mary or Elvis.

For shamans it is completely ordinary for a single past-life spirit to be split or divided and be included in multiple reincarnated people, especially ancestors. This leads to the question of whether or not we get to choose who we want to be in our next life while we are in the in-between time after death. Is it possible we can choose our parents? Our bodies?

The shaman's answer would be different cross-culturally, but in general it's safe to say that shamans believe that higher level spirits, including shamans, can return of their choosing while lower level individuals cannot, except in extreme cases where a spirit has left such a strong imprint of an unresolved issue that the spirit wills his or her way back. Most spirits are lower or middle level and are somehow placed in their new life situation according to how they have led their previous life. This can be related to the principle of karma in Hindu and Buddhist traditions. The definition of karma differs slightly throughout traditions, but in general we can say that the law of karma affects all of our actions and past, present, and future experiences, thus making everyone responsible for his or her own life and the pain and joy it brings to him or her and others. Here is a condensed excerpt from my *Shamanism for Beginners* book that succinctly explains shamanic spirit levels:

Lower Level Spirits

Since there are more new spirits coming than old ones leaving, many people will only have a conscious level of the underlying oversoul with no conscious awareness of advancement through karmic episodes in previous lifetimes. As one proceeds through various incarnate lifetimes, there are a multitude of opportunities for advancement in consciousness or, on the other hand, remaining the same or even digressing. Spirits at a lower level of consciousness are therefore in that situation for two main reasons. First, they could simply be very young spirits with few incarnations, or they could be relatively old spirits that have incarnated maybe many hundreds of times but have remained undeveloped for one reason or other. A new spirit that for example is murdered or raped or experiences some other form of deep trauma may take many, many lifetimes to break free from that episode. On the other hand a new spirit may encounter love, wisdom, and life lessons that in just a few lifetimes rapidly advance his or her consciousness.

Lower level spirits tend to be self-centered, as they have not yet experienced and embodied an expanded view of consciousness. They are easily swayed by the consensus of others, will fiercely defend their limited point of view, and show true compassion for only an immediate group of people. The same can be said for lower level spirits that a shaman may be in contact with. There could be many reasons for a shaman to meet a lower level spirit, and oftentimes this can be a good thing. Advancement in consciousness is learned through experiences; if this were not so, then there would be no opportunity to progress.

However, malevolent spirits almost always come from the lower level and can be quite dangerous. These are usually spirits that have incarnated many times without advancement and have turned to evil deeds as a way of placating their frustration and what they perceive as unfair treatment by the world around them. In shamanic cultures, these spirits take revenge on incarnate people by stealing the souls of babies, creating diseases or psychological illness, tricking, deceiving, and otherwise appearing as that which they are not. Beginner shamans often endure many trials with these angry or delusional spirits.

One of the main themes found between lower level spirits and beginner shamans is similar to difficulties that arise in sex and marriage in the waking world. A beginner shaman will be much more easily swayed into a codependent relationship with a lower level spirit that needs this type of attention and approval. Appearing in a way that captures the shaman's attention and then by helping the shaman at certain times, the spirit gains the confidence of the shaman but will ultimately disappoint or even injure the shaman by its immature nature. Beginner shamans are frequently powerless over these lower level spirits and require the assistance of a more advanced shaman to get rid of them and help move them along to rejoin the continuum.

Middle Level Spirits

At this level spirits basically appear and make themselves accessible to shamans for positive reasons as they have reached a level of maturity at the incarnate level to avoid most of the trappings of self-centered actions pervading the lower levels. That is not to say that middle level spirits have shed all aspects of anger, jealousy, or other lower level traits. They have simply advanced into beings of higher moral character and have experienced the positive side of karmic actions and so have the desire to keep growing.

Spirit guides at this level often help shamans in co-creation with the planet. This means helping to balance or restore relationships between the community and that which provides for life: our home biosphere. Having passed through various lifetimes of knowledge and experiences that have expanded their consciousness, these spirits are often the close companions of shamans, as many shamans will be at a similar level of consciousness as their middle level spirit guides.

At this level it is common for spirits to want to experience the myriad essences and energies of the natural world, and they may become animals, trees, clouds, rivers, hills, rocks, and so on for periods of time. For this reason the shaman and the community in general are made very aware through the history, traditions, and taboos of the tribe to act with respect toward nature and be accountable for their actions. Throughout shamanic lore we find middle level spirits occupying forms of nature that become extremely angry when they are abused or mistreated. They often enforce the karmic consequences of hunting more animals than is necessary or felling more trees than is needed, by causing some type of harm or even death to the wrongdoers. At a global level this may be what is currently happening between humans and the spirits of nature.

The massive human suffering on our planet is directly related to the mistreatment of the biosphere, overpopulation, and insane uses of technology, of which war and starvation are simple karmic responses.

Upper Level Spirits

Spirits at the upper level are often guides for shamans but are surprisingly few and far between. It's quite normal for us to want, believe, and hope that we are one of these rare spirits that have reached a high level of conscious advancement. The truth is most people, or spirits, aren't even close. At this level the spirit, whether incarnate or not, is virtually invisible. Upper level guides walking Earth as living beings do their work in a most unassuming manner. They focus on the improvement of the human condition. When you encounter one of these beings, your life is changed forever; the stimulus of the unconditional honesty and the pure energy radiated is beyond explanation or words. They stick out singularly to those around them, but they are not "public" people. Normally they are involved in the most significant ways by guiding and nurturing events in a behind-the-scenes way that is unobtrusive or even intentionally clandestine. In the dreamscape, upper level spirits tend to appear only as guides. They can be extremely helpful but also very brutal in their teaching methods.

We will return to shamanic spirit guides in a moment, but first it's pertinent to look at what may happen in our normal lives. Let's begin with deceased loved ones and relatives. It is not uncommon for us to see and communicate with these people in our dreams; however, in most cases this is happening in a normal dream completely in the hands of our subconscious. During a spontaneous lucid dream, it is possible to encounter one of these spirits in a more tangible way. This can also happen during intentional lucid and shamanic dreaming. From a shamanic perspective, encountering the actual spirit of a deceased relative or loved one is rare except for in the days or weeks (cultures differ on time period) directly following death. During this intermediate state between two lives on Earth, the spirit is still available; after that the

spirit moves on and is normally out of reach. This is why in some shamanic cultures such as the Huichol, a powerful shaman will place a
small part of his or her life force (iyari) into a tiny piece of quartz before
death. The family keeps this sacred item wrapped and hidden in their
ceremonial temple (*rirriki*).

If you have attained a good level of proficiency in dreaming with
your spirit animal(s), you may decide to intentionally seek out human
spirits in the dreamscape, or one or more may spontaneously appear. In
either case you will most likely encounter a guide from the second level
that is ready to pass to the third level or an actual third level guide.
Lower level spirits are either new or underdeveloped spirits that don't
have the capacity to cross over to you in the dreamscape. But nothing
is carved in stone, and encountering a lower level spirit that has passed
through many incarnations and is still underdeveloped can happen.
These spirits are often angry and malicious and should be avoided.

Although possible, it is extremely difficult or impossible to *find* a
specific human spirit in the dreamscape: difficult if they are still in the
intermediate state or if they are an upper level spirit that has decided to
stay in the spirit world; almost impossible if they have been incarnated
again. If you decide you want to try to find a deceased person in the
dreamscape, first you must be completely honest with yourself about
what level the spirit is on. Unless the person is very high on the middle
level and is acting as a guide for lower level spirits in the spirit world, or
the person is a third level spirit who has decided to stay for the same or
other reasons, you will not find him or her.

If you feel it is possible to find this deceased person, my suggestion
is to go about it in a similar way as you would with your spirit animal.
In this case, instead of your jicara being your portal, use an item from
the person that was special to him or her. If you are proficient in finding your spirit animal in the dreamscape, your training and experience
will guide you in the steps necessary for you to try to find this person
by changing the dream with a portal.

When you become an experienced dreamer, there will most likely come a time when you will spontaneously encounter an upper level spirit guide in the dreamscape, especially if you are doing healing work on people or the environment (including animals). This can be a very exciting moment, and anything could happen. Be open to all possibilities. An upper level guide may appear in any form and in any dreamscape. The guide might have a single message for you, or you may find a lifelong guide. I have every confidence that if you have made it this far in the practices, you will know exactly what to do if or when this situation arises.

PART FOUR

SHAMANIC PRACTICES FOR QUANTUM HEALING

13

Shamanic Viewing

I am assuming that by reading this you are most likely not a shaman living in an indigenous community separated from the modern industrial world. For this reason I have been and will continue providing bridges (information and practices) that we as modern people can use to travel back and forth between the modern worldview and the shamanic worldview.

With regard to the shamanic practice of shamanic viewing, there are more than a few starting spots in our modern view that can help us cross to the shamanic view. The two most helpful are remote viewing and quantum theory. These two modalities have both similarities and differences, but each includes useful information we can use to wrap our mind around the reality and practical applications of shamanic viewing.

Before getting into these two modern streams of thought, let's briefly identify and define shamanic viewing to set the stage for this chapter and the actual practice. Shamanic viewing is the *learned* ability to detect and interpret multidimensional phenomena. The uses for shamanic viewing include shamanic healing of people and places and the gathering of information related to multidimensional phenomena in both local and nonlocal space-time for said healing. In this chapter I will mostly concentrate on the concepts and practice of direct shamanic viewing as it relates to shamanic healing.

REMOTE VIEWING

A brief discussion on the modern modality of remote viewing can help us construct a bridge to shamanic viewing. *Remote viewing* is a term coined by the CIA for a system that enables a person to transcend space and time, to view persons, places, or things remote in space and time, and to gather and report intelligence information on the same. David Morehouse, a former army major who was a "psychic spy" in the late '80s and early '90s in the U.S. Army's Intelligence Security Command, wrote about the history of the program in his book *Remote Viewing: The Complete User's Manual for Coordinate Remote Viewing*.

In late 1972, CIA scientist Sidney Gottlieb, chief of the technical services division, procured a rather large monetary endowment to initiate the research project that began U.S. involvement in the study of Remote Viewing. If the Soviets and others were as heavily involved in this research as was being reported, the national security of the United States could be in jeopardy. The simple notion that this eerie capability might really be out there, and the possibility that we could do it, as well, almost certainly drove the CIA's decision process.

Stanford Research Institute (SRI) in Palo Alto, California, ultimately became the proving ground for what was to eventually be one of the intelligence services' most controversial, misunderstood, and often feared special access programs. The two men initially charged with the responsibility of overseeing this testing and evaluation program were Russell Targ and Harold Puthoff, Ph.D., both laser physicists working at SRI.[1]

Throughout the '70s and '80s, until 1995, the original remote viewing project of the CIA went through various incarnations of producing psychic spies. As Morehouse notes in his book, these included the Defense Intelligence Agency (DIA) under the program code name

Grill Flame, the U.S. Army's Intelligence and Security Command (INSCOM) code name, Center Lane, the Directorate of Science and Technology (DS & T) code name Sun Streak, which later had its code name changed to Star Gate.[2] During Star Gate in 1995 the remote viewing program was declassified, and the whole world found out what it was all about.

Shortly after its declassification, the program was "officially" canceled. During its lifetime, the remote viewing unit collected intelligence against a broad range of targets: strategic missile forces, political leaders (theirs and ours), counternarcotics operations, research and development facilities, hostage situations, military weapons systems, secret installations, technology developments, and terrorist groups. Having read extensively on this subject I feel, like many others, that the official canceling of the program came about due to the publishing of Morehouse's *Psychic Warrior*. There is hardly a doubt in many people's minds that, in some form and code name, the program exists in secret to this day.

Today, Morehouse and others, including co-creator Russell Targ, promote the psychic modality of remote viewing as a personal growth tool. Morehouse states that remote viewing "is an empowering art and science that will open the possibilities within you, creating doorways to levels of understanding never before thought attainable."[3] This notion of remote viewing as a personal growth tool is based primarily on the fact that we live in a multidimensional universe and that our consciousness is multidimensional as well. By embracing this reality we become aware that our consciousness is not limited to our body, brain, and mind. Multidimensional consciousness provides our mind with information beyond our physical body and beyond our conventional knowledge acquired through everyday mental activities in linear time.

QUANTUM THEORY

Quantum theory in the science of physics revolves around the concepts of complementarity, superposition, uncertainty, entanglement, and the measurement problem. A full explanation of these concepts is beyond the scope of this book, but there are many resources available for those who want to study them. The point here is that quantum theory points to the mysterious fact that something unaccounted for (in classical physics) is connecting otherwise isolated objects. That human beings are also part of this quantum interconnectedness correlates remarkably with what shamans and mystics have known for millennia. Modern experiments in quantum theory demonstrate that the worldview of classical physics is wrong. The acknowledgment of this has staggering implications for modern humans. Every day it becomes clearer that the rigid boundaries between science, metaphysical philosophy, and the practice of shamanism are quickly dissolving. Many aspects of quantum theory actually help prove the existence of phenomena such as telepathy and remote viewing.

Shamanic viewing (SV) is accomplished by entering an integrated state of consciousness (ISC) and viewing multidimensional phenomena that can then be interpreted. Shamans in different cultures have varying techniques to enter an ISC that allows for shamanic viewing. Some cultures employ the ingestion of plant entheogens such as ayahuasca, peyote, psilocybin mushrooms, and Datura, among others. I have personally employed these four entheogens (separately) on many occasions to enter an ISC, but there are other methods. The method I suggest is employing the five points of attention as described in this book. This highly advanced technique is the perfect vehicle for SV because you can maintain a sober and clear-minded ISC that is necessary for accurately interpreting multidimensional phenomena in hyperspace.

As noted earlier in chapter 4, many who study physics today agree that there are multiple dimensions beyond the four dimensions of space-time, but there is disagreement on how many there might be. Whatever the number, which may be infinite, these multiple dimensions constitute the hyperspace of our larger reality. SV is possible because embedded in the hyperspace are fields of consciousness. This is important for SV since our lifetime of experiences is not stored solely within the brain but in what can be called a *holographic field* that embeds the brain and the body. This field has staggering storage capacity and resolves the puzzle of adequate information storage within the brain.

During SV the shaman can access this holographic field of information. Ervin László, famous supporter of quantum theory and twice nominee for the Nobel Peace Prize, has this to say with regard to the storage capacity of the holographic field and how it is possible to access it:

> The brain does not have the capacity to store all the perceptions, sensations, volitions, and emotions experienced by an average individual in a lifetime. Computer scientist Simon Berkovitch calculated that to produce and store a lifetime's experiences the brain would have to carry out 1024 operations per second. Dutch neurobiologist Herms Romijn has shown that this would be impossible even if all 100 billion neurons in the brain were involved—and they are not: there are only 20 billion neurons in the cerebral cortex, and many of them have no evident cerebral function. . . . How this occurs is explained by the interactive process known as phase conjugation. Phase conjugation means a relationship between two waves that are equal but opposite in phase to each other. Two equal waves traveling in opposite directions create a single standing wave within which they are in resonance: they are phase conjugate. Applied to the brain, this means that when the brain receives information from its vacuum-hologram, it is in a phase-conjugate relationship with it. It emits a virtual outgoing wave that is conjugate with the incoming wave from the hologram. In this way the brain can read out the information it has created. This information is conserved in the vacuum hologram, so that our read-out embraces the experiences we have had throughout our life. The two-way phase-conjugate communication between the brain and the vacuum resolves the puzzle of adequate information storage within the brain. This accounts for our own long-term memory, but not for our connection with the consciousness of other

people. That phenomenon can also be accounted for, however, by adding a proviso to the read-in/read-out phase-conjugate relationship. We need to allow that this process has sufficient bandwidth to provide access not only to our own hologram, but also to the holograms of others. The "alien" holograms people can occasionally access generally prove to be those of persons with whom they are, or were, physically or emotionally bonded: sisters and brothers, parents and children, spouses and lovers, or simply persons with whom they had evolved ties of friendship and sympathy. Experience shows that altered states of consciousness are particularly conducive to reading alien holograms—providing access to other people's experiences.[4]

SV requires that we take László's "occasional access" of the holographic field to the next level through intentional access via our ISC, called direct shamanic viewing (DSV). This is especially necessary when working with clients in the capacity of healer. However, in learning SV, it is much easier to access the multidimensional hyperspace, which includes the holographic field, by first experiencing this with simpler life-forms such as plants, trees, and animals and elements such as fire, water, air, and soil.

I will give two personal examples of being in DSV. Throughout my life I have had numerous spontaneous events very similar to DSV. The difference here is that these experiences were intentional.

Personal Stories of Direct Shamanic Viewing

My first experience with intentional DSV happened when I was visiting the giant sequoias of Calaveras Big Trees State Park in Northern California near where I used to live. One day while walking among these ancient and magnificent trees, I sat down next to one of the largest trees and after a while began to nod off. In a half-asleep state (hypnagogic) I experienced sort of a "message" from the trees, telling me there was much more for me to see and feel that I was missing.

With this realization I became fully awake and intuitively knew that I should enter an ISC by raising the level of my attention to the five points. A couple of years previous, I had learned about the five points from my Huichol teachers, and it had radically changed my life for the better. But I really hadn't used this level of awareness outside my normal activities. It was simply a profoundly different and more mature way of interacting in the world—or so I thought.

As soon as I fully entered the awareness of the five points among the giant sequoias and passively desired to see and feel more, as the sequoias had suggested, everything changed. What I was now seeing (viewing) was an interconnected field of strings of light and luminous cocoons. The luminous cocoons were surrounding the giant trees and were enormous. Somehow I could perceive cocoons underground surrounding the roots of the trees. The strings of light were attached between the trees and were thickest at the roots and the tops.

After a few moments I also heard and felt a low pulse or droning sound that reverberated through everything, including myself. The pulses of sound were very slow and barely perceptible but were definitely happening. I had the impression that I was experiencing the slow and steady heartbeat of the forest. I got up and began to walk, retaining my ISC, and as I walked through the forest I began to see something I hadn't first noticed. The roots of the small trees and shrubs underneath the sequoias seemed to have a different quality of radiance from the roots of the sequoias, and I felt instinctively that they were not helping the sequoias. On the contrary they seemed to be somehow smothering them. I wouldn't use the word hurt *because I didn't feel or perceive any kind of pain. But I also knew that the small trees and plants weren't helping the trees either.*

The next day while at the grocery store I stopped at the bulletin board and saw a flyer for jobs at Big Trees State Park. They were hiring chainsaw operators and helpers to clear the small trees and brush underneath the sequoias. Based on my experience with chain saws, I was hired and trained and worked for the park that summer clearing brush and supervising controlled burns. In the process I learned the physical reality of what I had seen in my DSV.

The small trees and shrubs take water and nutrients that the massive sequoias need. Natural fires in the parks check their growth; the sequoias need fire to propagate and thrive. But humans have prevented these fires, with the result that the plants have proliferated. Though controlled burns are controversial, I learned through my ISC before, during, and after my work in the park that they are necessary, along with brush clearing, and I know I helped the sequoias. Looking back on it I can clearly see during my first day of DSV with the sequoias that they were both teaching me and asking for my help. My natural affinity for these trees helped to expand my experience with the five points of attention in a way that I could directly view what was happening in the forest. As a result I later found myself helping these beings in ways I would have never imagined.

A month or so after that experience, I was lying on my couch reading. It was fairly late on a warm summer night. My canine companion Sophie was with me. Earlier that year when I moved from Sedona, Arizona, to Northern California I brought not only Sophie with me but also our little friend El Gato. El Gato Bandito de Kitty-Cat-O (his full funny name) came to us as a stray kitten, not more than five inches long. We found him sleeping on our porch one night, and after extensive searching for the owners and putting up flyers with no luck, we adopted him. Sophie and he became very close, like brother and sister.

El Gato was more or less an outdoor cat that would come home every few days to eat cat food and sleep with us. On this night I had not realized he was out (the screen door was slightly open) as I had just seen him in the house.

While reading quietly I heard a gut-wrenching scream of agony from outside and knew right away it was El Gato. We lived in the woods surrounded by thousands of acres of forest. My main fear for El Gato at this place was the coyotes, and from the sounds I was hearing it appeared he got caught. Not worrying that I was in my underwear (we had no neighbors close enough to see me), I jumped up and grabbed a flashlight, and Sophie and I were out the door in two seconds.

Following the screams, we ran down the wooded slope behind the house at full speed with Sophie in the lead. After a hundred yards or so Sophie stopped, and in the light of my flashlight I picked up five sets of eyeballs looking at us. That was the moment I realized I was in my five attentions. The severity of the moment automatically caused my resources to emerge.

I looked down at Sophie and an incredible thing happened: she took off straight for the coyotes and my perception went with her. I had intentionally experienced this before with other animals but never before with Sophie. I was seeing through her eyes as she ran. Her sight was amazingly different from mine, so I staggered for a few seconds until I got used to it.

Sophie was a big confident dog that had fought with coyotes, javelinas, and other dogs her whole life and had never lost. She was raised in the woods and had no fear. As she approached the coyotes at full speed, I felt her adrenaline and fearlessness, but some part of me was still aware of myself and in that moment I felt afraid for her. I didn't want her to get hurt.

Those feelings brought me back into my perception but in a way I didn't expect. I was viewing the scene in hyperspace. The darkness meant nothing. I could clearly see the coyotes in the dark without my flashlight. Except the coyotes weren't coyotes. The most aggressive one was a wasp, two were flies, one a rat, and one a fox. All were the same size as a coyote. Sophie was a brown bear about twice her normal size.

The coyotes took one look at her running toward them and they ran off, wanting no part of a fight. Sophie didn't chase them, as she figured her job was done. My normal perception was restored, and I watched Sophie walk up the hill to me. But where was El Gato?

In my normal state I had the feeling that unfortunately El Gato had been taken by the coyotes. I sat down in the dark and was overwhelmed by the sadness of never seeing my little buddy again. But Sophie had other ideas. After giving me a kiss, she began walking back to the house; however, she was not walking normally—she was tracking. Sophie was an experienced tracker and could find me hidden in the woods over five

miles away. Once I knew what she was doing, I followed her and joined my
perception once again with hers. It took her less than two minutes to find
El Gato, who was curled up under a log and severely injured.

I'm thankful to say that after two surgeries for internal injuries and
many months of healing, El Gato made a full recovery. After that incident
he rarely left Sophie's side. It was actually quite humorous that when the
three of us were outside, he would actually walk right under Sophie's belly.

The zoomorphic type changes that my perception experienced with the coyotes and Sophie while viewing in the hyperspace may seem bizarre or imaginative to those who have not experienced something similar. However, this is not uncommon to the Huichol and other indigenous shaman. The Huichol often use a term that could be roughly translated to "spirit" in these situations. For example, it is common for them to see the spirit of certain flowering plants as different kinds of spiders. The powerful Datura and Solandra hold the wolf spirit; the sacred peyote transforms into Kahullumari, the blue spirit deer, who is the guide, messenger, and guardian of the sacred desert of Wirikuta. There are many other examples that can be cited, including those from nonshamanic modalities, such as the Holy Spirit as a white dove in Christianity and the many zoomorphic Egyptian gods, among others. In terms of intentional SV, once we are in an ISC and are viewing in hyperspace, it is necessary to be open to all possibilities of what can be seen or felt beyond our normal senses.

Upon returning to Mexico and telling my Huichol teachers about my viewing experiences while integrating the five points of attention, I entered into a new level of training. It seems that they were waiting for me to find this ability on my own, but now that I had, they were going to teach me how to use it. I believe that when they teach me, they do it in a way slightly different from their own people. I am not Huichol. The manner in which I will describe the practice of DSV is a combination of how they taught me and what I have discovered on my own and through teaching other people.

With slight modifications that I will explain as we go, the basic outline, or steps, to the practice will be similar for whatever you are attempting to view. As I said at the onset, this is a learned technique. Practice, including successes and failures, is the only thing that will make you proficient.

Listed below are the main components to direct shamanic viewing:

- **Integrated state of consciousness (ISC).** Without first entering an ISC, intentional DSV is not possible. As previously stated, an ISC cultivated by the five points of attention is the recommended technique for DSV.
- **Passive volition.** We are not trying to force our viewing but rather set ourselves up for success and passively view what is there.
- **Viewing target.** This is the plant, tree, animal, person, or element that you desire to view.
- **Viewing focal point.** Similar to an adjustable lens on a camera, we can view at a wide angle, normal view, or zoom.
- **Viewing physical data.** In the clear-minded ISC fostered by the five points of attention, we are still cognizant of the physical world and information received by our physical senses.
- **Viewing hyperspace and holographic field data.** This is information we receive that is not limited to our physical senses.
- **Decoding of viewing data.** We determine the meaning of what we are viewing.

Practice 30
PHASE-CONJUGATE MIRRORS OF THE MIND

Entering and holding an integrated state of consciousness is the most challenging aspect of direct shamanic viewing. Once you are adept at the practice of the five points of attention, DSV is a natural progression, especially with instruction and practice. To begin this instruction I'm going to plant a seed—a modern concept—that has helped my students learn DSV. Why I am sharing this here will be apparent shortly.

I previously discussed the concept of phase conjugation as it relates to the holographic field in hyperspace. Now we will look at phase conjugation from another point of view—mirrors and mirrors in the mind. Jean Millay, Ph.D., in her book *Multidimensional Mind: Remote Viewing in Hyperspace,* brings to light a fascinating correlation between phase-conjugate mirrors and remote viewing based on the work of researcher Ray Gottlieb, O.D., Ph.D.

Gottlieb explains that perceptual unity has long perplexed neuroscientists. How does the brain gather scattered sensations such as shape, size, color, distance, motion, name, associated memories, and effective meaning instantaneously into whole, meaningful perceptions? Gottlieb postulates that phase-conjugate mirrors suggest a possible mechanism for this unity. He cites the experiments of the pioneers of holography, who constructed four phase-conjugate mirrors from three lasers. Two lasers meet head-on; when a third is aimed into this configuration, it reflects much like raindrops reflect sunlight to make a rainbow. In *Multidimensional Mind,* Millay explains how the reflections from millions of p-c mirrors synthesize information in the brain.

> Ordinary mirrors reflect light according to the angle the light strikes the mirror, but P-C mirrors "self-target"—the reflection retraces the path back to its source at any angle of incidence. . . .
>
> The reflection merges spatial and temporal information from all three input beams so data from several sources can be combined and fed back to a specific location. Mirrors of different light frequencies cannot interact so many can function at the same site. Mirrors form and vanish instantly as the lasers go on and off. No threshold power of the object [third] beam is required for conjugation to occur. . . .
>
> Here we see how this light apparatus might mirror actual brain function. Imagine millions of coherent packets of light traveling through white and gray matter, meeting in strategic places, creating millions of P-C mirrors that synthesize and reflect information automatically and accurately to meaningful sites. . . .

And where might we find an ideal medium for such light works? The ventricles come to mind. They're four in all, linked into a winged structure. The two lateral ventricles are centered in the cerebral hemispheres, the third between the two halves of the thalamus and hypothalamus, and the fourth between the cerebellum and the brain stem."[5]

Gottlieb's concept is interesting and thought provoking: the brain communicates with itself via phase-conjugate mirrors, and coherent light energy is involved with the process of translating information from hyperspace into sensory memory and then into awareness and the ability of expression. However, I bring it up here simply because when I read Millay's description of Gottlieb's theory, I had already "viewed" this phenomenon and was extremely surprised to learn of a scientific explanation for it. I just sat there with my mouth open in disbelief.

I will explain. During my shamanic viewing training with Huichol shamans, I was very fortunate to be able to view my teachers as they were viewing in hyperspace. What I have viewed on several occasions is so close to what Gottlieb describes that it can't be overlooked. While in an ISC sitting in circle with shamans and the Sacred Fire, I viewed millions of tiny reflections of light in the area of the brain of multiple shamans while they were in an ISC trance state during various ceremonies. It was like viewing a whole galaxy of stars in the night sky inside the mind of the shaman.

This viewing of millions (or billions) of tiny light reflections was also the precursor to my viewing the holographic field of the shamans and so viewing what they were viewing. And I know for sure that they were doing the same thing with me. There were even times when I viewed two shamans viewing me while I viewed them, and we created four phase-conjugate mirrors just like the three lasers in Gottlieb's hypothesis. These four phase-conjugate mirrors appeared like doorways in each of the cardinal directions with the Sacred Fire in the middle. The multidimensional doorways were similar to the doorways and windows experienced in shamanic dreaming.

The major point here is that when you are in an ISC, you can passively intend to view the p-c mirrors of your own mind, which is a gateway to DSV. The easiest time to begin viewing your own p-c mirrors is in the moments right before and after sleep. As previously discussed, the hypnagogic state and hypnopompic states are terms used to describe the borderline state between wakefulness and falling asleep and being asleep and waking up, respectively. During these states, but especially the hypnagogic, the phosphenes and colored specks of light you can see even with your eyes closed are akin to viewing p-c mirrors while in a fully awake ISC. I didn't mention this during the chapter on shamanic dreaming so as to not distract from the dream work. However, once you practice viewing the p-c mirrors in a hypnagogic state with eyes either open or closed, it is easier to passively intend them in a fully awake ISC.

Although it is common to view p-c mirrors spontaneously during an ISC, the natural progression in training to *passively intend* to see them has proven to be very helpful in developing this ability. First practice in a hypnagogic state, then in an awake ISC with closed eyes, followed by an awake ISC alternating eyes open and closed, and finally in an ISC with eyes open. Viewing p-c mirrors with eyes open is easier in the dark. When you can passively intend to view them at will in daylight, you have mastered the technique.

Practice 31
TARGETS OTHER THAN PEOPLE

Once you have mastered viewing p-c mirrors at will, the next step is viewing natural objects. I suggest you train outdoors when possible and in a natural setting that is both inspiring and free from the distractions of people and noise and light pollution (if practicing when dark). If this is not possible, you can train indoors with natural items from this type of place.

In this step choose various viewing targets over the course of weeks or months, but for the time being resist the temptation to view people.

Until you learn the technique, the viewing of seemingly inanimate objects such as rocks or animal parts (feathers, bones, etc.) is more difficult, so I suggest starting with live plants and trees or even animals if you see them. Here is the basic practice:

1. View your target and collect physical and emotional data with all of your senses, intellect, and feelings.
2. Engage the five points of attention to enter an ISC.
3. While in the ISC bring forth your p-c mirrors.
4. Passively view your target with the intention of viewing it in hyperspace. Many situations can happen in this step depending on which dimension you are viewing. You may see the target's field of energy; it may morph into something completely different; it might connect or communicate with you through your normal senses or nonverbal communication. Remain open to any and all possibilities.
5. If or when you feel inclined for whatever reason, change your focal point of viewing.
6. Continue viewing and collecting information about your target from hyperspace. Your target may remain the same as when you first began viewing, or it could change once or many times. Be patient, and receive whatever you view or feel.
7. While still in an ISC, attempt to decode the information you are receiving.

The last step can be, by far, the most difficult. Sometimes the meaning of the information will be apparent, and you will understand immediately, as in my example with the sequoias. But often the meaning of what you view will be baffling. Why has a flowering plant turned into a spider or a deer into a blue jay? As in my example with the coyotes: Why did each morph into a different animal? In this step you may understand the meaning of what you are viewing in the context of hyperspace, which may or may not have any meaning to you in normal reality.

In the coyote example, I understood the meaning to be that I was viewing characteristics that each coyote shared with another species. I was more or less viewing the personality traits of each coyote. When I viewed a running deer morph into a blue jay, it didn't make much sense to my mind while viewing in hyperspace, but my rational mind knew that the blue jay is an ally to the deer. Throughout many years of hunting deer when I was younger, I know that the loudmouthed blue jay is a security guard for the forest and will alert all the animals of threats. A running deer with its white tail up does the same job as the blue jay by signaling to any other deer around that there is an intruder nearby.

It's common, especially when first learning, to not immediately ascertain what is viewed in hyperspace. Don't worry; this is normal, and many times the meaning will appear later. For example, once when I was first learning DSV, I was sitting quietly in a large abandoned lot next to the railroad tracks near my house. I was in the process of viewing a flowering dandelion and had just pulled my focal point back to view the whole field of dandelions when suddenly a turkey vulture landed in the lot. These birds are quite common for that area, so it was not surprising to see it. However, upon switching my viewing to make the vulture my target, it gradually changed into a beautiful and large willow tree.

Upon flying away, the vulture changed back to its original form, and I was left wondering the meaning of the morph into a willow tree. In both my ISC and later in my normal state, I couldn't decode what I had viewed. Many months later while reading the local newspaper, I discovered the lot I was viewing was an old dumping spot for manufacturing companies and was recently made part of the federal government's Superfund Act or CERCLA (Comprehensive Environmental Response, Compensation, and Liability Act) designed to clean up sites contaminated with hazardous substances and pollutants. Years later, after extensive cleanup, the lot was turned into a park with a ball field and playground and was planted with willow trees on the border of the railroad tracks. When I asked a local official I met one day at the park why they planted willows, he told me of their ability to remove toxins—which is the same role the turkey vulture plays in removing carrion.

Although this type of DSV can be a highly enjoyable practice, as shamans we engage in it for relevant information from multidimensional hyperspace. The meaning behind what we are viewing is what's important. If I had viewed the hazardous lot more accurately, I would have known why I had to jump a fence to get into it. If I see a plant turn into a spider, I should ask what kind of spider is it? Is it a poisonous variety? Or vice versa, if I view a certain known type of spider and it turns into a plant, what does that tell me about that plant?

A more experienced shamanic viewer might have viewed what I did with the vulture and willow at that abandoned lot and been able to accurately decode the viewing experience that I couldn't at the time. As you gain more experience collecting information, you will gradually learn to decode it with greater accuracy. It is also helpful to learn DSV with a more experienced partner. Those with more experience can help beginners decode information, which helps the novice viewers advance to a deeper understanding of what they are viewing.

Practice 32
DIRECT VIEWING OF RANDOM PEOPLE

Applying DSV to people brings forth ethical concerns we must think about, assess, and make commitments toward. In certain situations, DSV could be a direct invasion of a person's privacy, which is certainly not the intention here. The goal of this practice is to view a large number of individual people over the course of many weeks or months so that we can develop our viewing abilities when working with people on a one-on-one basis for healing.

In this practice you view *strangers* in public spaces that you have *no intention* of interacting with. Under no circumstances, no matter what you view, are you to interact with these people during or after viewing them. It is not ethical to intrude on people with what you view, even if you see that they need help. By viewing these strangers, you will be developing your skill as a viewer so that you can help other people that *ask you to* in the future.

1. Find a suitable public place where it is extremely unlikely you will see anyone you know, such as a park, mall, city street, or plaza—basically anywhere people are walking around or gathering is fine. The idea is to simply blend in so you can view people quickly and then move on to the next person. I like to find a comfortable place to sit where it feels completely normal for me to be there. Think of it as "people watching" but at a different level.

2. As you settle in to where you will be viewing, collect physical information about the place and what is going on there. What is the general feeling or "vibe" of the place in that moment?

3. Engage the five points of attention to enter an ISC and bring forth your p-c mirrors. At this point in your training, you should have no problem accomplishing this even with other people around. If you don't, then either sit patiently and try again or move to a different location.

4. As people come and go, begin by selecting a random target person and passively view that person with the intention of viewing his holographic field in hyperspace. As in the first practice, many situations can happen in this step depending on which dimension you are viewing.

5. If or when you feel inclined for whatever reason, change your focal point of viewing.

6. Continue viewing and collecting information about your target from hyperspace. It is important to view each person for a very short time— twenty to thirty seconds maximum. Even though you are spending a short time viewing, your target may remain the same as when you first began viewing her, or she may change in appearance once or many times. Be patient and observe whatever view or feel you are receiving.

7. While still in an ISC to attempt to decode the information you are receiving about the person in a nonjudgmental way. Do not try to

psychoanalyze him or attach any personal feelings to what you view. You are simply viewing and are not there to get involved in any way, which includes being affected by the people you are viewing at a conscious or subconscious level. This is another reason not to spend more than thirty seconds on each person.

8. Depending on where you are, you can view dozens or even hundreds of people in one sitting, but don't overdo it. When you begin to feel you have had enough, even if this is after just a few people, stop.

Comments and Suggestions

In step 6 you may see the target's field of energy or she may morph into something completely different. Remain passive and nonjudgmental about whatever you view. You may simply view the target's field of energy, which mystics and luminaries have often described as a luminous egg, golden aura, oval egg, or oval membrane. If this is the case, remember what this looks and feels like so you can compare it to others that you view. In the case of morphing, it is important not to get stunned by what you view and lose your ISC. There is no telling what you might view. Zoomorphic-type viewing is common in this scenario, where you don't know the person. A complete morphing into an animal or a hybrid of the person and an animal can occur. It may happen that instead of anything visual, or in combination with a visual shift, you view a person's holographic field of thoughts by actually hearing or feeling him. If this happens, abort immediately if you feel this could harm you. In any case, be sure to let go of the person's holographic field once he passes you by. If you are sitting and the person is sitting close by, only view the field for a short time—one minute at most.

In step 5, for this practice don't widen your focal point beyond the single person you are viewing. However, zooming in your focal point can reveal data not available otherwise. This is especially the case when viewing a person's energy field. The immensely complicated human organism is so multifaceted and multidimensional that DSV of people is one of the most challenging endeavors, at so many levels, that you could ever enter into.

If you successfully complete the practice of viewing single random people, it is enlightening to open your focal point and view crowds. I use the word *crowd* because opening your focal point to include just two or three people or a single person plus a crowd can be confusing and is usually not successful unless you are very experienced or in the company of an experienced shaman who can help you. I am suggesting that you view just the crowd. By doing so, you can view the collective holographic field that the crowd is experiencing; you will view the shared intent, feelings, and mind-set of a group of people. Decoding the viewing information of a large holographic field created by many people is an educational experience and will further your knowledge about hyperspace.

Practice 33
DIRECT VIEWING OF A CLIENT OR PERSON YOU ARE HELPING

Although direct shamanic viewing (DSV) can be employed in a variety of situations for a broad spectrum of reasons, I consider this practice the most important and what the previous practices have prepared you for: DSV of another person for the purposes of healing or strengthening. The actual healing practices will be discussed later. With this type of DSV we are simply gathering information and decoding. For simplicity I am going to use the word *client* as the viewing target for this practice, even though your target may simply be a friend or relative. Also, I am sure that many of you reading this are probably already practicing some form of healing modality for other people.

In this practice you will be employing knowledge gleaned from all your previous DSV experiences, plus learning more as you practice. In a best case scenario, you would begin learning this practice by viewing other DSV practitioners or even an experienced shaman. In lieu of that, begin practicing with people interested in the technique, who you feel comfortable with and they with you.

DSV as a modality for healing is a diagnostic technique that can be very valuable for both physically derived information and more importantly information from the holographic field and p-c mirrors. There are successful indigenous shaman-healers I know that could actually care less about the names of organs in the body or medical diagrams or the modern vocabulary for diseases. They work more or less exclusively with data from the holographic field and p-c mirrors to decode a client's ailment. The prescribed treatment given by these shamans is normally an energetic sucking technique (explained in the next chapter) or a specific healing ceremony. On rare occasions these shamans will refer the patient to someone else, such as a bone setter or even a medical doctor.

It is important to note that in indigenous shamanic communities not all shaman are healers and not all healers are shaman. I know very powerful Huichol shamans who can speak directly with Grandfather Fire, are expert dreamers, and can at times even affect the clouds and rain but who do not practice the vocation of healing people. Their function is to serve the community in other ways. However, I have had the privilege of knowing and being a student of shamans that are healers. The most effective of these shaman-healers work both in the realms of the holographic field and p-c mirrors but also have extensive knowledge of human physiology. The latter knowledge is not normally derived from a modern medical school but simply through a lifetime of experiences and the accumulated knowledge handed down from healers of countless generations.

The practice of DSV is for diagnostic purposes, as part of shamanic healing. In many cases the viewing data we receive from the client from the holographic field and p-c mirrors will suggest needed changes in behavior, nutrition, or thought patterns before the imbalance manifests as an actual illness. In other cases, we find severe energy drains from previous experiences that are still affecting the client. Almost everyone has significant energy drains, and some people have severe ones. Physical illnesses that are already manifesting in the client are usually fairly easy to view in hyperspace. However, knowledge of anatomy and physiology can be indispensable when pinpointing illness and even more importantly for decoding information related to healing. In an ISC we have not left our rational mind completely behind. In decoding treatment for physical illnesses, our knowledge of the human anatomy and physiology will make us more effective in diagnosis.

Before getting into the actual practice, it's important to realize the many factors that can influence this type of DSV. The factors listed below can affect both the shaman and his or her client.

- **Setting.** It is extremely important that the immediate space is free of distractions. DSV can be conducted with the client lying down, sitting, or standing, but in all cases he or she should be comfortable with the surroundings whether indoors or out.
- **Confidence.** It is vital that the client has confidence in the ability of the shaman either by having worked with the shaman before or by having been referred by someone the client trusts who has previously worked with the shaman.
- **Physical body.** The client should feel physically comfortable. Some factors that might make that difficult and will need to be addressed include illness or pain, hunger or overeating, sleepiness, discomfort in a physical position (lying down, sitting, standing), needing to use the bathroom, uncomfortable clothing, or being too hot or cold.
- **Emotions.** Determine the client's initial emotional state, which may be mad, sad, glad, or contemplative.
- **Mentality.** Aside from emotion, determine where the client is coming from mentally and intellectually. Even if a client is confident of your ability and the process, in some cases very intellectual clients may try to overanalyze and so stay closed mentally to the practice.
- **Memories (this incarnation).** In most cases of DSV with a single client, the reliving of memories of past events is a key tool.
- **Memories of past or other lives.** Whether the client believes in past lives or not is not important. Information from memories

that seem to be the client's but with a different body or in another life can help resolve current dilemmas.

As we have seen with experiences of DSV with random people, there are countless viewing situations that can arise. I have found that in DSV of clients, three basic viewing situations arise:

1. Viewing the holographic field of the client at the level of thoughts, emotions, feelings, and memories via their p-c mirrors.
2. Viewing the multidimensional hyperspace of the client. In this case we often view either the luminous cocoon of the client and can decode energy drains and obstructions or view the morphing of the whole person or specific physical areas of the body.
3. Alternate viewing of both the first and second situations.

Steps for Viewing

Step 1. Depending on the client and situation, the client may be viewed while sitting, standing, or lying down on his back: different circumstances require different strategies. However, unless it is physically uncomfortable for a client to stand or lie down, I normally don't have a client sit the first time I view her. I prefer, when possible, to view the client standing up. This allows me to view the entire physical body and energetic cocoon while I walk around the client. If the client is lying down, he may have to turn over and back again many times, which can be distracting. I usually, but not always, perform healings with the client lying down. If I have viewed the client before and have decided to view him again primarily through the holographic field, then sitting comfortably is sometimes the best option.

Step 2. As you are getting the client situated, or even before, you are collecting data through your normal perception of the senses, feelings, and intuition. Some practitioners of DSV like to converse with the client to know what's going on with her; others do not. Experience will dictate for you how you go about viewing each individual client. I have effectively viewed clients with or without conversation; it all depends on the circumstance at hand. For some clients, talking first seems to them absolutely necessary. But many times with this type of client, I have intentionally avoided much or any conversation before viewing. When you later tell the client what you viewed and it was what the client was going to tell you first, this has a profound effect on his level of confidence in your viewing and subsequent healing efforts. In any case, during this step you are using your perceptual abilities without yet entering an ISC.

Step 3. When you and your client are both ready, engage the five points of attention to enter an ISC and bring forth your p-c mirrors. This I have numbered step 3; however, due to your experiences of the previous practices and the first practice in the book, you may have naturally or intentionally already cultivated the five points. In either case, now is the time to bring forth your p-c mirrors and be ready for viewing. I mention "be ready" because right now something you wouldn't expect is likely to occur. Before you even passively intend to view your client, it is not uncommon to view the p-c mirrors of your client. This is an extremely positive sign because it shows your client is open and confident to receive your viewing, which is one reason this DSV practice is so different from viewing random people. In an ISC you have previously viewed the holographic field of random people, but you were not interacting with them; and they were in a normal state of consciousness, so more than likely you did not view their p-c mirrors. Now that you are interacting with your client, your mere presence or the situation of your client simply being involved in the viewing can alter the client's consciousness and induce powerful emanations from her p-c mirrors.

Step 4. Whether you spontaneously viewed the client's p-c mirrors or not, now is the time to passively view the client with the intention of seeing his p-c mirrors in their holographic field or his energetic hyperspace. I prefer to begin viewing with the client standing in a relaxed position with eyes closed. Make sure his shoulders are down, hands are open and not clenched, thighs are relaxed and not tightened. You can even have the client gently shake out his arms and legs before beginning if he seems tense. Slowly walk around the client at a distance, where your focal point can view his whole body and luminous cocoon. I usually begin with a distance of one arm length and one step back. Most luminous cocoons extend about an arm's length from the body, but some can be larger, so you must adjust as necessary. For whatever reason, people tend to feel more comfortable if you walk around them counterclockwise. However, most beginning viewers feel more comfortable viewing while walking clockwise. Since the point at this stage is for you to learn, you can choose which direction, but I suggest clockwise to start.

Step 5. Begin viewing by standing in front of the client. As in the last practice, at this point anything can happen. It may happen that your viewing begins with thoughts, feelings, and emotions in the p-c mirrors of the client's holographic field. In this case you collect as much data about what's going on in his holographic field as necessary to decode the information for healing and advice after the session.

Step 6. It also may happen that right away you begin to view the client's field of energy hyperspace. Even if you began with viewing the holographic field, this scan should also be done. While slowly walking around the client, scan her entire field and note the location of any drains (leaks) and discolorations, especially dark or opaque spots. Once you have thoroughly viewed the client's whole field, it is usually necessary to zoom your focal point to these areas in order to decode them. When later performing an energetic healing on the client, these are the areas you will be working on. Right now you may be getting lots of information from these areas, and you will get even more during the actual healing. For now, collect as much as you can from your decoding.

Step 7. As in the previous practice with random people, your client may morph into something different while you are viewing him, and this is vital information to decode. However, unlike before, you are now also viewing specific areas of the energetic field, and each of these areas may morph into something different. This is also vital information to decode for the actual healing.

Comments and Suggestions

When you have completed the viewing, you now have enough information to perform a healing, a ritual, or a verbal consultation. Remember that technique is all about *viewing*. We are not intentionally extracting or adding anything to the client. That can happen later with healing techniques and counseling. This also means we are not talking to the client while viewing unless she becomes distraught or some other situation arises where it is absolutely necessary to stop the viewing and speak to the client.

In the process of DSV, be careful not to internalize anything that you view or feel, as that will hinder a full and proper viewing. No matter what you view, you must remain calm and passively focused. In the early stages of learning this technique, this can be quite difficult. Intentionally viewing another person's p-c mirrors and hyperspace can be at times revolting or alluring if we do not remain detached from our own personal feelings, biases, and judgments. That is one of the main reasons this is such a highly advanced technique and why I introduced autogenic training in this book before DSV. You can't passively view another person if you haven't practiced and mastered passive volition with yourself. Normally, I have found that once a shaman can enter an ISC, especially via the five points of attention, this is not an issue. However, it is best to always keep in mind that DSV is a diagnostic tool and not a form of healing or therapy.

In step 5 while viewing the client's p-c mirrors of the holographic field, you must remember the decoded information to effectively move on to the healing phase. While viewing you can even discreetly write down viewed information for later use. This is also applicable to steps 6 and 7, although during these steps it is usually easier to remember what you view because they are more visual and do not deal directly with the thoughts or emotions of the p-c mirrors.

In steps 6 and 7 energetic drains caused by past experiences still affecting the client will be easily viewed. Many people think that because they've gotten over a past relationship or traumatic event either through their own personal growth work or therapy, they are no longer affected. This is not usually the case because the energy drains have not been patched and then sealed in their hyperspace field. Just because you don't think about a past experience anymore doesn't mean it is not still affecting your daily life and how you view the world. This is a tricky subject with some clients, as they will resist this reality. If you can view the drains, then they have not been patched and sealed. Of course, the experiences and situations from our past are learning experiences, and without them we would not be who we are. However, some experiences require energetic healing, not simply by processes of the mind. Through employing DSV to view the hyperspace field of the client to detect these drains, we can then use specific techniques to patch them. These techniques will be described in chapter 14.

When viewing the hyperspace of the client in steps 6 and 7, remember that the energetic field will also display the various conditions of the physical body, and this is another primary reason for employing DSV. While decoding what is viewed as pertaining to the physical body, keep in mind these key areas:

Brain, eyes, ears, nose
Teeth, gums
Neck, lungs, breasts, heart
Digestive tract
Liver, gallbladder, kidneys, spleen
Uterus, ovaries, cervix, vagina, prostate, testes, bladder, rectal area
Bones, joints, spine

As you decode any physical maladies from what you view in the client's hyperspace field, be careful not to become fixated on any one area, even if what you decode seems serious or even life-threatening, as this may cause you to miss another area that might also be serious. Also, sometimes one area of trauma may obliterate another or hide it from your view. This is another reason we zoom our focal point when we view anomalies in the field and walk around the client while viewing in order to view at different angles. For example, if the client has a large discoloration in his field that you view in the location of the spine from the back, you could easily miss an anomaly in one of the major organs. Similarly, in the case of viewing morphing, if you view a large snake in the area of the small intestine, you could miss the scorpion hiding in the anus.

It takes a lot of practice and patience to learn DSV for clients, so take your time, and don't expect too much too fast. The indigenous shamans who have taught me have spent a lifetime mastering this craft.

14

Advanced Shamanic Healing

Shamanic healing is the culmination of all the previous practices laid out in this book. To begin this chapter, a word of warning is in order. If you cannot enter an ISC at will, have not mastered shamanic dreaming, are not proficient at DSV, and have not obtained your animal jicaras and healing stones, please do not attempt shamanic healing on others. These five tools are the prerequisite for the shamanic healing I am about to explain. Without these tools you put yourself in danger doing this type of powerful work. Your p-c mirrors and your holographic field can be severely damaged if you are not fully prepared. I have seen it happen many times, especially to kindhearted healers who skipped over some of the practices that take the most time to accomplish. Then they must seek out a shaman who is fully initiated and experienced to be healed. Even with the best of intentions, if you are not fully prepared for this, you will do more harm than good to yourself and your client.

The shamanic healing techniques I will now describe are an extension of the advanced practices of DSV, with support from your animal spirits, healing stones, and Grandfather Fire. During the viewing of your client, you collected information to be decoded in order to facilitate the healing process. As previously noted this happens at the levels of ordinary consciousness and an ISC whereby you view the p-c mirrors and holographic and hyperspace fields. With viewed and decoded information, you can proceed to healing.

There is an infinite spectrum of information that you could have collected and decoded, due to the complicated lives of human beings and the incredible human organism itself. Sorting it all out and learning what to tackle first comes with time and experience. A client could have energy drains from past experiences still affecting her; misaligned, blocked, or opaque p-c mirrors; minor or life-threatening injuries or health issues; blockages and unwanted foreign energy; or all of the above; plus more. To say that human beings are complex is a vast understatement!

However, as healers we must start somewhere. My intention is to describe a few core practices that you can use and expand on as your experience grows. These practices can be used as a base in the creation of your own unique methodology. In any case our goal is to conduct ourselves with the utmost respect for our clients. Remember that if you don't know how to heal a particular issue, the best thing to do is refer your client to someone who can. For example, I'm not the best person to see for a broken bone, and when it comes to physical gynecological problems, as a man I have no experience and would refer the client to a female healer. The healing work I am presenting here is in the realms of p-c mirrors and holographic and hyperspace fields. This is the venue of healing that I am most versed in.

I am extremely happy to say that as the medical establishment has broadened its view in recent years, we now have lots of medical doctors who are naturopaths and doctors of integrative medicine and some that are learning the ways of shamanic healing. I am fortunate to have had the opportunity to train open-minded doctors and interns. It is my great hope that with the vast information of the medical field combined with the knowledge and practices of the shamanic arts, we may revolutionize the modern health care system toward holistic practices that embrace both science and spirit.

Practice 34
CLEANING THE HOLOGRAPHIC FIELD

The shamanic healing I will be describing always occurs in three distinct steps for the practitioner and one more step for the client. As previously discussed, the first step is DSV of the client, which includes decoding. This diagnostic procedure provides the healer with the information necessary to facilitate proper healing techniques. The second step is the cleansing of the holographic field and p-c mirrors of the client. The third step is infusing energy into the cleansed areas, which may include placing an energetic "patch" on the injured area. The fourth step is solely for the client as he walks through his life and through his actions permanently heals the patched area.

This practice is for step two. When thinking about energetically cleaning a client, the analogy of cleaning a floor is helpful. Sometimes we simply sweep a floor or mop. Other times we may vacuum. At times it is necessary to remove bigger items from the floor. In any case, we first look at (view) the floor and decide what needs to be done in order to clean it. Our DSV procedure is analogous to viewing the floor, and our decoding is like deciding the best way to clean it. Obviously, the holographic field and p-c mirrors of our clients are infinitely more complex than a floor, but as in cleaning a floor, we need to choose the correct tools and techniques when engaging in shamanic cleaning.

The first technique is sweeping, and the tool is a large vulture feather. If it is decided after DSV with your client to proceed to healing, the first technique I almost always employ is sweeping of the holographic energetic field and p-c mirrors. Even if a deeper clean will follow, sweeping first always helps in many ways. The sweeping technique is a procedure of removing unwanted and unhealthy energetic debris from the luminous cocoon and p-c mirrors that lie on the surface. In most cases the debris has been collected recently and has not sunk in very deep yet, or the debris was initially not so intense as to have penetrated deeply. By using this technique, we accomplish an initial cleansing, and from there we can view even more clearly those areas that need deeper attention. During and after the sweeping, we can view the client to decode even more clearly our client's needs with regard to further healing.

I prefer to sweep with the client standing, but it can be accomplished lying on the back first and then turning over if standing is not an option. The cleansing qualities of a vulture feather as a shamanic tool is most effective if you have collected it yourself from a bird you are familiar with, but if you are given one from a bird you don't know, the cleansing energy of the feather will still assist you. Be sure when first acquiring a vulture feather that you physically clean it. Vultures cleanse the natural world by eating carrion that could be potentially harmful to other species, so bacteria can be an issue with vulture feathers, and all birds can potentially carry parasites such as mites and lice. Even though vultures spread their wings in the morning sun for cleansing and tend to be fastidious at preening, we still must clean their feathers before employing them as tools for our work.

There are many ways to cleanse feathers; however, with vulture feathers we need to be even more careful than with other bird feathers. Cleaning vulture feathers can be more aptly described as sanitizing. In no way will our cleaning affect the core energy of the feathers. The energy they contain is not on the surface; it lives inside the feathers. Here is my preferred method for cleaning feathers, especially those from the vulture:

1. Put on gloves, and put a handful of mothballs and the feathers in an airtight container. Store the container outside for at least twenty-four hours; the mothballs will kill any parasites. Mothballs can be dangerous to pets, children, and wildlife, so be careful where you store them.
2. Now we want to take care of any bacteria and viruses. Soak the feathers for at least a half hour in a fifty-fifty mixture of isopropyl alcohol and hydrogen peroxide. This mixture will kill the bacteria and render most viruses inactive. Bleach is more effective but will make the feathers

brittle and can diminish their color. Hydrogen peroxide not only oxidizes bacteria to death but also serves to brighten up the feathers without leaving them brittle.

3. After soaking, hand-wash the feathers with a mild organic soap. Gently lather up each feather, making sure to remove any remaining stains or debris with your fingers, and then gently swish the feathers in a basin of water. This step also removes any remaining chemicals or oil that may be on the feathers while keeping them soft to the touch.

4. Finally, put the feathers in a warm, sunny place to dry and be infused by the sun and wind. When a feather is almost dry, you can use your fingers to smooth together any gaps in the anterior or posterior vanes of the feather to restore it to its original shape. It is important that the feathers dry quickly to avoid any fungal or mold infestations.

The second tool for this procedure is necessary when working indoors. If working outside you can sweep energetic debris off and into the atmosphere, as the elements will naturally neutralize and dissipate it. When indoors we need a vessel to sweep the debris into so we can dispose of it after the procedure. The two containers I recommend are:

1. A gourd or clay bowl six to twelve inches in diameter: basically the same as we use for our animal jicaras. Make sure there are no holes in the bottom. Inside the bowl place a healing te'ka (see practice 6).

2. Any kind of bowl, similar in size to the above, that will hold water. Fill the bowl one-third full of water and add about one-half cup or so of salt and stir.

Below are the steps for this shamanic cleaning procedure. Here I will describe the preferred process with the client standing. If standing is not an option, the procedure can be accomplished with the client lying down on her back and then rolling over onto her stomach.

1. With your sanitized and energized vulture feather in your dominant hand and your debris vessel ready, enter an ISC and begin DSV while also remembering your initial DSV session with the client.

2. Beginning at the top of the head, begin sweeping with the vulture feather and "flicking" energetic debris into the air (if outside) or into your vessel (indoors). If you are using a vessel, it will be in your nondominant hand so you can put it into position to receive the debris from the sweeping and flicking as you move up and down and around the client. Sweep off every part of the client's body, starting in the front and moving to the back. Take your time, and don't miss any areas. Some areas will require more sweeping than others: use the tool of DSV to see what is happening. As stated earlier, no one can know what you might see during DSV. Use your experience in DSV to clean the client as best you can.

3. Stop cleaning, step back, and focus solely on DSV; inspect your work while walking around the client. A full second pass of sweeping or sweeping specific areas is usually necessary.

4. Most likely there will be some areas you cannot sweep clean. Make note of these areas: they will be dealt with later during a deep cleaning procedure.

5. When you are satisfied that you have removed all of the energetic surface debris that you can in that moment, talk to your client about removing any deeper energetic blockages and negative foreign energy and patching energetic drains. Ideally, this next level of treatment happens right away, but if time does not allow in that moment, try to schedule the procedure for as soon as possible. The blockages, foreign energy, and energy drains you viewed for your client will not go away on their own; they will still be there when the client returns.

6. The procedure for cleaning your vessel can be accomplished in two ways, depending on the circumstances. If you are going to use it again right away—as sometimes occurs if seeing multiple clients in one day, or for me when I give healing workshops and trainings to groups—the vessel must be cleaned right away. For a gourd and healing te'ka, rinse

both with salt water. For a bowl with salt water, simply dump the water in a drain or on the ground (soil, not concrete) and then rinse with salt water. If you aren't going to use your gourd and healing te'ka until the next day or longer, simply remove your te'ka from the gourd and place it outside; the elements will naturally cleanse it.

Practice 35
EXTRACTION OF THE HOLOGRAPHIC FIELD AND PHASE-CONJUGATE MIRRORS

As stated at the beginning of this chapter, shamanic healing, especially this procedure, should not be attempted without mastering the previous practices. To facilitate this procedure, it is you, the shaman-healer, who will be the main tool. For this reason, you must be sure that you are energetically clear, clean, and strong. You must also be completely detached from emotions and the controlling aspects of the ego. During this procedure, you will be acting as an energetic transfer mechanism. In the physical dimension you are analogous to a backhoe digging to extract earth and rock from the ground and then moving it somewhere else to be dumped or a vacuum cleaner sucking up debris to be deposited elsewhere. And just like a backhoe or vacuum cleaner, you only hold the extracted material for a short time—in this procedure for a second or less. It is imperative to dump out absolutely all of the material you extract. If you don't, you will become ill and need to be healed. Only you (or a highly experienced healer) can know if you are ready. If so, please continue. If not, take your time and work on mastering the previous techniques until you are ready, however long it takes.

Shamanic extraction healing work will require all of the energy, power, and wisdom you have collected through learning to cultivate an ISC at will via the five points of attention, mastering shamanic dreaming and DSV, obtaining your animal spirit jicaras and uniquely powerful te'kas, and embodying self-healing through the dichotomy of passive volition, death, and rebirth and connection to the Sacred Fire.

The basic procedure for energetic extraction cleaning is very straightforward and simple; it's all the variables that come up, and how to handle them, that make it complex. I'm going to describe the procedure as simply as I can so you can begin practicing to fill in the gaps that I can't really explain in words. First, I will describe the procedure in narrative format and then in a step-by-step list.

In this procedure you are going to use the decoded information you obtained through your initial DSV of the client and during the surface cleaning to remove embedded energy blockages and foreign energy from your client to initialize healing toward a healthier state of being on energetic, emotional, and physical levels. You will be removing energy blockages and foreign energy by sucking them out of your client and expelling them into a vessel. At the physical level, this is accomplished via enormously deep inhalation and exhalation of your breath. At the level of energy, this happens simultaneously with your breath work via your holographic field and p-c mirrors.

You will be prepared for this intense and challenging task through your experiences of the previous practices and mastery of previous procedures. In your first attempts at this procedure with friends, colleagues, and family members, it is best to be very methodical and systematic. As you gain experience and confidence and see the tangible results of your work, you will become more fluid and dynamic in your approach and the manner in which you conduct your healing work.

In preparation for your first few sessions, I suggest you either sit quietly somewhere you are extremely comfortable or go for a walk in nature. (I prefer the walk, even after years of doing this, simply because I do my best personal growth and creative work while moving, not sitting, but that might not be the case for you.) Recapitulate or relive some of your experiences with the previous practices. Bringing forth the memories and energies of previous experiences with your jicaras, te'kas, dream journeys, and so on will round up your power and confidence that you are ready for this next step as a shaman-healer. While actually performing the extraction procedure on a client, I have found it is not necessary to directly call to spirit helpers or te'kas because they are already with me.

However, when we perform the third step of the healing—infusion of energy—I have found it to be more powerful to directly summon some helpers, usually just the ones I feel could help the most for that particular client. I will explain this further in the next practice.

Here is a step-by-step list of instructions for the extraction procedure:

1. If you are moving to this procedure right after your initial DSV and sweeping of the client, you can move directly to step 2. If not, perform a DSV and sweep-clean of your client.
2. Prepare your extraction vessel as in the previous practice.
3. Prepare your client physically by having him wear as little clothing as he feels comfortable with. I prefer to have the client nude with a sheet over his body that I move aside briefly as I work on different sections of the body. If the client is not comfortable with that, simply have him wear clothing that covers the genitals and for women the breast area as well. Seldom will you ever extract directly on the breasts or genital area. When working on the areas of the sternum or solar plexus, a garment can be moved slightly for the extraction; the same goes when working on the areas of the cervix, navel, or base of the spine. When ready, have the client lie down comfortably on his back with legs extended and relaxed, arms relaxed and at his sides, and hands open with palms down.
4. If you are not already there, enter an ISC via the five points of attention.
5. From your DSV and sweeping you should already know which areas of the holographic field you will be working on and if you will be working on their p-c mirrors. This step of this procedure is undoubtedly the most difficult for the novice healer simply because of the infinite number of things a healer can view in a client. From opaque or different colored blobs, to treacherous animals or zoomorphic creatures, to areas that look to be covered in fog, dust, sand, or even colored gelatin (these are usually but not always found clouding the p-c mirrors), to dangerous plants or arachnids and insects—there are

countless energy forms that can appear to the healer in myriad ways.

However, in this step the extraction procedure remains the same for whatever you are dealing with. Choose your first blockage or foreign energy to extract. But remember, in the final procedure, you will be infusing energy, so it is vitally important during this extraction step that you remember, or even write down, what and where each extraction occurred so you can later patch the extraction area with the appropriate resonance or type of energy.

If I view work that needs to be done to clear the p-c mirrors, I usually go for them first. I will continue this explanation as if that were the case because it usually is.

6. Kneel close to the client's head with your vessel right next to you.

7. Without touching him, lean your head closer to his and instruct him to breathe out as you breathe in and breathe in when you breathe out. The first time you do this with a client, it may seem a little tricky, but once the client gets the hang of it, it's simple. Then with exaggerated breaths, breathe in while he breathes out and breathe out while he breathes in. Practice this for roughly ten breaths in a row or until the two of you are synchronized and you are sure that when you are ready he will breathe out as you are sucking in your breath on his skin during the extraction. When you are sure the client can synchronize with you, then stop for a few moments.

8. Explain to the client what is going to happen next: with exaggerated breathing you will synchronize your breathing (while you breathe in, he breathes out). Now that you have practiced this, the healing should only need a few breaths. When you are ready, exhale forcefully and then place your lips on his forehead and suck out whatever you see blocking his p-c mirrors. Your physical sucking action should be like you are sucking through a straw as hard and as long as you possibly can.

9. When you have taken in as much as you can, exhale as hard as you can into your containment vessel while viewing the energy of the blockage leave you. This step is often accompanied by retching, spitting, or coughing as the foul energy is expectorated.

10. Quickly inspect your work with your DSV. Oftentimes it takes more than one round of sucking and expectorating to extract an area but never more than three. If it takes you more than three, you are not performing the procedure correctly or you are not yet ready to provide this procedure to clients. If I'm sure I didn't get it all, I simply say "again" to the client, begin breathing, and when synchronized after a few breaths, perform the sucking extraction again, followed by exhaling again into the vessel to expectorate.

11. Inspect your work again. Normally one or two sucking passes is sufficient to remove a blockage or a foreign energy. If not, perform another pass. If what you are trying to extract is still there after three passes and you are a novice, either move to the next area and perform the procedure to see what happens or abort the session and continue with the previous practices until your energy is strong enough for this procedure. At the end of these steps, I will explain what to do if you can't extract an area properly after three sucking passes.

12. When you have completely extracted one area with one to three sucking passes, then simply move to the next area. If you are a novice I suggest you do no more than five areas of extraction with a client during his initial session. When performed correctly, extraction is hard work, especially if each area takes two or three sucking passes, and you need to have adequate energy to properly perform the next step of infusion for the client to end the healing session. If more than five areas need extraction, make an appointment for the client to come back at a later date. Rarely will you have clients that need more than two sessions if you perform the sweeping cleaning correctly. Once you become experienced at this procedure and your stamina increases, you will be able to suck out ten or more areas in one session if needed. When you get to this level, one session with a client is usually sufficient for a full deep cleaning.

13. When you have completed the extractions for a session, take a *short* break. Drink some water, but avoid chitchat. During the break you will make ready your tools for the next step—the infusion.

If after three properly performed extractions on a particular area, you are still not satisfied it is cleaned, then we need the help of the client in diagnosing the blockage or foreign energy while at the same time we use all our resources to decode this area. If you have an area like this, as described in step 11 (I rarely do, but it does happen), simply continue extracting the other areas. Continuing on successfully with other areas will gain you and your client momentum, and your client will have more energy available now that those other areas are cleaned. More energy now available to your client, combined with elevated confidence in your work (the client *will* feel a positive change in his energy from the extractions), will help you work *together* with your client in decoding a problem area.

Almost always these extra stubborn blockages are due to foreign energy, such as a particularly strong energetic event with another person from the client's past. A severe energetic event like this, likely life changing, is usually fairly simple to decode with the help of the client.

First, have the client stand and thoroughly perform DSV again on that area. Be sure to zoom in and walk around the client to view him from all angles. I have found that sometimes in these cases you will find out that there is actually another blockage in that area that can be missed during viewing that hinders either of them from being extracted. In this case there is a special technique to use, which I will explain next. For now, let's say you have one severely stubborn blockage of foreign energy to extract.

It is your job as shaman-healer to gather and decode as much information about the foreign energy as you can via DSV. What do you see? How does it feel? What does it mean? Even though this event in the client's past may have exacerbated other similar events that, through the years, may have fortified this blockage, we still need to extract the original core event. During your viewing, while you ask yourself the above questions, you *will* receive information. After you have viewed thoroughly and collected as much information as you can, have your client lie down.

In many if not most cases like this, I can gather and decode sufficient information that I can tell what type of event is the core of the blockage. Usually, it was an extremely traumatic violent event (being mugged, being shot or shooting another person, domestic violence); sexual abuse, including rape; humiliation by a relative, classmate, teacher, or boss; witnessing a violent death, including suicide; or not being able to help someone during a natural disaster, such as a flood, hurricane, or tornado. These are some of the events I have found in my healing work, but obviously there are others.

With your client now lying down again (on his back), begin to gently explain to him what you have viewed or felt about the traumatic event during your DSV of the blocked area. The idea here is to speak to him in a kind but deliberate and strategic manner to find out what specific event from his past is still blocking him. Each of the above examples of energetic trauma will provide you with different qualities of information: decoding information about rape will be totally different from shooting someone; being personally humiliated will be totally different from watching a suicide. Many times my strategy will be to begin by asking a question based on the information from my viewing of the blocked area. For example, I might say, "May I ask you a question? Do you have a traumatic event from your past in which you were abused by someone?" or "Have you ever seen someone die—but not from natural causes?"

You base these questions, this conversation, on information you received from your viewing. You are not fishing in the dark. What you want to do as delicately as possible is get to the specific event that caused the trauma and therefore the blockage. It is important not to mentally or psychologically analyze the event at all or even discuss the event too much. We are working with energy, not psychotherapy. All we need to know is what the specific event was in order to extract it energetically from the client's holographic field or p-c mirrors. Once you know what the event is, and preferably the specific person involved, you can move on to the extraction, which will have one more added component to the procedure.

Since you have already successfully extracted blockages or foreign energy in other areas of your client, he will already be familiar with the procedure. The procedure is the same for this extraction except that before you begin the synchronized breathing in step 8, you will ask the client to close his eyes and remember the event. Once he has the event in her mind, tell him that when you start breathing together you want him to *relive* the event. Tell your client to use the synchronized breathing (you breathe in while he breathes out, you breathe out while he breathes in) to go even deeper than ordinary memory, to try to feel as if he were actually there again. To facilitate this, do a few more synchronized breaths while he is reliving the event, and then suck the event out and expectorate into your vessel. As before, do this as many as three times, but with this technique I rarely have to do it more than once.

Practice 36
ENERGETIC INFUSION OF THE HOLOGRAPHIC FIELD AND DECODING CLIENT AILMENTS

There are numerous ways we can infuse energy into our holographic field, p-c mirrors, and physical body. We can use fire, smoke, wind, earth, water, infused or essential oils, many various kinds of holistic healing modalities, or even just simple encouraging and nurturing words or an authentic loving hug.

There are more than a few specific energy-infusing ceremonies I have been taught to impart by my indigenous shaman mentors that revolve mostly around the five elements and living beings in nature. There are two reasons I chose to use this particular one here: (1) I have already included a section of this book on te'kas and (2) I have found them to be the best medium of infusion for patching (mending) areas in the holographic field and p-c mirrors after extracting blockages and foreign energy. After extraction there will be a hole or void that is distinctly noticeable through DSV that needs to be filled for the client to be healthy and whole. That is the goal of this procedure.

An energetic infusion of your client into the specific areas of extraction should always be done at the end of every extraction procedure.

When employing te'kas for aid in energetic infusing I like to have a variety of te'kas at hand to energetically patch the void left by an extraction. Each te'ka has specific and unique qualities of energy, and almost all te'kas you will encounter (depending on where you find them) are ancient, usually between ten thousand and two billion years old and therefore are perfect tools for our shamanic work.

I placed the section on te'kas in this book close to the beginning in hopes that when you got here you would already have collected some to work with. I will proceed as if you have a nice selection to choose from. If you don't now, I hope you will in the future. I usually have between five and ten different te'kas on hand when doing this type of infusion for extractions. In all situations the luminous te'ka is the default te'ka for this procedure if you don't have the specific one for the job. The luminous te'ka is like the adjustable wrench or adjustable pliers when installing a bolt. When installing a bolt, you like to have the right size wrench or socket for the job, but sometimes you don't, so you go with an adjustable wrench or pliers. It might not be the perfect tool, but it still gets the job done.

There are times when I will use more than one te'ka to fill a void and secure a patch—kind of like dressing an open wound with gauze and then using tape to hold it on. But this is not usually the case: if you have the proper te'ka for the job, you normally don't need two—just know that it's an option.

First, what we need to do now is choose one of the extraction points or areas on the client that we are going to infuse. I like to start with the head or upper body of the client and work my way down the extraction points toward the feet, but you can infuse them in any order you like.

Once you have chosen an extraction area to infuse, in an ISC remember what you viewed, felt, and decoded from that blockage or foreign energy during your DSV and the extraction procedure. This information is vital to the infusion. Now you must choose the proper te'ka for the infusion. As a novice this might seem tricky, but as you gain experience, you won't even have to think about which one to use: you will simply know, or a specific te'ka may actually tell you to use it. At any level of experience with this procedure, if you have truly come this far with the practices in this book, I have no doubt you will have the ability to properly execute the infusions.

I'm going to give you an example that required me to use a shadow te'ka. Novice extraction healers are often uncertain or hesitant to use a shadow te'ka, preferring to go for a luminous, guardian, or magical te'ka, which are extremely powerful and proper to use in the right situation. But the shadow te'ka should not be avoided; often misunderstood and so often overlooked, it can be a unique and powerful tool.

The client in this example never spoke to me about this blockage caused as a result of a foreign energy, but in viewing and decoding, I could pretty much tell exactly what had happened to him. Remember that even though I explained the extraction technique for the extra deep and stubborn blockages, most blockages that you cannot sweep off are deep but not as deep as those and don't require the help of the client to remember or talk about it. In many cases, like this one, DSV revealed to me the exact nature of the trauma without my ever speaking to the client about it. That is the preferred method in this kind of healing work. Minimal talk. Get in there and do your energy work in a friendly, loving way but at the same time remain detached.

This particular case was humiliation that gradually grew into self-loathing and later severe depression. When I extracted this particular blockage from the client, I viewed what had happened to him while I was expectorating (this can also happen during the sucking). I saw that he had been devastatingly humiliated by his teacher and classmates at around age ten. I viewed the kids' and the gym teacher's energies that were fixed to him fly into the vessel. When I turned back to him after expectorating, he was smiling and actually giggled; not a full-on laugh, which sometimes happens, but he knew he was finally free from that tragic episode from early in his life, and he was happy.

Without talking about it, he knew that I knew what had happened. No words necessary. After the extractions I knew immediately that I would use the shadow te'ka to patch that particular event. After I completed all the infusions, I had him make a strategy for his everyday life in order to make the patches permanent. I will explain this last step in practice 37.

Here are the steps for the infusion procedure:

1. Gather your te'kas near to you (where you are working on the client who is in the same position he was in during the extractions).
2. Choose an extraction point to infuse with an energy patch. I usually begin with the head and upper body and work down to the feet, but if you feel one area is best infused first, use your intuition and viewing. You can apply the patches in any order you see fit.
3. Having chosen the extraction point, use the memory of the extraction and your viewing and decoding information to help choose the appropriate te'ka to aid you. This step is tricky to describe in words. Sometimes, especially as you become more experienced with the procedure, you will just "know" which te'ka to use. If this is not the case, your knowledge about, and connection to, your individual te'kas will guide you in choosing the appropriate one: you know your te'kas and the individual energies each contains.

   If I'm not positive about which te'ka to use, I will use DSV of my te'kas to help me choose. It is common for a particular te'ka to "show" you or give you a sign for you to use it. While employing DSV on your te'kas in the moments right before infusing a particular extraction point, one te'ka may appear brighter or morph into something else. In the case of morphing, it is not uncommon to view a te'ka as an animal or plant whose energy infusion would be best for patching that specific extraction point.

   Sometimes when a te'ka morphs to show you to use it, the morph you view will seem to make perfect sense logically but other times not.

For example, in the case of a young woman who had been sexually molested, my guardian te'ka morphed into protective energy that appeared as a German shepherd dog, which seemed completely logical. However, with another young woman who had a similar experience, my magical te'ka morphed into the energy of a beautiful willow tree. I used that energy for the patch but honestly wasn't sure exactly why that te'ka chose to patch here. Without the client's knowing what type of energy I had used in the infusion, she expressed to me a newfound feeling of confidence after the infusion. I have learned not to question my ancient te'kas; in many respects, they know way more than I do.

4. Once you have chosen a te'ka for the infusion, or one has shown you to use it, inform the client that together you are going to synchronize your breathing again: when you breathe in he breathes out, when you breathe out he breathes in. The only difference from the extraction is that there are two focal points to the procedure this time. Both your inhalation (sucking) and your exhalation (blowing).

5. With the chosen te'ka in your hands, begin synchronized breathing with the client. When ready, suck energy as hard as you can from the te'ka (while the client breathes out) and then immediately blow the energy of the te'ka into the extraction void of the client (while the client breathes in). Do this up to three times if necessary, but normally you can infuse a sufficient amount of energy with just one or two infusions at a specific extraction point.

6. Repeat this procedure for the other extraction points.

7. With the infusions complete, move on to the final step.

Practice 37
MAKING THE ENERGETIC PATCH PERMANENT

Once you have extracted blockages and infused them with energy, the client must do his own work to keep the patch on and make it permanent. This is really the only time we speak to the client briefly about the extractions and infusions. The idea here is to help the client develop strategies for his everyday life so the blockages and foreign energies don't repeat. This may seem tricky, but it is actually very straightforward if the client is honest with himself. Although the client may not be at fault for what happened to him, as in the previous example of humiliation, if he continues to harbor negative feelings toward an event, it will tend to grow into an energetic blockage. The same goes for a foreign energy blockage. If the client continues to interact with the person who caused the foreign energy to infiltrate his holographic field or p-c mirrors, the blockage will continue to grow.

If you have successfully accomplished the first practice in this book, you can help your client in making the patch permanent by offering suggestions through your own experience. You may not have any similar events as your client, but the general practice is the same for any energy draining event: identifying the event, clearing it, patching it, and making a strategy so it doesn't happen again (making the patch permanent). Review practice 2 for coming up with a legitimate plan of action that will keep the client on a healthy energetic path.

Permanently healing patches has a snowball effect in terms of energy. The more patches you permanently heal, the more energy you will have for healing others. Similar to practice 2, have your client start with permanently healing patches that he knows he can heal, or at least make a viable attempt to heal. For example, asking for forgiveness from someone (whether alive or deceased) or forgiving someone that hurt him can be a powerful first approach to healing patches when applicable. It will be up to the client to decide if that means talking to the actual person or not. Many times talking to the person is either not a good idea or impossible. That is why a good strategy is to teach your client to work with the sacred flame of Fire (even if simply with candles). Similar to practice 1, you can teach him how to use Fire for specific events that you have patched and infused.

If you were able to extract all the necessary blockages and foreign energies during the extraction, then with the completion of the infusions and making strategies, you are finished with the client. If there are more extractions to be done, schedule another session for as soon as possible.

15
The Five Points
of Attention

I sincerely hope that if you are reading this you have mastered the practice of the three points of attention and now you are ready to move to five. Mastering the shamanic technique of the five points of attention opens for view an unfathomable amount of opportunities, as you will now be able to fully utilize a natural integrative state of consciousness in your shamanic work.

I'm going to begin the explanation of the five points of attention with an edited excerpt from my book *Teachings of the Peyote Shamans: The Five Points of Attention*. This excerpt describes the night I received the last two points of attention in a ceremony performed at the base of Hauxamanaka, a mountain in Mexico that is the sacred site of the north for the Huichol. On this night I was seated at the fire with the *marakame* (singing shaman) Jesús, his granddaughter Maria (a shaman apprentice), and Marcelino and Rafael, who were *jicareros*—five-year temple members who keep alive the sacred traditions. At this point I had practiced the three points of attention sufficiently that I was going to receive the final two.

Personal Story
of the Five Points of Attention

Maria took a muvieri *(a wand) from her* takwatsi *(basket) and drew the symbol of the five directions in the dirt between us. She looked to her grandfather, and he nodded his head in agreement.*

"Grandfather told me before this trip that if you were ready he wanted me to unveil the two remaining points to you. The two remaining points are below, or underneath, and above, or beyond."

Maria then pointed to the five points on the drawing. The center was me, the right point the object, the left point the place, the bottom point the underneath, and the top point the beyond.

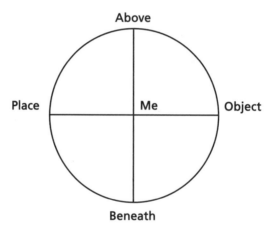

Fig. 15.1 Five points of attention

"Now as you can see, all the points are connected. You can also imagine that if I were to pull up the center point, the curved lines of the circle would straighten, and we would now have a four-sided pyramid with a point at the top."

As soon as Maria said that, a vague memory suddenly came clearly into my mind. Jesús had taken me to Teakata (the central sacred place of the Huichol), where we visited cave shrines. In one of the cave shrines was a small pyramid sitting among all the other offerings. The pyramid was about a foot high and seemed to be made of compacted dirt or clay. It was fashioned to have five distinct levels, and I remember wondering to myself what it was doing there. It seemed so out of place with all the usual beaded gourd bowls, arrows, candles, and yarn drawings that were typical of Huichol offerings. I had never seen a pyramid of any kind in all my time with the Huichols except on that one occasion. It also occurred to me that I had heard of Huichols visiting the pyramids at Teotihuacan outside Mexico City, but I never knew why, and I really didn't think to ask.

Somehow reading my thoughts, Maria continued, "The five points of attention and the significance of the number five were well known to the exceptional ancient people that built many of the pyramids throughout Mexico. I'm guessing that you know some of them?"

"Yes," I replied, a little surprised that we were having this conversation. "I have had interesting and sometimes even amazing experiences at the pyramids of Teotihuacan, Uxmal, Palenque, Chichen Itza, and others."

"Have you ever visited the pyramids in Egypt?" she asked.

"No, not yet. Maybe someday," I replied. "I haven't really had the urge to go there."

"I have not been there either, probably for the same reasons as you, but I have seen photos, as I'm sure you have too. Do you recall any major differences between the great pyramids in Egypt and the ones we have here in Mexico and Central America?"

The answer did not come right to my mind. Normally because of that, I would have simply just said something lame like, "No, not really" or shaken my head no in order to receive the answer. But since I was aware of my three points of attention, my thought process was much clearer, and I was able to pull my mind back and quickly survey the situation. Almost immediately images from different places, many that I had been to and some that I had only seen in photos and videos, came to mind, and I had the answer.

"The Egyptian pyramids are pointed at the top, and they don't have steps. They were not built for people to get to the top."

"Exactly," Maria said with a smile. "The Egyptians made their pyramids for different reasons even though they obviously understood the power of the five points. The exceptional ancient ones over here made their pyramids flat on top. And many times they even had an open chamber up top with a roof. And always they had steps on the outside so you could go up there. That's because that is the center point that connects all the others. The ancients that made the pyramids that you have been to didn't make them just to look at or as a monument to the dead. Oh no. They made them to be used for focusing attention on the five points.

"Once you fully comprehend the five points of attention, not just intellectually but with your pure essence, it's simple to understand why the ancient people went through so much work to construct them. The ancient people that built the four-sided pyramids with platforms on the top and steps to reach them were living in a totally different reality than most people do now.

"Even with all the tourists, my favorite is still Chichen Itza. What an inspiring creation that pyramid is—beautiful steps on all four sides leading up to the center. You can climb up the north and come down the south or climb up like Father Sun in the east and later come down as the setting sun on the west. When you are standing or sitting at the top, you are the fifth point of the four-sided pyramid. You are the center of the universe. That is exceptional!"

I had to agree that what she was saying did ring true and that I had even thought about the five points of the four-sided pyramids before when I had climbed them. It's certainly not difficult, if you are open to it, to experience "something" different in your perception when you are at the top of one of those ancient pyramids, even if you know nothing about them. Listening to Maria I wished that I had had knowledge of what she was telling me when I had visited them in the past.

"Don't worry, I'm sure you'll go visit some of them again," Jesús said. "You're way too curious not to!"

"That's right," Maria added. "Maybe I will even go with you. Someday when I get my passport, I want to go to Tikal too. But let's not *focus on that now. Grandfather Jesús has asked me to explain this to you so I have to try and do an exceptional job. I have just told you about the two remaining points of attention, but that doesn't mean you understand them. It should be obvious to you that we recognize the concept of the pyramids, and sometimes exceptional Huichols employ that shape in offerings or power objects. But in general all Huichols prefer to view the universe as well as consciousness in forms that are round and circular. That is why our temples are round and not square. For this discussion, let's move on from the pyramid and go back to the circle with five points. In order to understand the points below and beyond, we can add this visual aide to our circle.*

"You see, for us, we conceive the world as a giant jícara, a great big ceremonial gourd. In the middle of this gourd is where we live. The place of the five directions. Then there is also what is under and what is over. Someone who is very good at drawing could make this diagram in three dimensions and it would look nicer, but I'm sure you get the idea. Right?"

I nodded affirmatively and was truly excited to hear what she was going to say next. I had waited a long time for this!

"Okay. Let's start with the attention of below or under. This can also be called the root attention. But before we go any further, I have to tell you about a truth. This truth is similar to the truth about the first three attentions. The truth is this: the fourth and fifth attentions are a pair that work together just like the first three work together. Nobody knows why it is almost impossible to focus awareness on yourself, the subject, and something outside of you, the object, at the same time without adding the third point—place. You have already confirmed this for yourself, and anyone with the proper intent can confirm it as well. In this same respect it is virtually impossible to add either of the other two points of attention to the first three without adding them both together. Understand?"

"Sure. Okay. You don't go from three to four; you have to go from three to five."

"For that simple but incomprehensible reason, I'm going to help you understand the next point of attention, which in this case will be the

attention of the underneath, but don't even bother trying to add this point to your other three points until I have explained to you the essence of the fifth point. Just be patient, listen, and try to comprehend without moving your attention from the three points you are currently living. If you do, you will just drain your energy and probably not get to experience all five points together. I hope I am making myself clear. Some people who don't listen to this advice never make the union of the five points. They live in the awareness of the three points, which can be a nice life. But that is not the objective. To be exceptional, we have to cross the boundary from three to five."

Jesús suddenly broke into the discussion and told me to arrange the fire in a new way as Maria explained to me about the fourth attention. He instructed me to take the arrows (sticks) of the fire that were pointed toward our destination (the top of the Cerro Gordo) and make a teepee or pyramid with them and other new sticks. I could move the pillow log or keep it where it was; it didn't matter.

I immediately figured he was having me do this to distract me from trying to add the fourth point to the first three without the fifth point. In retrospect it was the perfect distraction because, first of all, I love playing with fire, and secondly, the numinous quality of the flames made it easier to be calm and patient as I held my three points of attention in balance.

Maria began her instruction. "The fourth point of attention we will now speak of is that which is seemingly below or underneath our normal states of perception. This includes awareness of the physical world that we do not see during our normal day. The roots of trees that allow them to grow, worms that give life to the soil, seeds that are waiting to sprout, leaves and branches decomposing into the ground, underground rivers, minerals, fossils, magma, crystals, bones, dead people, lost cities, ants and woodchucks and tarantulas, snakes and rabbits and bears in their dens. Sewers, subways, electric and gas lines, tunnels and mines, rats and homeless people, landfills, toxic waste, secret stashes, hidden bunkers, nuclear missiles, basements, oil, and garages. These are a few of the things beneath us every day, but we don't normally attend to them. We do not normally place conscious awareness to what is under us. But why not?

"On the other hand, there are countless senses, intuitions, and conditions of primal awareness or instinct that we don't normally attend to either. As an example, let's begin with the mother of the fourth attention—intuition. How would you define intuition?"

"Knowing something without knowing how I know it?" I replied.

"The eminent psychologist Carl Jung defined it as perception by way of the subconscious," *Jesús stated very slowly and in a mock tone of a college professor, which made everyone chuckle and lightened the mood.*

"Yes!" Maria declared emphatically. "Knowing without knowing how you know, subconscious perceiving, knowing without using logic or reason. Intuition is underneath our normal rational awareness and sits squarely in the point of the fourth attention.

"So how about other examples?" she asked.

"Humor!" exclaimed Marcelino while pointing a finger at Jesús.

"Excellent example," Maria replied happily. "What makes something funny? Why do some people laugh at something and other people don't? Maybe they just don't get it. Or maybe they do get it, but they don't consider it funny. Whatever the case, the essence of what makes something funny is hidden underneath."

"Fear," Rafael added in a mock scary voice.

"Exactly," Maria agreed. "How do we know to be afraid of something? Maybe we learned that certain things or situations are dangerous. But the core essence of fear lies underneath reason. Like the pure instinct of survival, to fight or run with no time to think about it."

"Sexual attraction," Jesús added, trying to sound sexy but failing miserably.

"Okay, Grandpa, that's a good one," Maria replied sarcastically. "Attraction is as mysterious as intuition or anything else involving the mind of the fourth attention. We don't know why we are attracted to certain people or food or trees or animals; we just are. Attraction lies underneath reason.

"Are you getting the theme here, James?" Maria asked with more seriousness.

"Yes. But wouldn't I be aware of these things while I'm being attentive of myself, or attentive of the object or place?"

"Good question. But remember everything in the circle is connected. In our attempt to raise awareness, we intentionally place our attention on the various points at the same time so that we don't get lost in just one attention. Placing our attention on three points and then five enables us to be five times more aware than when we are in dreamless sleep. However, since the points are all ultimately connected, they will and do bleed over and onto each other to a certain degree. But those of us who are exceptional at this can place attention onto all five points at once with very little or no perceived overlap. As you know, attention to yourself is a separate point to attention to your object, just as attention on yourself or the object is separate from your intuition or instinct or what is below you that you cannot perceive with your senses. Your ego or your personality or your emotions or your physical senses are not intuition or instinct. They are two completely different points. The object of your attention is not intuition. The place where you are is not instinct. This is why we designate the perception of the subconscious and the unseen, what lies beneath, as the fourth point of attention. But as I said earlier, you will not be able to truly verify that until you also add the fifth. So let's explain that now.

"The fifth point of attention is the beyond, signified as being above. The best way to begin to grasp this point of attention is to first not associate it with any other point. In explaining the fourth point to you, you automatically asked if it is part of the other three. This is a normal response. But the answer is no. All the points are separate even though they are connected. If you are in the east, you are not in the west. If you are in the north, you are not in the south. But you are still on planet Earth. Ultimately, all is connected. In this sense we place our fifth attention in a separate place that can be described as the beyond. The beyond is not your intuition; it is not what you call yourself; it is not any object, circumstance, or place.

"The fifth point is completely dispassionate and indifferent. It can be likened to how the sun or stars or moon would think or feel about us; they do not think or feel anything about us. They are beyond us. We use the analogy above simply for understanding purposes and also for practicality in learning. This attention is a point outside anything that we know. But when we are aware of the reality of this point, we gain perspective of our true essence because it is not influenced at all by who we think we are or even what we do. The fifth point is the so-called companion of the fourth point because, just like the first three points, they only work together. Intuition and instinct are underlying states whose essence is only fully comprehended by awareness of the fifth point of attention, the beyond. Conversely, attention of the beyond is only truly accessed when coupled with the point of attention of what lies beneath."

Jesús added, "It might not appear so to you now, but the fifth point is actually the closest point that we can place our attention on. In this same regard we can describe the fourth point as the farthest. The fourth point includes awareness that is 'brought to light' through attention or circumstances of life. The fifth attention simply is. *It is there always just waiting for you to catch it!*

"James, there will be many more chances for discussion about these things in the coming days, and it is normal to have questions. I believe tomorrow will be very important to you as you begin to apply your awareness of the five points of attention all together during the light of day, traveling, conversing, sensing, and all that. But for now my suggestion is to work with the fire for a while. A good task would be to place the pillow and arrows back to pointing to our destination for tomorrow and to feed the fire some more wood."

Jesús looked toward Maria, and she added, "Tatewari, Grandfather Fire, is the best guide for integrating the five attentions. Now that our preliminary explanation of the remaining two points is concluded for the moment, you will no doubt be testing out whether you can perceive and combine all five. The fire can help you because it embodies all five attentions. While working with the fire, you place attention on the first

point by being aware of how and what you feel. Am I warm? Do I feel
sleepy? Don't burn myself! Am I confused? Happy? Whatever.

"The fire is an awesome object outside yourself to direct the
awareness of your second point of attention. The fire also illuminates
the place where we are so our attention is aware of our third point.
Awareness of the fourth attention is exuded by the warmth of the fire as
it brings forth the energy of the wood that lies within it. There are not
many entities or phenomena that bring out the fourth attention of our
primal feelings, instinctual knowledge, and intuition more profoundly
than fire. And of course the element of fire perfectly reflects indifference
and insignificance toward human beings and their affairs; it lets us know
clearly that we are not the center of the universe, which is the essence of
the fifth attention."

For the rest of that night, I carefully tended the fire while expand-
ing my attention to five, and for the first time I truly understood what
this practice was about. My primal mind was awakening but not at the
expense of my personality or ego. I felt in a state of balance that I had
never experienced before and that is difficult to put into words. I was
one with everything but at the same time myself.

Practice 38
THE FIVE POINTS OF ATTENTION

Let's review the fourth and fifth points:

The fourth point of attention is that which is seemingly below or
underneath our normal states of perception. There are countless senses,
intuitions, and conditions of primal awareness or instinct that we don't
normally attend to. The mother of the fourth attention is intuition:
knowing without knowing how you know, subconscious perceiving,
knowing without using logic or reason. Intuition is underneath our
normal rational awareness and sits squarely in the point of the fourth
attention.

The fifth point of attention is the beyond, signified as being above. The best way to begin to grasp this point of attention is to first not associate it with any other point. All the points are separate even though they are connected. If you are in the east you are not in the west. If you are in the north you are not in the south. But you are still on planet Earth. Ultimately all is connected. In this sense we place our fifth attention in a separate place that can be described as the beyond. The beyond is not your intuition; it is not what you call yourself; it is not any object, circumstance, or place. The fifth point is completely dispassionate and indifferent. It can be likened to how the sun or stars or moon would think or feel about us; they do not think or feel anything about us. They are beyond us. We use the analogy "above" simply for understanding purposes and also for practicality in learning. This attention is a point outside of anything that we know. But when we are aware of the reality of this point, we gain perspective of our true essence because it is not influenced at all by who we think we are or even what we do. The fifth point is the so-called companion of the fourth point because, just like the first three points, they only work together. Intuition and instinct are underlying states whose essence is only fully comprehended by awareness of the fifth point of attention, the beyond. Conversely, attention of the beyond is only truly accessed when coupled with the point of attention of what lies beneath.

When beginning to learn the three points of attention I suggested you perform a novel practice (crawling in nature). Although working with Fire shouldn't be a novel experience for you by now, just as the Huichols taught me, I suggest you first practice the five attentions outside with a fire built in a sacred way (practice 1) or at least five candles set in a pattern of the four directions with one in the center.

The attentions when with the sacred flame:

- **First attention.** Be aware of how and what *you feel*. Am I warm? Do I feel sleepy? Don't burn myself! Am I confused? Happy? Whatever.

- **Second attention.** The Sacred Fire is an awesome *object* outside yourself. Gaze into the flowing flames.
- **Third attention.** Attend to the illumination of the *place* you are in and why you are *there*.
- **Fourth attention.** The Sacred Fire brings forth the energy that lies inside the wood, while at the same time bringing forth your primal mind, instincts, and intuition that lie *beneath* your normal awareness.
- **Fifth attention.** Attend to the unfathomable mystery of the universe and how the Sacred Fire connects us to the stars above as it rises toward the sky. We are simply one tiny point of light in a numinous reality.

When you have passed through your initial attempt at raising your awareness to the five attentions, the next step is to begin doing it alone at home or in nature—somewhere without a lot of distractions, especially other people. From there, gradually begin practicing during all the many facets of your life. This is not easy. But with practice, time, and patience, I hope you will be successful.

The profound and extremely useful ISC produced by living the five attentions at the same is a remarkable accomplishment that may take a lifetime to perfect. As for me, throughout many years of practice, I can say that I spend most of my time at the level of awareness of the three attentions without having to consciously think about it, and living in the three attentions has enhanced my life in countless ways. I have advanced my awareness to the five attentions so that I can employ this profound awareness at will in special moments such as when I do my shamanic work or when connecting with nature, or during challenging situations that require me to make special efforts. Sometimes I find myself in the five attentions spontaneously, like right now as I am writing this. My Huichol shaman mentors tell me that the more we practice intentionally being aware of the five attentions in special moments, the more we will find ourselves in that level of awareness during our "normal" lives until one day it is possible that we stay there.

In the meantime, when we learn to cultivate the five attentions at will, we have available to us an integrative state of consciousness that we can use to benefit all of those around us, especially our clients and shamanic community.

EPILOGUE

What's Next?

I'm going to conclude by first stating a point I made at the close of my last book on autogenic training, which includes forty practices. I know full well that most people, including me, don't complete all the practices and techniques available in instructional books. If you truly have completed all the practices in this book, congratulations are in order. However, for those of you who are more like me, you might want to try the practices that you skipped. I've found that many times the things we avoid are precisely the things we need the most. Also, there are so many practices in this book that require long periods of time to complete or become proficient in that I always suggest to my students to keep practicing. This not a race; take your time and enjoy the new experiences, feelings, and knowledge included in the practices.

As always with my practical books, what's next includes my sincere hope that you share what you learn with others and make a positive impact in your community as you embody the ways of the shaman. Many of you are probably already involved in some modality of the healing arts. It is my hope that you personally refine or tailor techniques to your specific healing modality and also create new ones (feel free to share them with me!). This phenomenon that we call shamanism is for indigenous cultures a lifelong calling and pursuit. In this, as in most things, we can never stop learning.

APPENDIX

Ethics and
Shamanic Practitioners

Globalization is a term that describes the process of expansion of the human population on our planet and the growth of "civilization" that has accelerated dramatically in the past fifty years. Because of entities such as the World Trade Organization and World Bank, instant communication worldwide via satellites and the internet, homogenization of language (English is now the dominant technical language worldwide), cultural diffusion as people give up their local traditions to compete in a global marketplace—among countless other considerations—the world is getting very small very fast. Whether we support or are critical of globalization, no one can dispute that this process is affecting all levels of industry, finance, politics, information, language, culture, ecology, technology, and ethics.

At this moment there can be no doubt that what we refer to as shamanism is going through a global metamorphosis as well. On the one hand, we see the steady decline of traditional shamanic tribes as they are assimilated into modern culture and their young people lose interest in keeping the ancient shamanic traditions alive. On the other hand, there are many tribes throughout the world that have been previously assimilated in whole or part that are reclaiming and rebuilding their shamanic traditions. Into this mix we have a new wave of modern-industrial people interested in learning about shamanism and who are feeling the call to learn to become shaman.

The situation is very complex. However, one important facet of all this rises immediately to the top, and that is the topic of ethics. Historically, a shaman was an integral part of a tightly knit tribal community. His or her knowledge and experience was culturally formed and grounded. Trained within the cosmology of the tribe and highly scrutinized for both successes and failures in his or her role, the shaman was under the watchful eye of the community just like everyone else.

But in the many places of the world where we see a revival or even a new beginning of shamanic practices, such as the New Age shamans of Western society, we now have shamanic practitioners with little or no cultural shamanic background. Most of these practitioners are "self-appointed" shamans with second- or thirdhand training from workshops or seminars, or they may have only learned their "craft" from reading a few books! Eleanor K. Ott, Ph.D., folklorist and environmentalist, writes about the problems and challenges these new shamans face in an essay in *Shamans through Time*.

> This isolation from the checks and balances that a supportive and also critical community provides places these new shamans in the ethically questionable situation of doing certain traditional shamanic practices, such as attempting to heal illnesses of the body, mind, or spirit, outside of the bonds that informed and tied the earlier shaman to a cultural community. They are, in fact outside of any long-standing tradition altogether. This same isolation is the cause of many problems that face the new shamans. Especially this is true in issues of ethics, which depend on a cultural context for their resolution.[1]

The marketing of "shamanic training" and of travel to exotic locations to learn from "legitimate shamans" has become big business. Both these circumstances end up doing more harm than good and can even be extremely dangerous. Let's take a brief look at the potential problems of this situation.

TEACHING AND SELLING OF SHAMANIC PRACTICES THAT AREN'T SHAMANIC

This is the least harmful in terms of physical or psychic injury to an individual or group, but it does significantly impact the overall view of shamanism and misleads an unknowing and susceptible public that have the good intentions to learn. I have been to enough "shamanic" ceremonies led by modern self-appointed shamans with minor training for other modern people that were so far from legitimate shamanic practices that I certainly base my comments here on personal experience.

The problem here is that though someone may have good intentions, if there is no peer group, then anyone can make up a few business cards and flyers, give himself a cool name that includes some type of animal, and put "shaman" in front of his name. If he is a good salesperson, he will tap into a market of honest people who want to learn, and he will probably be successful. But that doesn't make this person a shaman, as I hope I have already explained in this book.

Only you can know what level of shamanic work you are on and if you are ready to teach shamanic practices or perform shamanic healing. The practices in this book are powerful. It is my hope that you will fully master them before attempting to teach them or employ them in healing work.

CARELESSLY OPENING THE SPIRIT WORLD

For those with the intention, will, and skills to delve into the spirit world and call forth spirits to influence happenings on this plane, there must be adequate attention placed on the shadow side of the spirit world that may do more harm than good. There have been shamans throughout time, more properly referred to as sorcerers, who are more interested in personal gain than serving their community and who have been known to injure and even kill through their malicious manipulation of the spirit world. And who is to say that an inexperienced shaman, especially without the support and guidance of an experienced shaman, might not "accidentally" through a momentary loss of attention let a malevolent spirit cross—and then what will he do if he doesn't have the skill to send it back?

Without a professional peer group to keep a watchful eye on a new shaman, which was the case (and still is in certain tribes throughout the world) in ancient shamanic communities, there is a high risk of being taken when the spirit world is opened. Opening the spirit world does not guarantee a benevolent outcome. In addition, a modern neoshaman without the support of a shamanic community and peers may unknowingly let personal subconscious or secret fears, intents, or desires come into play when working with the spirit world, which could cause dire and dangerous circumstances for both the shaman and his or her clients.

SHAMANIC JOURNEYS TO EXOTIC LOCATIONS

I love to explore this magnificent planet we are so fortunate to live within. I have been a traveler my whole life and I hope will continue to be for many years to come, and I encourage anyone with the time and resources to expand his or her mind and spirit through feeling and experiencing the energy of new places and cultures.

However, with the rise of interest in shamanism, a new trend has been developing that combines "exotic travel" with working with indigenous shamans. This trend has potentially dangerous consequences and should certainly be mentioned here in an advanced guide to shamanism.

First, there are some authentic indigenous shamans around the world, a few of whom I have met and worked with, who understand the necessity of sharing their knowledge outside their cultural boundaries. As the human enterprise continues to degrade the planet, these shamans are willing to work with outsiders or even travel to foreign countries to help accomplish a calling from Mother Earth to evolve consciousness toward holism.

But these shamans are the exception to the rule. Most authentic indigenous shamans on the planet are involved in upholding their part of the "world tree"—first, for the health of their community, which includes the health of the biosphere, and second, to keep alive their tribe's traditions, values, and way of life. American and European seekers of "shamanic experiences" make about as much sense to them as the Huichol sacrificing a bull in a church on Easter would be to a practicing Catholic! In other words, these shamans have no use for or desire to become part of the tourist trade. In fact, many shamanic tribes that in the past one could visit with proper respect and a few choice gifts to tribal elders are now vehemently guarded and strictly off-limits to outsiders, which is a real shame.

This circumstance has been created in part by people with good intentions, such as me; by people with exploitive intentions, such as certain authors (when I began visiting shamanic communities I wasn't an author nor had even thought about writing a book); by photographers and anthropologists; and mostly by the recent influx of tourist groups seeking exotic experiences with indigenous shamans. This last group is not only the most dangerous to these shamanic cultures, threatening their very existence, but also to the tourists themselves.

Unfortunately, right now there is an exploitive element to the "shamanic travel" being sold to the public, especially to destinations in South America where the trip includes an ayahuasca ceremony with an "authentic" shaman. These trips are sold to honest people, mostly American and European visitors, who want to be healed of something, or advance their spiritual development, or even become a shaman. There are two main things to consider in this situation.

First, the ayahuasca brew is extremely psychoactive. If a participant has a "bad trip" and an authentic ayahuasca shaman is not present to help him or her come to terms with those visions and experiences, that person could suffer permanent psychological damage.

Second, many of the men (women are almost nonexistent as ayahuasca shamans) in these South American countries who claim to be ayahuasca shamans are *mestizos*. These people live in the city and not in the exotic places where they take people; they have received no formal training and do not have the cultural background of an authentic ayahuasca shaman. This lack of training combined with the powerful ayahuasca brew can lead to precarious and even dangerous situations.

For these and many other reasons, all of us interested in, and working in, the field of shamanism need to consider the ethical factors involved in healing others, leading ceremonies, ingesting plant medicines, and preserving sacred sites and ancient cultures.

ETHICAL RESPONSIBILITIES
FOR SHAMANIC PRACTITIONERS

Here are some of the considerations I feel are most important:

- **Service.** The only reason to be a shaman is to serve individuals, groups, communities, humanity in general, and the planet and all her species. If you have not been called to do this unconditionally, then you should pick a different vocation. Service requires complete attention to the health and safety of clients and respect for their personal values, space, and beliefs. Clients should be made fully aware of the treatment you will be facilitating so that they enter into it completely voluntarily, knowing of any risks (if any) and also the potential benefits of your service. An agreement of confidentiality should be made between shaman and client(s).
- **Integrity.** A shaman is in a position of power when a client comes to him or her. The client may be in a highly vulnerable or sugges-

tive state. In this regard, the shaman must always be aware of how his or her actions will affect the client and act with the utmost integrity and with the well-being of the client in mind, regardless of the personal feelings of the shaman one way or the other.

- **Expertise.** A shaman has the ethical responsibility to support others with practices that he or she has fully mastered and been trained to perform.
- **Peer review.** A shaman shall be held responsible to the community he or she serves by being open to, and even seeking out, counsel and advice from other shamans for continued growth and to insure high ethical standards within the shamanic community.
- **Reasonable exchange of energy.** Shamans throughout time have received some sort of compensation for their work. Be ethical in what you ask for, and make accommodation for those that may have little means at the time they seek your help.

Notes

PREFACE.
WHY ADVANCED SHAMANISM?

1. Endredy, *Ecoshamanism,* xv.

CHAPTER 2.
STATES OF CONSCIOUSNESS

1. Green and Green, *Beyond Biofeedback,* 55.

CHAPTER 3.
PSI AND SHAMANISM

1. Radin, *Entangled Minds,* 14.
2. Endredy, *Lightning in My Blood,* 49–52.
3. Radin, "Frequently Asked Questions."
4. International Association for Near-Death Studies, "Key NDE Facts."

CHAPTER 5.
FUNDAMENTAL PRACTICES: PART 1

1. Endredy, *Teachings of the Peyote Shamans,* 68–69.

CHAPTER 6.
FUNDAMENTAL PRACTICES: PART 2

1. Metzner, *The Unfolding Self,* 136.
2. Burke Museum, "The Science and Legends of Birthstones."

CHAPTER 7.
LUCID DREAMING

1. LaBerge and Rheingold, *Exploring the World of Lucid Dreaming,* 36.
2. Hamilton, "Why it's best to write your goals down."

CHAPTER 8.
MASTERING DREAM CYCLES FOR LUCID DREAMING

1. Dement, *Some Must Watch While Some Must Sleep,* 37.
2. Psychology World, "Stages of Sleep."

CHAPTER 12.
SENTIENT BEINGS IN THE DREAMSCAPE

1. Lupa, *New Paths to Animal Totems,* 16.
2. Lupa, 252.
3. Ecology Global Network, "Birth and Death Rates."

CHAPTER 13.
SHAMANIC VIEWING

1. Morehouse, *Remote Viewing,* 21.
2. Morehouse, *Remote Viewing,* 26.
3. Morehouse, *Remote Viewing,* 27–28.
4. Laszlo, *Science and the Reenchantment of the Cosmos,* 57.
5. Millay, *Multidimensional Mind,* 191, 192.

APPENDIX

1. Ott, "Shamans and Ethics in a Global World," 281.

Glossary

altered state of consciousness (ASC): A change in one's normal mental state (usually temporary) without being considered unconscious. Altered states of consciousness can be created intentionally, or they can happen by accident or due to illness.

autogenic training (AT): A method of rational physiological exercises designed to produce a general psychobiological reorganization.

autonomic nervous system (ANS): Also known as the visceral nervous system, or involuntary nervous system, is a part of the peripheral nervous system and acts as a control system that functions largely below the level of consciousness to regulate visceral functions such as heart rate, digestion, respiration, salivation, perspiration, pupillary dilation, micturition (urination), sexual arousal, breathing, and swallowing.

central nervous system: The command center of the human organism, which includes the brain and spinal cord.

direct shamanic viewing (DSV): The learned ability to detect and interpret multidimensional phenomena.

electroencephalogram (EEG): A neurological test that uses an electronic monitoring device to measure and record electrical activity in the brain.

electromyogram (EMG): A diagnostic procedure to assess the health of muscles and the nerve cells that control them (motor neurons).

ganzfeld experiment: A technique used to test individuals for extrasensory perception and telepathy.

holographic field: Our information storage field, which is embedded in both brain and body and contains our lifetime of experiences.

hyperspace: A term used to describe dimensions beyond the four dimensions of space-time.

hypnagogic state: The transitional state of consciousness from wakefulness to sleep.

hypnopompic state: The state of consciousness immediately preceding waking up from sleep.

hypothalamus: A section of the brain responsible for the production of many of the body's essential hormones and chemical substances that help control different cells and organs within our body.

integrative state of consciousness (ISC): A learned state of consciousness that provides enhanced access to normally unconscious information through integration of different brain systems, which induces emotional, behavioral, and cognitive integration; passive manipulation of our autonomic nervous system; and psychic-energetic integration with our environment via our holographic field and p-c mirrors.

jicara: From the Wirrarika language—refers to a bowl used to hold sacred items of an animal spirit guide.

lucid dreaming (LD): To become aware you are dreaming while you are dreaming.

medulla oblongata: Located in the lower brainstem, it controls major body functions that include respiration, cardiac regulation, vasomotor activity, and certain reflex actions such as coughing, sneezing, vomiting, and swallowing.

near-death experience (NDE): A profound psychological event that may occur for a person close to death or, if not near death, in a situation of physical or emotional crisis.

nierika: A Wirrarika word for a sacred item that assists you as a portal to the dream world.

NREM (non-rapid eye movement) sleep: Dreamless sleep.

out-of-body experience: The experience of your consciousness leaving your body.

parasympathetic nervous system: A subsystem of the autonomic nervous system often considered the "rest and digest" or "feed and breed" system.

passive volition (PV): Planting a seed in your mind and simply letting it grow in your subconscious and throughout your body, without active volition.

peripheral nervous system (PNS): Our nerves and ganglia outside of the brain and spinal cord.

phase-conjugate mirrors of the mind (p-c mirrors): Coherent light energy that produces the process of translating information from the hyperspace into sensory memory and then into awareness and the ability of expression.

psi: A term used to represent parapsychological or psychic faculties or phenomena.

REM (rapid eye movement) sleep: A state of sleep where you have more dreaming and bodily movement and faster pulse and breathing.

shamanic viewing (SV): The learned ability to detect and interpret multidimensional phenomena for healing of people and places, and the gathering of information related to multidimensional phenomena in both local and nonlocal space-time.

somatic nervous system: Part of our nervous system that allows us voluntary control of body movements via skeletal muscles.

sympathetic nervous system: Part of our autonomic nervous system, it is considered the "fight-or-flight" system that activates a physiological response for quick mobilizing.

te'ka: A sacred stone that comes to you while in nature to assist you with shamanic healing work.

Bibliography

Burke Museum. "The Science and Legends of Birthstones." Accessed September 22, 2016. www.burkemuseum.org/blog/curated/science-and-legends-birthstones.

Dement, William. *Some Must Watch While Some Must Sleep*. New York: W. W. Norton, 1974.

Ecology Global Network. "World Birth and Death Rates." Accessed September 24, 2016. www.ecology.com/birth-death-rates.

Endredy, James. *Advanced Autogenic Training and Primal Awareness: Techniques for Wellness, Deeper Connection to Nature, and Higher Consciousness*. Rochester, Vt.: Bear & Company, 2016.

———. *Earthwalks for Body and Spirit: Exercises to Restore Our Sacred Bond with the Earth*. Rochester, Vt.: Bear & Company, 2002.

———. *Ecoshamanism: Sacred Practices of Unity, Power & Earth Healing*. Woodbury, Minn.: Llewellyn, 2005.

———. *The Flying Witches of Veracruz: A Shaman's True Story of Indigenous Witchcraft, Devil's Weed, and Trance Healing in Aztec Brujeria*. Woodbury, Minn.: Llewellyn, 2011.

———. *Lightning in My Blood: A Journey into Shamanic Healing and the Supernatural*. Woodbury, Minn.: Llewellyn, 2011.

———. *Shamanism for Beginners: Walking with the World's Healers of Earth and Sky*. Woodbury, Minn.: Llewellyn, 2009.

———. *Teachings of the Peyote Shamans: The Five Points of Attention*. Rochester, Vt.: Park Street Press, 2015.

Gerber, Richard. *Vibrational Medicine: The #1 Handbook of Subtle-Energy Therapies.* Rochester, Vt.: Bear & Company, 2001.

Green, Elmer, and Alyce Green. *Beyond Biofeedback.* Santa Barbara, Calif.: Knoll, 1977.

Hamilton, David. "Why it's best to write your goals down." Accessed September 22, 2016, http://drdavidhamilton.com/why-you-should -write-your-goals-down/.

Harner, Michael. *The Way of the Shaman.* New York: HarperCollins, 1990.

International Association for Near-Death Studies. "Key NDE Facts." Accessed September 22, 2016. http://iands.org/ndes/about-ndes/key -nde-facts21.html.

Jung, Carl G. *Psychological Reflections: A New Anthology of His Writings, 1905–1961.* Princeton, N.J.: Princeton University Press, 1953.

Kalweit, Holger. *Shamans, Healers, and Medicine Men.* Boston: Shambhala Publications, 1992.

Kellert, Stephen R., and Edward O. Wilson, eds. *The Biophilia Hypothesis.* Washington, D.C.: Island Press, 1993.

Kelzer, Kenneth. *The Sun and the Shadow: My Experience with Lucid Dreaming.* Virginia Beach, Va.: A.R.E Press, 1987.

LaBerge, Stephen, and Howard Rheingold. *Exploring the World of Lucid Dreaming.* New York: Ballantine, 1990.

László, Ervin. *Science and the Reenchantment of the Cosmos: The Rise of the Integral Vision of Reality.* Rochester, Vt.: Inner Traditions, 2006.

Lupa. *New Paths to Animal Totems: Three Alternative Approaches to Creating Your Own Totemism.* Woodbury, Minn.: Llewellyn, 2012.

Maslow, Abraham. *Religions, Values, and Peak-Experiences.* New York: Viking Compass, 1970.

Metzner, Ralph. *The Unfolding Self: Varieties of Transformative Experience.* Novato, Calif.: Origin Press, 1998.

Millay, Jean. *Multidimensional Mind: Remote Viewing in Hyperspace.* Berkeley, Calif.: North Atlantic Books, 1999.

Morehouse, David. *Remote Viewing: The Complete User's Manual for Coordinate Remote Viewing.* Boulder, Colo.: Sounds True, 2008.

Motoyama, Hiroshi, with Rande Brown. *Science and the Evolution of Consciousness: Chakra, Ki, and Psi.* Brookline, Mass.: Autumn Press, 1978.

Ornstein, Robert E. *The Psychology of Consciousness*. San Francisco: Freeman, 1972.

Ott, Eleanor. "Shamans and Ethics in a Global World." In *Shamans through Time: 500 Years on the Path to Knowledge*, edited by Jeremy Narby and Francis Huxley. New York: Tarcher/Penguin, 2001.

Psychology World. "Stages of Sleep." Accessed September 23, 2016. https://web.mst.edu/~psyworld/sleep_stages.htm#3.

Radin, Dean. *Entangled Minds: Extrasensory Experiences in a Quantum Reality*. New York: Paraview Pocket Books, 2006.

———. "Frequently Asked Questions about Parapsychology." *The Scientific and Medical Network Review* 61 (1996): 5–11; DeanRadin.com. "Frequently Asked Questions, Part 2." Accessed August 31, 2017. Last modified January 2007. www.deanradin.com/para2.html.

Rinpoche, Tenzin Wangyal. *The Tibetan Yogas of Dream and Sleep*. Ithaca, N.Y.: Snow Lion Publications, 1998.

Sanchez, Victor. *The Toltec Path of Recapitulation: Healing Your Past to Free Your Soul*. Rochester, Vt.: Bear & Company, 2001.

Sleepdex. "Stages of Sleep." Accessed September 23, 2016. www.sleepdex.org/stages.htm.

Talbot, Michael. *Mysticism and the New Physics*. London: Routledge & Kegan Paul, 1980.

Targ, Russell. *Limitless Mind: A Guide to Remote Viewing and Transformation of Consciousness*. Novato, Calif.: New World Library, 2004.

Wolf, Fred Allen. *Mind into Matter: A New Alchemy of Science and Spirit*. Needham, Mass.: Moment Point Press, 2001.

Index

BOOKS OF RELATED INTEREST

Advanced Autogenic Training and Primal Awareness
Techniques for Wellness, Deeper Connection to Nature, and
Higher Consciousness
by James Endredy

Teachings of the Peyote Shamans
The Five Points of Attention
by James Endredy
Foreword by José Stevens, Ph.D.

Earthwalks for Body and Spirit
Exercises to Restore Our Sacred Bond with the Earth
by James Endredy
Foreword by Victor Sanchez

The Lost Art of Heart Navigation
A Modern Shaman's Field Manual
by Jeff D. Nixa, J.D., M.Div.

Shamanic Healing
Traditional Medicine for the Modern World
by Itzhak Beery
Foreword by Alberto Villoldo

Speaking with Nature
Awakening to the Deep Wisdom of the Earth
by Sandra Ingerman and Llyn Roberts

The Accidental Shaman
Journeys with Plant Teachers and Other Spirit Allies
by Howard G. Charing
Foreword by Stephan V. Beyer

Becoming Nature
Learning the Language of Wild Animals and Plants
by Tamarack Song

INNER TRADITIONS • BEAR & COMPANY
P.O. Box 388
Rochester, VT 05767
1-800-246-8648
www.InnerTraditions.com

Or contact your local bookseller